BUCCANEER BOYS 2

Buccaneer Boys 2

More True Tales by Those Who Flew

'The Last All-British Bomber'

AIR COMMODORE
GRAHAM PITCHFORK MBE, FRAeS

FOREWORD BY

AIR MARSHAL SIR PETER NORRISS KBE, CB, AFC, FRAeS

Grub Street • London

Published by
Grub Street
4 Rainham Close
London SW11 6SS

Copyright © Grub Street 2021

Copyright text © Air Commodore Graham Pitchfork 2021

A CIP record for this title is available from the British Library

ISBN-13: 978-1-911667-18-6

Typeset by Francesca Mangiaracina

Printed and bound by Finidr, Czech Republic

WING COMMANDER DAVID HERRIOT

(1949–2020)

Throughout the preparation of *Buccaneer Boys 2*, David Herriot was my 'chief of staff'. When we discussed the idea for another volume, he immediately encouraged me to start the project. From that day, until a few days before he passed away, he proof-read all but two chapters, in addition to sourcing material and photographs for me, just as he had done in the first volume of *Buccaneer Boys*. Until his final days, his trademark enthusiasm never wavered.

David Herriot was the epitome of a 'Buccaneer Boy' who knew how to balance his professionalism with the world of fun. A superb navigator and tactical instructor, his zest for life was infectious and his contribution to the unique brotherhood of the Buccaneer world was immense.

I dedicate this book to his memory – a brilliant airman, a fine officer and a great friend.

CONTENTS

FOREWORD

AIR MARSHAL SIR PETER NORRISS KBE, CB, AFC, FRAeS

When Graham Pitchfork asked me to write the foreword for *Buccaneer Boys 2*, I initially wondered if the chapters could match the wonderful tales of the 2013 edition of *Buccaneer Boys*. I should not have worried, as the authors have more than risen to the occasion, and Graham has created a fine book to read.

My first direct involvement with the Buccaneer was in November 1971 when I was posted to No. 15 Course on 237 Operational Conversion Unit at RAF Honington. However, I had previously had indirect connections through my father, who was a production manager at Blackburn Aircraft working on the Beverley, and at various air shows in the summer of 1971, where I was displaying the Jet Provost. My father had been aware of some of the teething problems experienced during the aircraft's development and so was intrigued to see some of the engineering solutions on the aircraft when I showed him round one in the hangar at RAF Laarbruch. The Air Day at Lossiemouth not only enabled me to get physically closer to the aircraft, but it also introduced me to the splendid *joie de vivre* for which Buccaneer aircrew are renowned.

Hailed as the last all-British bomber, the Buccaneer proved itself to be a highly adaptable and versatile machine. It was designed initially to operate off an aircraft carrier and to toss a nuclear store at a Sverdlov-class cruiser, but initiatives by Royal Navy personnel enabled its weapon-aiming system to be used for the delivery of conventional weapons from a variety of attack profiles. The South African Air Force subsequently made serious use of the Buccaneer's attack capabilities during the Bush Wars. Following the Wilson government's decision to cancel both the TSR-2 and the F-111, the Buccaneer entered service with the Royal Air Force in the maritime and overland strike/attack roles, and its operational development continued, with new weapons and capabilities being introduced during its life.

Little did I know in 1971 that over the following 12 years I would achieve some 1,500 hours on the Buccaneer and 600 on the Hunter during three tours: one as a squadron pilot with XV Squadron, one as chief flying instructor on the OCU, and one as the squadron commander of 16 Squadron. The flying was exhilarating and challenging. Carrying out Fam1 sorties with pilots new to the aircraft, when you did not have a dual-controlled aircraft, often caused the adrenaline to flow, as did my few deck-landing practices on *Ark Royal*. As the Buccaneer display pilot in 1975 I had some 'interesting moments', not least at the Toronto Air Show when a light aircraft with a wing walker appeared in front of us at crowd-centre as we ran in at 550 kts.Rebuilding the squadron following two structural failures, including the Red Flag accident in February 1980 that led to the fleet being grounded for nearly five months, brought different challenges, and it is a testament to the resilience of the crews that less than 15 months after the restoration of flying, with limited aircraft availability, the whole squadron took part in that year's Red Flag exercise and performed splendidly. During that tour I was also privileged to form and lead the five-ship formation display team, the Black Saints, which carried out a number of displays at air shows in Germany.

The chapters in this new book cover the whole gamut of what Buccaneer life was like, for aviators and interested readers to enjoy. The authors bring out loud and clear the commitment to what they were doing, the fun they had doing it, and the strong bonds among those who flew and serviced the aircraft, irrespective of the service to which they belonged. Those bonds exist to this day and manifest themselves in a number of ways, not least the annual Buccaneer Blitz, a December lunchtime gathering in London of those who have flown the Buccaneer whether on squadrons or in supporting roles such as test pilots.

While the Buccaneer Aircrew Association was officially formed after the 'final hurrah' at Lossiemouth in 1994, there were early stirrings some 10 years previously when a small cohort of aircrew met up for a reunion in a Greek restaurant one lunchtime, and this event grew into a very popular curry and beer bash at the Nag's Head in Knightsbridge, an event that was soon known as the 'Blitz'. Attendance grew to a point where more space was needed, and so HMS President has now become the annual port of call for some 130 of us. In parallel Buccaneer ground crew now hold an event in Norwich to which local aircrew also go along.

So sit back and soak up the tales of the Buccaneer Boys who flew a remarkable aircraft over its 35-year life and who believed in what they were doing. They lived life to the full and, despite the ageing process, many of them still do. While calling them 'Boys' may be something of a misnomer, it is said that flying keeps you young at heart, and when you see them at play, you'd have to agree it appropriate. Enjoy the read!

ACKNOWLEDGEMENTS

Following the success of *Buccaneer Boys*, and the encouragement of the committee of the Buccaneer Aircrew Association and the publisher, I accepted the challenge of trying to match the earlier volume. This attempt to achieve that aim could not have happened without the great support I have been given by my colleagues, 'The Buccaneer Boys'. They have trawled their memories, logbooks and sought the recollections of other chums in order to provide the chapters that follow. Their names appear with their own chapter and I trust they will accept this as due recognition for their superb narratives.

I want to thank my old colleague and the president of the Buccaneer Aircrew Association, Sir Peter Norriss, for his eloquent foreword and the support he gives to the Buccaneer Aircrew Association. My old friend Tom Eeles has been a great help with ideas, support and proof reading. Finally, I want to single out the help and support of David Herriot. I have paid a personal tribute to him at the beginning of this book. It was an immense pleasure working with him, just as it was for the 24 years we shared steering the Buccaneer Aircrew Association. My great regret is that he will not see this book that captures so much of which he was proud. I hope you would have approved David.

The vast majority of photographs have been provided by the authors and from my own collection. I am grateful to Angie, widow of Willie Steele, for the photograph in Chapter Twenty. I also want to thank Colin Buxton, 'Skids' Harrison, Podge Middleton, Mark Rahaman, Norman Roberson, Steve Ryle and Terry Thomas for their help in sourcing and providing additional photographs. Every care has been taken to identify and seek the permission of their copyright holders. However, if I have unwittingly transgressed, I apologise.

Finally, I must thank the Grub Street team. As always, the support and help given by John Davies, Francesca, Natalie and Tess has been outstanding. It is a pleasure to work with them.

"What an incredible bunch of people we all are and a more unified group of aviators there cannot be across the world."

Colonel Jan Guyt, South African Air Force

"Being a Buccaneer Boy was certainly memorable. Even now, long after the last aircraft has flown, Buccaneer ground crew are immensely proud of our role in making the Buccaneer the most formidable aircraft, crewed by elite aircrew, and no matter which squadron we served on."

Corporal Mark Rahaman, 16 Squadron and 237 OCU

CHAPTER ONE

ENTER THE BUCCANEER

GRAHAM PITCHFORK

In November 1940, 21 elderly Swordfish bi-planes took off from HMS *Illustrious* and effectively destroyed the Italian Fleet at Taranto. Just six months later, in May 1941, the torpedo-carrying Swordfish of HMS *Ark Royal* crippled the *Bismarck* and sealed the fate of the mighty German battleship. Within a few months, carrier-borne aircraft of the Imperial Japanese navy had wreaked havoc at Pearl Harbor and, three days later, sent two of the Royal Navy's battleships, HMS *Prince of Wales* and HMS *Repulse*, to the bottom of the South China Sea. As the war came to an end in 1945, aircraft carriers operating in the Pacific had formed the cornerstone of the Allied victory against the Japanese. The reach and devastating power provided by carrier-borne aircraft had been amply demonstrated, and the aircraft carrier had quite clearly replaced the battleship as the capital ships of the Fleet.

The end of World War Two may have seen the demise of the menace of Nazism and Japanese imperialism, but it would soon herald an uneasy peace, and the outbreak of the Korean War in 1950 emphasised the dangers inherent in the new world order of the 'Cold War'. The Soviet navy had previously been limited to coastal operations geared to the defence of the Soviet Union, but a significant increase in their warship-building programme highlighted the emergence of a global capability posing a great threat to the security of the vital sea-borne trade of the Western Powers. Pre-eminent in the Soviet shipbuilding programme was the development of the 17,000-ton, heavily gun-armed Sverdlov cruiser.

During the war years there had been major developments in radar technology, and the capability to detect high-flying aircraft at long range had been achieved. However, the shape of the earth dictated that an aircraft flying just above the surface would not enter the 'lobe' of enemy radar until it reached a range of some 26 miles. Flying at very high speed and very low level, an attacking aircraft would give a target as little as three minutes' warning of an impending attack. The surprise element of such an attack had been recognised by the staff of the Naval Air Warfare Division and in 1952 they realised that this was the answer to the threat posed by the Sverdlov. The following year the Navy Board issued Specification M.148T for a two-seat, carrier-based strike aircraft capable of delivering nuclear and conventional weapons over long ranges and at high speed. Naval Air Requirement NA.39 was issued the following year.

The primary role of the aircraft, as specified in the requirement, was to be effective at attacking ships at sea, or large coastal targets, which would be radar-discreet and identifiable at long range. The primary weapons were listed as the 'Green Cheese' anti-ship homing bomb and a tactical nuclear bomb, with an additional requirement to deliver a large range of secondary weapons. The aircraft also would have the ability to act as an air-to-air refuelling tanker. The operational profile envisaged a 400-mile radius of action, with a descent from high level to very low level just outside the detection range of a target's radar, followed by a high-speed low-level dash to and from the target. Stringent weight limits were imposed so the aircraft could operate from and be supported by the Royal Navy's current aircraft carriers. This meant having maximum take-off and landing weights and ensuring the aircraft's size enabled it to be lowered to the ship's hangar by the lifts.

The naval requirement set a daunting technical challenge, but most of the major British aircraft companies submitted designs. At the end of March 1954, five companies were invited to tender for the order of 20 development aircraft. The Blackburn and General Aircraft Company at Brough were successful with their B.103 design and the initial go-ahead for production was given in July 1955. Although a small company compared to other British aircraft manufacturers, Blackburns had a long history of producing aircraft for the Royal Navy, but B.103 was their first venture into the jet age.

Achieving the necessary landing speeds for carrier operations posed a particularly difficult challenge and most companies utilised the benefits of 'jet deflection', which was at the early stages of development. Blackburns investigated the benefit of boundary-layer control, achieved by blowing high-pressure air, bled from the engines, over the leading edges of the wing and tailplane and over the flaps and ailerons in order to obtain increased lift and thus reduce landing speed. The net value of these measures was an approach speed with full flap and aileron droop some 17 knots slower than an 'unblown' approach. This method provided significant advantages over the jet deflection method and also allowed the Blackburn design to employ a smaller wing – an important feature for high-speed low-level flight. The need to generate high bleed-air pressure from the engines for the approach and landing phase resulted in a high engine RPM and an unacceptable landing speed. A large airbrake, forming part of the aft fuselage, was the answer. With it fully extended, the appropriate approach speed could be maintained and this became the standard landing configuration for the aircraft. A T-tail had already been selected but the position of the airbrake made this inevitable.

Another advanced feature was the embodiment of an 'area rule' design, which allowed a reduction in the amount of thrust required to maintain maximum cruising speed. This offered the bonus of a larger internal rear fuselage size for the storage of avionics and fuel.

The structure of the aircraft was based on two large machined steel spars used in the inner wing, with integrally stiffened machined skins on the thin wings and the all-moving tail-plane giving the aircraft added strength. Generations of Buccaneer aircrew have extolled the virtue of their aircraft's strength over the years. To some it was akin to the proverbial brick-built s*** house! The folding nose contained the radar, and the design of a 180-degree rotating bomb door for an internal bomb bay capable of carrying 4,000 lbs of stores was unusual and would provide an added bonus in later years when an external fuel tank was incorporated in the skin of the bomb door.

Selection of the engines presented some difficulties and, eventually, a scaled-down de Havilland Gyron producing just over 7,000 lbs of thrust was chosen. Two engines gave the desired sea-level cruising speed of Mach 0.85, and just sufficient thrust for take-off. It is interesting to note the comments made by an independent audit carried out by American officials who made the telling remarks, 'the airplane seems underpowered and pitch-up could be a problem'. Time would prove them right.

Just 33 months after Blackburns had been given the go-ahead, the first aircraft (XK486) was ready for taxi trials. For such a relatively small design and production team, on what

The Blackburn NA.39 takes off for its first flight.

for its day was a very advanced project, this represented a remarkable achievement, and particularly when compared with the ponderous progress we see on some projects today.

By March 1958, the aircraft was ready for engine runs and these were completed at the company airfield at Brough near Hull. The small airfield was totally unsuited to operate the NA.39 and so the company arranged to lease the former bomber airfield at Holme-on-Spalding-Moor, some 18 miles from the factory. However, the Ministry of Supply deemed that the 6,000-foot runway at Holme was still too short for the first flight, so XK486 was partially dismantled, covered in a shroud and transported by road to the Royal Aircraft Establishment's airfield at Bedford. Blackburns' recently appointed chief test pilot, Derek Whitehead, an experienced former Royal Navy test pilot, commenced high-speed taxi runs in April. These trials suffered an early setback when a tyre blew out and damaged the starboard inner wing skin, but the engineers soon had the aircraft ready for its first flight, which took place on 30 April with Whitehead at the controls and the head of flight testing, Bernard Watson, in the rear seat. The first flight was made without using the boundary-layer control system, and the 39-minute flight was a complete success. After a further three months of testing at Bedford the aircraft finally returned to Holme and the test programme continued. Further aircraft became available and they were towed along local roads, in the early hours of the morning, from the factory at Brough to Holme airfield where they made their first flights before being allocated to specific tasks for the flight test programme.

More pilots were converted to the NA.39 before joining the flight test team, and they included Lt Cdr Ted Anson, an experienced Royal Navy test pilot who went on to become 'Mr Buccaneer Royal Navy', filling every Buccaneer appointment up to captain of HMS *Ark Royal* before retiring as a vice admiral.

The NA.39 made its public debut at the SBAC Show at Farnborough in September 1959, when Derek Whitehead and 'Sailor' Parker demonstrated XK490. In the following January, deck trials took place on board HMS *Victorious* and Derek Whitehead, flying XK523, made the first carrier landing on 19 January 1960 in difficult weather conditions. A second aircraft, XK489, the first 'navalised' aircraft, joined the programme and 31 successful sorties were completed, together with important deck handling, aircraft lift and hangar stowage trials.

As more of the development batch aircraft became available the flight test programme gathered momentum. Lessons learned from earlier trials were embodied in the newer aircraft and minor structural changes were made. Hot weather trials were conducted in Malta, weapons trials commenced at West Freugh, and three aircraft were attached to A&AEE Boscombe Down for completion of the Controller Aircraft (CA) Release, obtained in April 1961. These trials by C Squadron at Boscombe included full carrier trials, some being conducted from HMS *Ark Royal* in the Mediterranean during January 1961. One aircraft (XK526) was then shipped to Singapore for tropical trials. In the meantime, the aircraft had finally been given a name and, on 26 August 1960, the NA.39 acquired the very appropriate designation of Buccaneer S.1, the 'S' indicating the aircraft's strike (nuclear) capability.

As the manufacturer's and Boscombe Down trials continued, the Royal Navy formed its

The officers of 700Z Flight with Cdr 'Spiv' Leahy standing in the centre.

first unit with the specific task of developing operational and engineering techniques and capabilities.

The Royal Navy's Buccaneer Intensive Flying Trials Unit, (IFTU) 700Z Flight, was formed at RNAS Lossiemouth (HMS Fulmar) on 7 March 1961, when Rear Admiral F.H.E. Hopkins CB DSO DSC, the Flag Officer Naval Flying Training, took the salute at the commissioning parade held in Hangar Two. Cdr Alan 'Spiv' Leahy DSC, a highly experienced ground-attack pilot and Korean War veteran, commanded the flight.

In April 1965, I joined Graham Smart at Lossiemouth on an exchange posting and we formed the first RAF crew to operate the Buccaneer. It was the beginning of three years of exciting flying that took me to the Far East, to Aden and to East Africa. After a year at sea, it was back to Lossiemouth to spend two years as an instructor with 736 Squadron – the Buccaneer training squadron – with later detachments to 803 Squadron conducting weapons trials. My abiding memory of this period of my service life was the opportunity to fly with some great aviators and make some marvellous friends.

Whilst I was with the navy at Lossiemouth, the first South African Air Force crews began their conversion onto the new, and only, export version, the Buccaneer S.50. They loved their new acquisition and flew it aggressively until 1992.

The plan for Graham and me was to gain experience on the new generation of 'fast jet' before heading for the TSR-2, but this was not to be. During our time at sea, two political

The first South African Air Force Buccaneer S.50 over Holme-on-Spalding-Moor.

decisions were to change my RAF career pattern. First, TSR-2 was cancelled, and then it was announced that the Royal Navy's new carrier programme (CVA-01) was also cancelled. This latter decision was to see the end of fixed-wing flying in the navy for the foreseeable future. As a result, an increasing number of RAF officers were loaned to the Fleet Air Arm to maintain the strength of their three Buccaneer squadrons until the eventual demise of navy Buccaneers in 1978.

The cancellation of TSR-2, and later its replacement the US-built General Dynamics F-111, left a huge gap in the RAF's tactical strike/attack capability. The answer was to inherit the navy's Buccaneer fleet, and order a new build of the aircraft to create six RAF squadrons – in the event there were only five plus the OCU. The RAF would then assume responsibility for providing tactical support of maritime operations (TASMO), and a strike capability operating from RAF Laarbruch in Germany and assigned to the NATO strike plan.

With the impending run down of the Fleet Air Arm squadrons, Lossiemouth was to close as a naval air station, with 809 NAS re-locating to Honington where the training of all Buccaneer crews, both RN and RAF, was to be carried out on the newly formed 237 OCU. The instructors were drawn from both services. It was this close professional, and social, relationship, initially on RN front-line squadrons, and then at Honington, that established the unique and lasting bond amongst the Buccaneer fraternity.

With the cancellation of the TSR-2, and then the F-111, there was a need for Buccaneer experienced crews to establish the RAF's Buccaneer force at Honington. From a cast of one, I was dispatched to Honington to join Wg Cdr Roy Watson to establish the operations wing pending arrival of 12 Squadron in October 1969, the RAF's first Buccaneer squadron. Little did I know that I was to spend another 12 years involved with the Buccaneer, culminating in command of 208 Squadron, the highlight of my 36 years of RAF service. The aircraft was to see a further 12 years of service with the RAF.

Finally, on 31 March 1994, the RAF said farewell to the mighty Buccaneer when 208 Squadron, commanded by Wg Cdr Nigel Huckins, stood down. In the intervening 33 years the aircraft went to war in the First Gulf War, and in the wars of Southern Africa, it deployed and operated worldwide, and it was a cornerstone of NATO's deterrence capability.

Above all, it generated a breed of aircrew and ground crew that were second to none. So, let the 'Buccaneer Boys' tell their own stories of operating and servicing the 'Last All-British Bomber'.

CHAPTER TWO

BUCCANEER INTO
NAVAL SERVICE

MICHAEL CLAPP

*Mike Clapp, on the right,
being greeted by Cdr Ted
Anson at Lossiemouth.*

In January 1950 I joined the Royal Navy to do my National Service as I was passionate about anything to do with the sea. There was one problem. No one told me I could join as a short service supplementary list officer, so I committed myself to a full career.

Serving in the Korean War as a midshipman was exciting. Shore bombardment to cut the logistic lifeline of the North Korean and Chinese troops made our contribution very popular with soldiers who used us as their holiday camp. We watched the Fleet Air Arm bombing inland targets and attacking MiGs.

In 1955, I was serving as a junior lieutenant in HMS *Comet*, a destroyer in the Mediterranean. One day, my captain told me that I was to attend No. 1 Long Observer Course in HMS Seahawk, RNAS Culdrose in Cornwall. This, he had been told, was because the navy badly needed general list officers in the observer branch.

I had absolutely no desire to fly. After the 'Long 'O' Course', we went to HMS Gannet, RNAS Eglinton, in Northern Ireland to learn about anti-submarine warfare from the air. We flew in the new Gannet aircraft, and I enjoyed the course very much. Life was looking up.

Soon, I came to respect and hugely enjoy the Fleet Air Arm, a branch of the Royal Navy that was too often seen as remote from the 'real' surface navy. Their history, however, showed that they had pioneered a large number of very useful capabilities, and were early developers of airborne weapons when others were still employed basically for reconnaissance.

In the late autumn of 1956, I found myself briefly in 751 Naval Air Squadron (NAS) at RAF Watton flying the Avenger and learning about electronic warfare. This again taught me

Buccaneer XK525 on a fast, low run over Holme-on-Spalding-Moor

something about the advantages of air power, and the different RAF operating procedures.

After a period flying AEW Skyraiders of 849 NAS, and attendance on the RAF's Staff Navigator Course, I was settling into 766 Squadron, the navy's All-Weather Fighter Operational Training Squadron at HMS Heron, RNAS Yeovilton, when I was sent at short notice to Ferranti Ltd in Edinburgh. The company had designed, and was now starting to test, the Blue Parrot radar for the Blackburn NA.39, as the Buccaneer was then called. The radar, with its unusually long pulse length and slow pulse repetition frequency (PRF), was fitted to a Canberra, WV787.

With my ex-RAF pilot, Colin Curtis, who became a good friend, we flew mainly from RAF Turnhouse across Scotland to West Freugh to use the large radar reflector in Luce Bay. During this time, we tested the radar, and later the whole navigation system with the Blue Jacket Doppler ground position indicator (GPI) and master reference gyro (MRG), another Ferranti designed, and made, piece of kit that was a considerable advance at the time. Later, I flew in a Meteor, which was testing the pilot's strike sight (an early head-up display) before the complete system was integrated and fitted to a Buccaneer.

We were told the idea now was for the Buccaneer, on its own, to detect a target at long range, dive below radar detection, and run in at sea level to toss a tactical nuclear bomb or drop a conventional bomb or rocket. There was much talk of a likely target being a Soviet Sverdlov-class cruiser, well defended with modern electronic warfare and anti-aircraft missiles. Based on my time with 849 Squadron, directing Sea Hawks and Scimitars, I could fully appreciate the advantages of this technique.

On 12 November 1960 I made my first flight in a Buccaneer, XK525, with Lt Cdr Ted

Anson, a test pilot from C Squadron, Boscombe Down, but now working closely with Blackburns at their airfield at Brough, not far from Hull. I thought the observer's cockpit rather cramped but it seemed to work. A series of weapons system shakedowns followed in the Buccaneer, together with pilot familiarisation flights. Colin Curtis and I then flew this aircraft on further trials.

In November 1961, I finally returned to the navy and joined 700Z Flight, the Intensive Flying Trials Unit (IFTU) in HMS Fulmar, RNAS Lossiemouth, under the command of the legendary pilot, Cdr 'Spiv' Leahy. C Squadron at Boscombe Down had already put the aircraft through its paces as a machine, but now it was becoming a fully fitted weapons system, the aircrew needed to be trained in its detection and weapon capabilities. This would then lead to developing operational tactics.

Spiv Leahy and I flew together four times. The sorties were basically system acquaintances with only one sortie remotely operational. On this occasion we took off from Lossiemouth and climbed up through thick cloud with the intention of targeting Rockall after a long low-level approach. This meant we had to let down through cloud over the Outer Hebrides. I had selected a route that took us between two islands and warned him that, when/if we broke cloud, what he could expect to see, low land to port and cliffs to starboard, so I offset a little to port. When we did break cloud, it was at about 200 feet, he swore at me and immediately climbed up turning back for Lossiemouth. Not a word more was said beyond: "Don't ever do that again! Report to me in my office."

Luckily, in the crew room I found John de Winton. As an all-weather fighter pilot, he was the only pilot in 700Z Flight who had flown regularly with an observer. He kindly came with me and explained to Spiv that what I suggested was only what any pilot having an observer working on the radar can expect. That was the whole point of carrying one as they allowed the pilot to concentrate on flying while the observer handled the navigation. "They have the radar and trust you fly safely. They don't want to die either," he said. Spiv calmed down and accepted John's advice. I suspect many of the other pilots who had mostly flown single-seat aircraft, felt the same, but they too learnt. They also learnt about attacks at night, which they could not do before.

As time went on we flew with drop-tanks, bomb-bay tank and in-flight refuelling, all adding to our radius of action. We also practised conventional and nuclear bombing profiles and rocketing. Photo-reconnaissance and tanking had yet to be practised. The single-sideband radio (SSB) proved rather a problem and, in my time, was rarely used. However the passive wide-band homer was a great advantage since it detected long-range radars and provided a homing capability.

The need to understand, and be able to work, the various very different roles was demanding but fun, and was typical of naval aircraft, which needed to be multi-capable to limit the number of different types embarked in a carrier. Squadrons cannot afford the luxury of a single role at which the aircrew are specialised. Any specialisation has to be sorted out within the squadron.

While checking the aircraft's performance and fuel consumption, essential for navigational planning, we maintained a connection with C Squadron as well as Ferranti Ltd.

An 801 Squadron Buccaneer S.1 arrives on Ark Royal *on 21 February 1963.*

Both were, of course, very interested in our results. Some of our aircrew had done time in C Squadron, particularly the senior pilot, Ted Anson, Andy Alsop, a test pilot, and George Oxley, an experienced all-weather fighter observer, who had trialled the aircraft without radar, but with the Blue Jacket Doppler navigation system and MRG at Boscombe Down. They knew the ropes and brought their experience with them to the advantage of the rest of us.

One day, flying with Robin Greenop on a low-level navex around the Western Isles in a Hunter we came over a cliff. The wind was strong and flipped us over. Robin recovered and we carried on the mission. That afternoon he flew the same route again, but in a Buccaneer. He reported that as he crossed the cliff there was a small judder but no more. My faith in the Buccaneer grew.

Mike Hornblower, an air warfare instructor, developed plans for attacking shipping with either conventional bombs and rockets or a tactical nuclear bomb. This is where the advantage of the strike sight became apparent as it allowed the pilot to manoeuvre without concerning the observer, as long as the radar was either locked on or was tracking a distinctive feature.

Mike was fun. He had a Bentley with the number plate NA 39 but had a reputation for flying a little riskily. This was generated when one day he returned to the squadron after a low-level sortie with some heather on the aircraft's pitot head!

On 2 July 1962, I left 700Z Squadron and went directly to 801 Squadron, under the command of Ted Anson, as his senior observer. During my time in 700Z, I had flown over 24 hours in the Canberra, with nearly eight hours in the Meteor trialling the radar and strike sight, and then over 85 hours in the Buccaneer proving the kit, teaching aircrew about the weapons systems, and developing attack procedures. Now it would soon be off to sea with new and exciting challenges.

Life continued with trials, but now it was less technical and more operational in preparation for embarking in HMS *Ark Royal* for a few weeks to conduct deck-landing and catapult-launch trials. While embarked, we also worked with AEW aircraft probing targets and practising profiles. The operations went very well and confidence was increasing.

Back in Lossiemouth, we pressed on with conventional dive-bombing and rocketing on Tain Range, as well as nuclear-bombing profiles on the buoy in Luce Bay. We also developed in-flight refuelling, photo-reconnaissance and weapon practice at the range. Finally, in mid-August 1963, we embarked in HMS *Victorious* in the Channel. She was smaller than *Ark Royal* and had a very happy, welcoming ship's company.

We spent little time in the Mediterranean. Our first brief stop was at Aden where we practised close air support for the troops, and I was invited to go on a convoy to an army camp inland. The whole journey was fascinating and I wrote home describing the convoy and pickets racing up the hills on either side. My father, who had served in the Indian army, was delighted as it was exactly the life he had led in the North-West Frontier, but without the motorised transport.

A month later we reached Singapore and disembarked to RAF Tengah. *Victorious* did not stay long before heading for Japan with most of the squadron re-embarked. I was left with three crews to continue tropical trials for nearly a month. By January 1964 we had met up again and we all returned to Lossiemouth.

The 801 Squadron crest was a trident with the squadron motto 'On les Aura' – 'Let's have them', which appealed to us. While embarked, Rob Woodard, a pilot, organised 'Flying Fork Lunches' at which we entertained members of the wardroom who had been helpful to us.

In December 1963, I left a very happy squadron, which had pioneered a wide range of capabilities. During this time in the Mark 1, I flew 128 hours. Then, after a commanding officer designates' course for ship's captains, I flew to Singapore to take command of HMS *Puncheston*, a minesweeper being used as a patrol craft just when the Indonesian Confrontation began.

It was an exciting time. One night off Horsburgh Light to the east of Singapore, we caught a fast sampan carrying 14 Indonesian soldiers attempting to land on the east coast of Malaya. I had used my Buccaneer back-seat experience to drive the ship, and make the interception, from the radar. Other commanding officers relied on a second officer, but

The flight deck of HMS Victorious *in 1966.*

none had the same luck – two sweepers even collided! My time in the Buccaneer and 849 Squadron had come in handy.

In October 1965 I handed over and flew home to take command of 801 Squadron in early January. By now it was the first Buccaneer Mark 2 Squadron. It had only just been formed, and John de Winton had been put in command waiting for me to return. My senior pilot was Brian Giffin a very experienced Scimitar and Seahawk pilot who, like me, had flown in 801 Squadron's Mark 1s. Several others had been in 700Z and 801 Squadron so we were very much a family team who got on well, and we were determined to make a success of the aircraft.

Two weeks later Alan Deacon and I flew to RNAS Brawdy for an air day. Alan was ecstatic about the new Spey engines and the much-improved performance of the aircraft. He wanted to show off the Mark 2's capability to me, so we flew at sea level around the north of Scotland and west of Ireland. Happily, there were no bird strikes and I was indeed impressed.

We worked ourselves up and went through the drills before embarking on 19 April 1966 in HMS *Victorious* once more. It felt like home – the welcome was just as before. What followed was an intensive period of launches and landings to work up the ship's deck handlers as much as us.

It was then backwards and forwards between Lossiemouth and *Victorious* to continue deck trials and weapons training, mainly in conventional attacks.

On 8 July we finally embarked and sailed. On our way to Suez, we rocketed and bombed Filfla, a tiny rock south of Malta, and carried out sorties over Sicily and Cyprus. It was then down the Suez Canal, calling at Aden and Gan on our way to RAF Changi, where we arrived in mid-August, and where tropical trials flying low over the Malayan jungle took up most of our time.

For a while it was backwards and forwards between *Victorious* and Changi, but in October we re-embarked and took part in Exercise Sword Hilt on our way to Australia and the Cocos Islands.

In early January 1967, Brian Giffin and George Oxley, my senior pilot and observer, flew home and were relieved by Johnny Johnston and James Ingham respectively. Johnny was an ex-RAF flight lieutenant, and a very good pilot as well as delightful company. He told me he had become bored by flying Hunters in Germany and wanted a more exciting life at sea. James was a steady and efficient senior observer. Amongst my RAF aircrew was Tom Eeles. I like to think we all worked well together.

Returning to the Singapore area in March 1967, Johnny and I diverted to Tengah to refuel. The result was alarming as we had not been given the small amount of fuel we asked for, which was all we needed for our return on board, but, unknown to either of us, the bomb-bay tank had also been filled. As we approached *Victorious*, Johnny did comment that the aircraft seemed unduly heavy, but we caught a wire and pulled it out, I believe, as far as it would go. We were nearly over the side. I had already tried to work out if it would be safer to eject or swim with the aircraft, but all was well. To our embarrassment we then discovered why.

We sailed up the South China Sea and fired Bullpup at the Scarborough Shoal off the Philippines. It was then homeward bound returning to Lossiemouth on 13 June, having clocked up just over 227 hours in the Buccaneer, mostly from *Victorious*. This made a total of just over 550 hours in the Buccaneers of both marks. Carrier time does not allow as much opportunity to fly as ashore, as the ship is normally visiting ports to give leave and for maintenance time.

I then handed the squadron over to Johnny and went on leave. My next job was at RAF Old Sarum as the instructor in naval fixed-wing aviation at the Joint Warfare Establishment. That was the end of my close connection with the Fleet Air Arm, and it was soon back to sea in command of HMS *Jaguar* sailing for the Far East and home across the Pacific calling in on some of our Commonwealth partners and many of our colonies on the way.

My final job in the RN was to command the Amphibious Task Group in the Falklands campaign. I had asked for a fixed-wing observer to be sent out to join my staff to cover intelligence on the Argentine air force and task the Harriers. Flt Lt Chubb, another Buccaneer

Boy, was sent from Lossiemouth. He joined us at Ascension Island. I suspect he was a little bewildered to meet an antique 'Buccaneer Boy', but together we tried to work out the Argentine aircrews' problems in attacking us.

This all helped me to choose San Carlos Water as the main landing area. The plan worked. The Argentine aircraft approached with far too little time to aim accurately and, although the number of bombs dropped was huge, few hit ships and even fewer had released their bombs in time to allow their fuses to run down long enough to explode.

I remain convinced that someone without our experience would have chosen a different place and dispositions for the ships, and probably lost a lot of lives and material.

Thank you to the Buccaneer, for giving me such a wonderful experience and education. We needed you badly in the Falklands campaign with your range of weaponry, your ability to tank, provide photo-reconnaissance and radar detection. We needed the *Ark Royal* with her catapults and arresting gear to help achieve that. If she had still been in active service I reckon the chance of the Argentines not attempting the invasion would have been much higher, and a large number of lives and equipment would have been saved, the cost of which would probably have paid for a carrier!

I am pleased that so many of the RAF have enjoyed the Buccaneer so much, and have seen what the Fleet Air Arm can design and achieve.

CHAPTER THREE

LIGHT BLUE ON
A DARK BLUE BACKGROUND

JOHN HARVEY

This chapter recounts some of the activities and events relating to a unique formation, which became known, almost by default, as the RAF Element 736 Squadron (RN).

The history leading up to the formation of this unit is complex but can be traced back to the cancellation of two important RAF aircraft programmes, the TSR-2 and the F-111, which created a large gap in the inventory. A decision was taken to plug the gap with the Buccaneer, which it was belatedly realised was not only a first-class aircraft, but would also become available as a result of the rundown of the fixed-wing squadrons of the Fleet Air Arm (FAA). There would, therefore, be a requirement to train RAF aircrew on the Buccaneer.

The navy, of course, already had a Buccaneer training squadron in the shape of 736 based at RNAS Lossiemouth, also known as HMS Fulmar, which was still fully operational with Buccaneer Mark 2s, the earlier Mark 1s having been placed in storage.

The navy agreed to take on the task of training the first courses of RAF aircrew, but only with the assistance of manpower from RAF resources. This would comprise three RAF instructor crews, all of whom had served on exchange tours with the Fleet Air Arm, together with a substantial assembly of some 86 RAF tradesmen and one engineering officer who were to assist with the additional maintenance arising from the RAF flying training programme. For want of a better title this unit was to be known as the RAF Element 736 Squadron. Apart from the aircrew, none of its members would have had any experience either working with the navy or on the Buccaneer.

While all this planning was going on, I was, in blissful ignorance, passing through the RAF's advanced flying training course on Gnats at RAF Valley with a view to completing an operational tour before returning to mainstream engineering. All this came to an abrupt halt when, on completion of the Valley course, the engineer pilots on it were informed that due to delays in the training system, and a shortage of engineering officers, we were all to return to engineering duties forthwith. Rather mysteriously I was invited to HQ Strike Command for a briefing prior to a posting.

I was to report to OC RNAS Lossiemouth, otherwise known as the captain of HMS Fulmar, to take over the responsibility for the RAF Element forming. I was to be responsible to the captain for all the actions of RAF maintenance staff when they were 'on board' his ship and to OC RAF Kinloss when they were not. It all sounded a bit complicated and Strike Command clearly thought so as well. I was given a 'hotline' number to ring in case of difficulty with the navy, who I was informed, could be a bit odd. And that was that.

I set off for the far north in a somewhat reflective mood but, to my relief, HMS Fulmar was expecting me. I was directed to the wardroom, given a cabin, found the bar, and everyone I met was friendly. Much was explained, particularly naval terminology mostly linked to the fact that the base was administered as a commissioned ship in naval service. This resulted in benefits I was not anticipating such as a monthly entitlement to duty-free tobacco to be taken in cigarette (known as blue liners), pipe, or chewing form. Intrigued, I kept an eye out for wad-chewing matelots and conveniently placed spittoons but was disappointed. I soon discovered there was a lively trade in this tobacco ration, which could be exchanged for virtually any useful service available on the base.

The introductory process culminated with an interview with the captain. I was ushered into his presence by a very pleasant 2nd Officer Wren secretary who then retreated closing the door behind her. I was not asked to sit down and I still, unfortunately as it turned out, had my hat on. The small man sitting behind the desk viewed my salute with displeasure, curtly informing me it was not the navy custom to do so, and went on to deliver what sounded suspiciously like a dressing down for some misdemeanour I was unaware of. I left his office, with my hat now off, to be met by a very apologetic secretary who said her boss was having a very bad day and that I was the first person he had seen that day wearing a light blue suit. That was my introduction to the famed 'Winkle' Brown, someone I then knew nothing about. I was somewhat put out at the time, but it was soon explained that he had just been informed of the cancellation of the navy's new fleet carrier with the consequent severe impact on the future of the FAA in general. He clearly held the RAF responsible for this disaster.

Fortunately, I was not the only light blue suit on the complement of HMS Fulmar at the time. The RAF instructor aircrew had already arrived and there were several others who were serving on exchange postings. We took to gathering in a corner of the wardroom bar, which became known as 'crab' corner, crab being the derogatory label attached to members of the RAF by the navy. It appeared that preparations were already well in hand to receive the first RAF training courses. The only slight cause for concern was the decision to bring a number of the old Mark 1 Buccaneers out of storage for our use due to a shortage of Mark 2s. I learnt that the Mark 1, although being an excellent flying machine, was bedevilled with unreliable, underpowered engines, the Gyron Junior. The navy had lost a number of Mark 1s due to engine failures of one sort or another and had been quite happy to consign the survivors to storage.

I was greatly encouraged by the reception I was given when I arrived on 736 Squadron. Plans had been made to get me up to speed on the engineering aspects of the Buccaneer with arrangements made for the on-the-job training of RAF maintenance staff when they arrived. 736 was accustomed to this as it was also a training facility for ground crew as well as aircrew. I gathered that I was to be a deputy air engineering officer once I had satisfied the engineering commanders that I was competent and after I had met the standards of an examining board. This was a bit startling as I had been away from engineering practice for a while and knew nothing about how the navy did things. However, all was well after I had hurriedly explained that I had earlier spent over four years front-line engineering on Lightnings. The navy decided I was competent and signed me up forthwith; omitting to tell me at the time that this was for any engineering duty on the station … sorry, ship.

I took myself off to RAF Kinloss, which was to be the administrative and domestic host for RAF maintenance staff and found that arrangements were well in hand. The planning had worked and a workforce of some 86 aircraft tradesmen was being assembled, including quite a number from the Shackleton force based at Kinloss. The day-to-day administration of this bunch was to be the responsibility of the excellent Flt Sgt P. Smith who was to be resident, like myself, at Lossiemouth. Service buses would be used for transport between the two sites. The Kinloss station commander and his wing commander admin were both anxious about how the operation was going to work, particularly over disciplinary demarcation lines. Once again, I received specific instructions on the need for diplomacy with the navy.

Back at 736 some setting up was required, mostly concerned with the navy gaining an understanding of the RAF's rank and trade structure so that equivalent ranks and experience levels could be established. It worked well. It had been assumed that the RAF maintainers would look after the old Mark 1s with the RAF establishing itself down one side of the hangar and the navy on the other. However, from the start it was agreed that integration of the two workforces would take place wherever possible. Clearly, initially, the RAF needed a lot of assistance in terms of on-the-job training anyway, and there was also a long-term need for the RAF to gain experience on the Mark 2. Apart from the engines and the electrical generation system there was not a great deal of variation of engineering between the Mark 1 and 2 so it was fairly straightforward to share tasks across both marks. The navy were very good in all respects from the onset and the system shook down in a very short space of time.

The Buccaneer was a very robust aircraft, but the Gyron Junior engines proved to be a challenge to aircrew and maintainers alike. It suffered from two major sources of trouble; compressor stall and centre-line closure. This former problem would manifest itself with a startling, seemingly minor explosion and abrupt loss of thrust, which would generally have any green onlooker on the ground running for cover. To aircrew it felt as if someone was hitting the side of the aircraft with a sledgehammer. Strangely, it did not appear to do any damage to the engine itself. It was a problem that took a lot of skill to avoid as the necessary adjustments to the inlet guide vanes were delicate and each airframe had its own unique inlet flow characteristics.

The RAF detachment at Lossiemouth with Buccaneer S.1 XN957 '630'.

Centre-line closure was a different and more serious matter. The Gyron Junior was basically an underdeveloped engine and was used as a stopgap power plant for the Buccaneer. Under certain temperature conditions the clearance between the rotating compressor and turbine and their outer casing could reduce to zero as blades expanded and casings contracted. This could result in catastrophic, possibly uncontained, engine failure. A somewhat unconventional solution was devised. The inside of the casings was lined with an abrasive which ground down the blade tips if any contact was made, thereby avoiding catastrophic binding. Inspection plugs were built into the casings through which checks could be made with endoscopes to look for the characteristic polished finish on blade tips that had been ground down a bit. These two issues, particularly the compressor stall, had resulted in a number of Mark 1 losses in naval service and was to recur while the aircraft was in use for RAF training.

Being an early sixties era design the Buccaneer had an analogue system with no digital hardware or software at all. It was full of intricate electro-mechanical systems which required constant adjustment if optimum performance was to be maintained. It was not unusual for this to be done in situ, particularly on the strike sight (early generation HUD) system, by removing the covers of the relevant boxes and tweaking the appropriate servo system to achieve the desired result.

After what was a remarkably short shakedown period of about two months the RAF Element settled in. The navy ran a conventional shift system, known as watches on a ship, to cover day and night flying activities. Shift work presented little administrative difficulty. The coach transport system between Lossiemouth and Kinloss worked well for the duration with the only memorable event being a whole shift, or should I say watch, getting lost in a snowdrift for several hours one stormy night somewhere between Kinloss and Lossiemouth. This was the one and only time I ever had to get fully buttoned up in an RAF greatcoat when I went out to look for them.

Flypast at Lossiemouth led by '630'. Note the late departing Lightning.

I am pleased to say that there were no serious inter-service issues. Everyone on the hangar floor got on very well, the job got done, and I never had any need to use the hot-line number given to me by Strike Command.

Although the RAF Element integrated well with their naval contemporaries and there was little friction, there was a certain amount of good-natured inter-service rivalry. Buccaneer XN957 '630', when extracted from storage with the Naval Air Support Unit (NASU), was already considered a venerable aircraft when handed over to the RAF for recovery. It was so old it still had the original retractable in-flight refuelling probe! The naval side of 736's shed made it clear that it would be a miracle if the 'crabs' could get 630 into the air again, and so the challenge was set. A large formation flypast of Buccaneers had been planned for the annual Lossie Air Day, and Lt Cdr Dickie Wren, OC 736, said he would lead this formation in 630 if it could be made ready in time.

Remnants of XN951 being lifted from the runway.

After many trials and tribulations, including the usual close-range somewhat hair-raising experience of the Gyron Junior compressor stall on ground runs, 630 was present on the flight line at the required time and the CO led the large formation with Mick Whybro in the back in charge of timing. The aircraft was also sporting an RAF fin flash, which had mysteriously appeared the night before.

It was reported that some senior naval personages took exception to this and an investigation was demanded but 736 took the jest in good humour and the fin flash was allowed to remain in place, to the puzzlement of many future plane spotters. Predictably the investigation drew a blank and the perpetrators were never identified. It is interesting to note that this aircraft now resides in the Fleet Air Arm Museum at Yeovilton, still complete with the fin flash.

The decision to use the Mark 1s appeared to have paid off until the closing phases of the RAF's training when the old problem of Gyron compressor stall and probably centre-line closure returned with catastrophic results with two accidents, one fatal, within a fortnight. The first involved Fg Off Ivor Evans on his first familiarisation flight. The instructor in the back seat was Flt Lt Tom Eeles. The port engine stalled when a low overshoot was initiated and both aircrew ejected successfully at very low level over the middle of the airfield watched by numerous spectators including myself in AMCO. Ivor Evans was uninjured, but Tom Eeles suffered a bad back injury as a result of having his shoulder straps loose; this was the standard practice during Fam. 1 exercises as it allowed the instructor to see what the pupil in the front was doing.

The empty aircraft careered across the airfield, narrowly missing some contractors working on an approach radar and came to rest with the cockpit broken off and the starboard engine still running at high power. Without the cockpit controls it proved remarkably difficult to shut this engine down, which was a good demonstration of the robust nature of the Buccaneer. The engine was eventually swamped with foam. Years later when idly looking through a complete history of all Fleet Air Arm aircraft I found an entry about this particular aircraft, XN951. It had apparently suffered from chronic compressor stalling problems throughout its service history. If only we had known!

The second accident occurred a week later. XN968 was climbing out after take-off when it had a catastrophic uncontained starboard engine failure, and both aircrew ejected. Unfortunately, the navigator was killed as his seat malfunctioned after being damaged when it broke the canopy on ejection. The nature of the fire after the engine failure pointed to penetration of the fuselage fuel tanks by fragmented turbine parts. Turbine fatigue, coupled to centre-line closure, was suspected and it was decided that corrective action was not worth pursuing. The Mark 1 fleet was grounded immediately, with the exception of a few delivery flights. The remainder of the RAF aircrew awaiting training completed it on Mark 2s, which were then becoming increasingly available from the new build programme.

The RAF aircrew training programme on 736 was a clear success, but receiving rather less acclaim was the fact that another product was 80 fully experienced Buccaneer ground crew. Indeed, when the time came to transfer aircrew training to Honington it seemed that the RAF Element had been forgotten, and I was afraid they would be dispersed. So, I made a quick trip to Honington and knocked on a few doors, which produced the desired result and most of the Lossiemouth team were transferred there.

Like myself, these airmen and NCOs had benefitted from exposure to FAA culture, which was different from that prevailing in the RAF at the time. By its very nature of isolated shipborne operations, FAA maintenance staff did not have the benefit of on-site manufacturers' representatives with a hotline for queries, and sometimes decision-making. Embarked in a carrier, engineers of all levels were expected to get things sorted. If you couldn't do this, you didn't last very long. The outcome was much more opportunity to use your own initiative and you were encouraged to do this. There was a recognition that mistakes could be made, which was accepted as an operational risk. This culture prevailed on FAA shore bases as well and the RAF Element was fully exposed to it. It was interesting to watch the initial reaction to it at all levels, including my own. Most had never had the opportunity to exercise their own judgement or skill and most relished the chance to do so. There was no shortage of opportunity.

When it was formed the RAF Element was not particularly well endowed with senior NCOs but had a lot of junior technicians and corporals who soon found themselves responsible for tasks they would have been unlikely to have had elsewhere. I remember the look on a corporal airframe fitter's face – I think it was Cpl Scott – when he was given the task of changing an outer folding mainplane that had been damaged by a bird strike. Astonishment, apprehension, and enthusiasm all featured in quick succession. With a small team he got the job done with minimum supervision and all the independent checks were passed with no difficulties. On another occasion a corporal completed a complex airframe insertion repair on the outer skin below the cockpit that would, in an RAF environment, have probably required an official manufacturers repair scheme authorised by Command. These are just two illustrations of how a different culture allowed for the rapid development of confidence and skill. The odd mistake might be made en route but, provided you didn't make the same mistake twice, all was well.

I had imagined that I would continue to be employed on the Buccaneer force, and I did in fact spend a short period at RAF Honington after leaving Lossiemouth. However, the RAF with its mysterious ways had other plans for me and I was whipped away onto the Advanced Maintenance Engineering Course at Cranwell, never to work on a Buccaneer again. Perhaps it was a good thing. I would probably have made myself most unpopular with the comment "we would never have done it that way in the navy".

CHAPTER FOUR

LEADING THE FIELD

PETER GOODING

As the sweltering heat of the summer of 1969 enveloped the tribal North-West Frontier of Pakistan, I was at the Pakistan Air Force Academy at Risalpur coming towards the end of what I would now call my 'gap year' as an exchange instructor teaching Pakistanis, Iranians and Iraqis to fly; the year was a rich experience, but not all beer and skittles! This had followed a shortened first tour instructing on the Jet Provost at Syerston, Nottinghamshire, during which I recall being impressed by a display at Gaydon in atrocious weather when the only flying event in the gloom was a high-speed pass by a naval Buccaneer almost entirely enveloped in a cloud of condensation. Somewhat tongue-in-cheek, I had then asked for a posting to Buccaneers, despite my advanced flying training having been on the mighty Vickers Varsity. I was bowled over when a signal arrived with my posting to No. 3 RAF Course at HMS Fulmar, Lossiemouth, before joining 12 Squadron at Honington in Suffolk. Following the controversial decision that the RAF was to take over the maritime air defence and strike/attack roles from the Royal Navy, 12 Squadron, with its appropriate motto 'Leads the Field' and fox emblem, was to be the first RAF Buccaneer squadron, primarily in the maritime role, before other Buccaneer squadrons replaced the Canberras in the overland role in Germany.

After a long summer break and, for me, a vital and formative 25-hour speed-up course on the Hunter on 79 Squadron at Chivenor, I joined 736 NAS at Lossiemouth in the winter of 1969. The deal between the services was that the first nine RAF courses would fly the Mark 1 Buccaneers, converting to the Mark 2 at the end of the course. The Mark 1 had been superseded in the naval front line by the Mark 2 and would have gone out of service but for the RAF courses. I was lucky to be teamed up with Ron Forder, an experienced and very able Buccaneer navigator who had previously served on exchange with

Peter Gooding with his navigator Ron Forder.

the navy. His competence and advice certainly gave me greatly added value to our student sorties together.

The Mark 1 was underpowered, but a delight to fly at light weights, as long as the Gyron Junior engines behaved. My recollections of flying on the course are of having to line up pointing into wind for a crosswind take-off, opening the throttles very gently and monitoring that the variable inlet guide vanes opened, before releasing the brakes and steering quickly back to the centreline. Once the engines had spooled-up you hardly ever needed to throttle back until landing. On landing we never used full flap and droop in case an engine failed on finals or we needed to go around. Weaponry was the highlight of the course; the most exciting being what the navy termed 'divisional dive-bombing'. After running in as a pair in a fairly close arrow formation, the leader tipped in, putting both aircraft in a 20-degree dive. As wingman, you then had to put your strike sight on the target, avoid the leader, as you tended to converge in the dive, and then individually release the 28-lb practice bomb before pulling up together; a real 'John Wayne' attack. Overall, the course was professional and sharp, led by some of the best aviators and instructors in both dark and light blue. I did notice that whereas in an RAF squadron the odd chap had had a previous ejection, in the navy most in the crew room seemed to have ejected at some time! After a great experience in Scotland, I left well equipped to start front-line life at Honington. I have two amusing memories of 736. One was the stern welcome from the senior pilot, John Manley, who confusingly briefed us that one of our student duties was 'securing the coffee boat'. Then there was my chum Jon Ford arriving one morning having

Officers of 12 Squadron visit Holme-on-Spalding-Moor.
Peter Gooding is standing fifth from the right.

cycled from the wardroom in a blizzard, covered with snow down one side of his body, but bone dry on the other saying: "I hate this place!" Years later he was to become RAF Lossiemouth's station commander.

We of No. 3 Course arrived at Honington early in 1970 to join the eight previously trained crews, including the boss, Wg Cdr Geoff Davies, and executives Sqn Ldrs Ian Henderson and David Edwards, who formed the nucleus of the squadron. We then set about working up to be proficient in the maritime strike and attack roles (strike the term for nuclear) when the squadron was largely left to itself, since the RAF had not been involved in those roles since the days of the Beaufighter and Mosquito in World War Two. As well as flying, we had to learn recognition of ships of all nations, and as much as we could of naval tactics and ship defences. Strangely, none of the pilots had flown with the navy front line, but luckily four of the navigators; Peter Huett, Ron Forder, Andy Evans and Peter Bucke had all served on exchange appointments. For the nuclear role, we had the British WE177. Our conventional weapons consisted of 1,000-lb bombs, the BL755 cluster weapon, and SNEB and two-inch rockets. The aircraft were initially Mark S.2As, but S.2Bs (with the strengthened wing to carry Martel) progressively replaced these. To fool

The RAF recruiting notice featuring Peter Gooding.

the Soviets, the weapons ranges had to pass the scores for simulated nuclear deliveries in code, but, for the identical releases simulating conventional weapons, scores were all passed in clear. We often wondered who devised these procedures.

We always welcomed the operations wing staff to fly with us when Wg Cdr Roy Watson (OC Ops) and his small team were frequent visitors. On one occasion we were short of 28-lb practice bombs, and Geoff Davies, the boss, had said there were none spare for Roy Watson's aircraft. Roy subsequently arrived at the squadron carrying a bomb under each arm – which he gave the armourers to load on to his aircraft. With his inimitable 'deadly eye', I am sure he scored direct hits with both.

The squadron was in No. 1 Bomber Group, which otherwise consisted entirely of the V-Force. The HQ initially managed its Buccaneers as if they were mini V-bombers. As an example, we had to transmit an 'Ops normal' call to 1 Group on HF every 30 minutes on all sorties. This proved totally impractical owing to the high intensity of our sorties, and the limitations of HF at the distances and heights that we predominantly flew. One staff officer who came to fly with us even suggested that it might be a good idea to equip the navigators with a telescope to aid ship recognition. Eventually 1 Group came round to the idea that the Buccaneer was more a maxi Hunter than a mini Vulcan.

Our day-to-day sorties were largely low-level formations over the sea to Scotland or across to Wales, with practice weaponry on coastal ranges or splash targets towed behind warships. Most sorties included strike progression with a bounce aircraft. Based at Honington, being far from ideally placed for naval exercise areas, either ours or those of the Soviets, we often used air-to-air refuelling (AAR) or deployed to forward operating bases to practise our maritime tactics.

With the aircraft being the latest to enter RAF service, the squadron inevitably attracted publicity. Ron Forder and I featured in several recruiting advertisements, one proudly stating that, as a 26-year-old pilot and instructor, I earned £2,793 a YEAR. Sadly, the young engineer only earned £1,953. That venture did earn us a few drinks in the Bell at Thetford with the production crew. Another press photo featured David Scouller and Peter Huett in front of an impressive array of weapons.

Quite early in the squadron's life we were detached to Malta for Exercise Lime Jug. Most of the RAF seemed to be there for this major event. I well remember the 'Ian Henderson

*A mixed formation of 12 Squadron Buccaneers and
43 Squadron Phantoms during Exercise Lime Jug in Malta.*

departure' from Luqa, putting on 120 degrees of bank and disappearing over the cliff just after take-off. Ian was the squadron display pilot, and throughout the life of the Buccaneer I never saw anyone display the aircraft better. There was one memorable occasion when I was duty aircrew officer. The cloud base was significantly below 500 feet, and Ian displayed for some visiting dignitary at Honington, the aircraft looking like a ball of condensation in the humid air with the nose sticking out in front. I must confess to holding my breath at times, but I wondered what was going through the mind of the station commander, John Herrington, who was standing right beside me in the tower, or of Doug Wilson, Ian's back-seater.

Detachments came thick and fast. We were regular visitors to Lossiemouth, for naval exercises, to Malta, Cyprus, and Ørland near Trondheim in Norway, which was a designated forward operating base. From Ørland, we had an exciting time stalking Danish fast patrol boats at night around the Danish islands, and encountering off north Norway the Soviet warships, about which we had learnt so much during our intelligence briefings. To identify and attack warships at night, we used the Lepus illuminating flare. This we tossed upwards, and it lit a large amount of ocean for a following Buccaneer to identify the target and make a visual attack. After a rapid change of weapon switches, during the tricky recovery manoeuvre after tossing the flare, the Lepus aircraft carried out a dive attack. This was some challenge to both instrument flying and weapon aiming. On one occasion, the Lepus burst into life, surprising an innocent merchantman going about its business. On returning from the far north on long night sorties out of Lossiemouth, often with a Victor tanker, it was comforting to pick up the Saxa Vord TACAN beacon at about 150 miles. On one such night, over solid white moonlit cloud, with the dark sky above, I remember a few seconds' illusion of flying upside down, being naturally used to light above and darkness below.

On one sortie, flying behind a Victor midway between Lossie and Stavanger, my wingman, Al Beaton, was withdrawing from the refuelling hose when the whole hose detached from the tanker and wrapped itself over his cockpit with the end thrashing around the tailplane. We turned for Lossiemouth, and experimenting with speed and flap settings, made the end stop its flailing. An ejection through the hose would not have been attractive!

On a visit to Goose Bay in Canada to evaluate the area for training, I flew with my new flight commander, Dan Needham, with Jon Ford and Andy Evans as the second crew. After a few drinks in the bar with the captain of a Canadian frigate that was due to sail north up the Labrador coast, we agreed to exercise our maritime role by 'meeting' a few days later; we did eventually find and 'attack' the ship, followed by the inevitable flypast, but we learnt why it was painted an almost duck-egg blue to make it blend with the similar-coloured icebergs scattered across the sea, and which looked the same as the ship on radar. The overland survival briefing at Goose if forced to eject in August was, "take your life raft, walk downhill when you will find a lake; get in your 'boat', and paddle to the middle – then you will not be eaten by the midges!"

The highlight of the first two years was undoubtedly what was intended to be the first of a series of annual detachments to Singapore to demonstrate Britain's commitment to the South East Asia Treaty Organisation (SEATO). Unfortunately, a change of government brought a change of policy, and the only detachment was in 1972. Four Buccaneers, with Victor tanker support, staged through Akrotiri, Masirah and Gan to operate from RAF Tengah for almost a month. Tengah was one of the 'crossroads' of air forces, and we added to the much-decorated officers' mess bar, with paintings of Buccaneers skimming along at skirting board level. The flying, by then with John Beard as my navigator, was largely theatre familiarisation over Malaysia, with weaponry at Song-Song Range off the coast, a mini-detachment to Hong Kong, and learning to avoid the thunderstorms – most spectacular at night. Off duty, Bert Neo, our Singaporean junior engineer officer, conducted us round the sights of downtown Singapore in his VW Beetle, and our operations officer, Benny Baronowski, an old Far East hand, introduced us to delicious street food. The Far East detachment was the swansong for the 'boss', Geoff Davies.

For some reason, Geoff's designated successor from the OCU course did not arrive, and the charismatic and energetic Wg Cdr Nigel Walpole had been raced through his OCU course, along with his competent young back-seater, Peter Rolfe, to take over the squadron in April 1972. With his fighter-recce background, Nigel quickly mastered the Buccaneer and almost immediately led the squadron to Gioia del Colle in southern Italy for an incident-packed NATO maritime exercise. On one pair's sortie against an 'enemy' frigate, the target presented a stern view, making it difficult to identify as we ran into the briefed position. Had it been for real, and the attack pressed home, we would have ended up with a 'blue-on-blue' incident; the debriefing was interesting. In those days, real-time intelligence of ship movements was usually non-existent, so in the intervening hours since crews had been briefed, the 'target' could be miles from the expected position. This incident highlighted the importance of cooperating with maritime patrol aircraft and other friendly forces, and the need for timely communications in the air.

The Gioia detachment was marked by uncharacteristically violent weather. One night I was duty ops officer when a violent thunderstorm hit the base just as our last aircraft were recovering. Our ATC officer, David Taylor, called to say that the control tower had been struck by lightning, and all the Italian controllers had abandoned it – he was the only one left. A loud crash in the background emphasised the point. On another occasion, four aircraft were recovering at night when No. 2 took the RHAG. Peter Warren and Don Thomas had to divert to Brindisi, where their arrival, below diversion fuel, and in a raging crosswind, was described as 'exciting'. In another unusual incident, Graham Pitchfork (he was standing in for 'Sparky' Powell who had broken his leg playing in a football match against the ground crew) received a significant shock having been struck by lightning in the rear cockpit. I experienced a windscreen fire and cracking caused by an electrical short from water ingress to the heating element.

On a lighter note, we were almost the only occupants of the Italian officers' mess. When the first one or two of us entered the dining room for dinner, a pitcher of local red wine was brought to our large table, enough for the eight or so set places. We found however, that if the next couple, instead of joining us, sat at a different table, they also gained a pitcher of wine, and so on as we spread out across the dining room. I think the staff soon rumbled our ploy! We also took the opportunity to visit nearby Taranto to study in awe the site of the famous Fleet Air Arm Swordfish attack of 1940.

Sadly, the first three years of RAF Buccaneer service on 12 Squadron were marred by three flying accidents. The wing weapons officer, Jock Gilroy, and his navigator Tom Willbourne were killed when their aircraft crashed into the Irish Sea as they left the weapons range at Jurby. Andy Marrs and Bob Kemp ejected safely after encountering difficulties behind a Victor tanker while holding over France before a flypast at the Paris Air Show. In 1972 George Vipond, a USAF exchange officer, and his young RAF navigator, Derek Walmsley, were killed when their aircraft flew into a totally calm sea on a formation descent to low level in 'goldfish-bowl' conditions of poor visibility and low cloud, perhaps looking for their formation leader who had levelled off. Not an accident, but John Beard and I struck a dense flock of seagulls on the run in to Wainfleet Range for a toss attack at 550 knots and 200 feet. The noise was incredible as the canopy shattered. Both engines' compressor blades were damaged and the leading edges of the wings were dented. Thanks to the rear cockpit blast screen, John was uninjured although covered in bird debris. Thankfully the windscreen was intact and the engines kept going to allow a safe landing.

By the end of 1972 a significant change had taken place on the squadron as a number left on posting or, as I did, to join 237 OCU as it built up its strength in the adjacent hangar at Honington to train replacements, new crews for the two RAF Germany squadrons forming at Laarbruch, and the recently introduced weapons instructor courses. Ian Henderson, an original flight commander, returned later as a wing commander to command 12 Squadron.

On reflection, I felt that we had certainly 'got the show on the road' in the first two years. Before long, coordination with the Nimrod force, and other international assets, enabled accurate, timely intelligence on maritime targets, making large coordinated attacks from different directions more routine and effective, especially with the introduction of Martel anti-ship missiles, and later the more advanced Sea Eagle missile.

My tour on 12 Squadron was a tremendous introduction to the excitement of flying and operating the Buccaneer. It was followed by two more tours on the aircraft: first as an instructor on the OCU, and then as a flight commander on 16 Squadron in Germany. All this was a marvellous background for later, when I was privileged to take command of IX Squadron, the first Tornado GR 1 Squadron, and a welcome return to Honington and Suffolk.

CHAPTER FIVE
AN RAF PILOT AT SEA

PETER STURT

Peter Sturt, at the bottom of the ladder, with his observer Peter King.

I left RAF Khormaksar in Aden in September 1963 following an exhilarating first flying tour as a very junior pilot on the Hunter FGA9, and I was posted to RAF Chivenor as a tactical instructor. Shortly after my arrival, I was selected to be one of the station's aerobatic display pilots (we had three in those days – to allow for sickness etc.).

So, after a year quietly enjoying myself flying displays in the Hunter, as well as carrying out tactical instruction for newcomers to the aircraft, I had a call from the officers' posting desk at RAF Adastral House in London. I was summoned with two of my Hunter colleagues to 'discuss' being a volunteer for Buccaneer flying with the Royal Navy. I was not too keen on this idea since I was thoroughly enjoying my tour at Chivenor, especially the aerobatic display flying, and had no wish to spend two or three years flying off an aircraft carrier bobbing about on the oceans.

So, the three of us went for the interview – Cliff, Jock and myself. Jock was the only true volunteer whereas Cliff and I knew nothing about the Royal Navy other than it involved taking us away from a very happy existence flying the 'queen of the skies' and fighting off the delights of life in sunny Devon.

Cliff came up with some cock-and-bull story about getting married or something. He persuaded one of his girlfriends to corroborate this tale, in return for a free dinner, if some senior officer from the Air Ministry rang her to check. We never did find out whether this lady got her free dinner! Jock spent his interview standing to attention trying to explain why he should be selected when all he had on his records were details of a misspent youth, including riding a donkey into the officers' mess at RAF Bahrain, and generally acting in what was perceived to be an unfit manner for any young man about to represent the RAF

Buccaneer S.2 of 809 Squadron lands on HMS Hermes *with a Wessex plane guard standing by.*

and fly with the Fleet Air Arm. We all thought he would have been an ideal rep for the RAF – certainly would have raised the tone! As I wasn't quick-witted enough to think up an excuse for declining the offer, I was obviously thought to be an ideal candidate and I was 'selected'. In the event, what a jolly good time I was to have.

I started my conversion to the Buccaneer in December 1966 at RNAS Lossiemouth. My first recollection is of trying to loop the Mark 1 on one of my early general handling conversion sorties. No one had told me this was not a good idea – it was also illegal. The mule-like kicking and banging of the stalled engines as I tried to recover from an unusual position pointing into space, gave me an early lesson that this was a machine that required a lot more respect and tender loving care than the Hunter I had previously been throwing around the skies.

In March 1967, I joined 809 Squadron disembarked at RAF Hal Far in Malta. I had never seen the deck of an aircraft carrier, not even the one marked out at RAE Bedford, and they had sent me to the smallest carrier in the world, HMS *Hermes*.

My squadron commander, Lt Cdr Lyn Middleton, gave me my deck-landing brief in Ronnie's Bar at Hal Far. This was the shortest, and most succinct, brief of my whole flying career. He cleared the locals off the dartboard, drew a deck and the circuit flying pattern on the blackboard and, in his inimitable Yarpie accent, spent the next two minutes telling me how to deck land a Buccaneer. Any questions? By this time, I was backed up against

809 Squadron. Lt Cdr Lyn Middleton seated in the centre.

the wall with his nose about two inches away from mine – I don't think he liked 'crabs' (naval slang for RAF personnel) very much. He must have thought that I had understood the brief because he then said that if I did what he had briefed my first deck landing would be my best, and the third, if I survived it, would be my worst. I stuck to his brief and his predictions were absolutely accurate – I survived the third landing, but only after having gouged a chunk out of the round-down with the hook – I had landed a bit short rather than the ideal of halfway down the deck to catch the No. 3 arrestor cable. After landing, Commander Air, known as 'Wings', grabbed me by the collar, marched me down the deck on his peg leg (the result, I think, of a naval flying accident), and showed me the error of my ways, and how easily overconfidence can creep in after only two sorties.

Being a small aircraft carrier, *Hermes* only had four arrestor cables (wires). If one caught the fourth on landing it was quite safe, but the cable held the arrestor hook so that the nosewheel, which was aft of the cockpit, ended up just a few feet short of the end of the angled deck. From the cockpit all you could see was the sea rushing by underneath you – a bit disconcerting the first time you ever did this. The other thing that was totally new to me was the landing. To be successful, the aim was to fly/crash the aircraft, from a four-degree angle of approach slope, straight on to the deck with no flare or round out as was normal for airfield landings. The Buccaneer was built robustly enough to withstand this harsh treatment.

Whilst all this was going on, some of the officers, and a few of the wives who were *Hermes* camp followers, were watching the aircraft land-on from the safety of Hal Far, commented that there was some chap trying to land on for the first time. It might be fun to see how he got on and whether he would make it in one piece, especially since he was light blue and had never seen a deck before. My new bride of just two weeks, Angela, was standing behind this group, chipped in and said that the raw recruit was me. The conversation suddenly became more encouraging.

809 Squadron Buccaneers fly over Crater in Aden in 1967.

My observer for most of my flying on 809 Squadron was Peter King. The Royal Navy had a custom that everyone on board should have a 'cobber'. A cobber would then be responsible for ensuring in the event of any major ship emergency, such as a fire, that he would seek out his other half to ensure their joint safety. It was a fairly obvious choice in a Buccaneer to have the crew as joint cobbers. Pete and I were thus joint cobbers, and this friendship has endured for many years, and well after our respective retirements.

On board, I found the wardroom rules interesting. On my first evening, it took one or two HNs (horses' necks – brandy and ginger) to discover that I had unwittingly been drinking triple strength. The old hands were ordering *one-third* HN, gin or whisky at a time. Treating friends to a drink was not allowed since the commander (the ship's senior administrative officer) had no way of determining from an individual's bar bill how much he had been drinking that month. The custom at sea was thus to ask friends what they wanted to drink, together with their bar number. Armed with half a dozen bar numbers, you gave them to the barman in return for the drinks, which you then carried back to your friends. The drinks were then added to the individual's bar bill. This custom rather fell apart when going for a run ashore.

Hermes was a happy ship. 809 was only a small squadron with some seven aircraft and eight crews. We hung around the Mediterranean, whilst Greece was kicking out its monarchy, and then held north of the Suez Canal, before departing for Aden where we were to meet *Victorious* to take over the east of Suez carrier commitment.

On a brief run ashore to my old stamping grounds, and in preparation for my forth-coming C Promotion exam, I managed to scrounge some 20-odd books and manuals from the publications store at RAF Khormaksar who were only too pleased to get rid of them as the station was winding down rapidly – I soon discovered why since I got them with a shed load of amendments. I subsequently took the exam on board in a force eight gale.

As background to the next phase of my time on *Hermes*, a brief bit of history of the region and the build-up to the British withdrawal from Aden might be appropriate. In January 1963, in response to growing nationalist unrest in the region, the British persuaded the sheikhdoms of the Aden Protectorates to merge with the Colony of Aden and form the Federation of South Arabia (FSA).

Inspired by President Nasser of Egypt, Arab nationalists had formed the National Liberation Front (NLF) in Yemen, which itself had designs on Aden and its surrounding territories. As the NLF escalated their attacks, a second nationalist group, the Front for the Liberation of Occupied South Yemen (FLOSY), also began terrorist activities against the security forces.

In February 1966 Britain announced that the Aden bases would not be retained after independence was gained in 1968. Few locals in Aden believed that the existing FSA government would survive without British support, and were therefore wary of being seen to support it.

The locally raised Federal Regular Army (FRA) and the Federal National Guard (FNG) defended Aden. The two were later merged into a single force, the South Arabian Army (SAA). Owing to heavy infiltration by the insurgents, Britain increasingly distrusted these forces. In June 1967, joined by the police, who had also been badly infiltrated, the SAA mutinied and attacked the British, forcing a temporary withdrawal from the Crater area of Aden. Britain realised that its presence in Aden would end sooner rather than later.

The prelude to withdrawal from Aden resulted in a memorable sortie on May 17 1967, a gigantic mass flypast to impress the locals of the might of British power. We joined forces with *Victorious*, which was now on the way home, and flew past Khormaksar with a mix-ture of Buccaneers, Sea Vixens and resident Hunters – some 55 aircraft. The flypast was nearly a disaster when the lead Sea Vixen crew from *Victorious*, who probably had never led anything larger than a four-ship, thought that we were 30 seconds early and, with little warning, slowed down from 350 kts to 300 kts. The cumulative effect on the formations, especially at the back end, was interesting to say the least. We eventually all got back, sort of together, as we overflew Khormaksar.

After a period flying off Aden, *Hermes* headed for the Far East in June 1967 when 809 disembarked to Changi for a month. However, we were soon heading back to Aden.

By June 1967, British forces had lost control and, though British troops re-occupied the Crater, the insurgents intensified their attacks. The Federal government collapsed in September 1967 and was replaced by a Marxist regime. With civilian government gone, a massive task force (Task Force 945) was assembled in the Gulf of Aden for the final British withdrawal. This task force included Sea Vixen and Buccaneer-equipped aircraft carriers

Hermes and *Eagle*, commando carriers, several destroyers, frigates and a submarine. As the November 1967 date for the withdrawal approached, the NLF and FLOSY began fighting each other for control of Aden, with the NLF gaining the upper hand. Following negotiations with nationalist groups over Britain's withdrawal, the remaining 3,500 men of the British garrison were evacuated in the last week of November 1967.

We then invited all the local dignitaries and dissident Arabs on board both carriers to view a firepower demonstration, with the Sea Vixens firing two-inch rockets as they carried out fast and low runs past the ship, and everyone beating s**t out of the splash target (towed some 600–800 yards behind the ship) with every bit of HE (high explosive) we could fire or drop. With the withdrawal from Aden successfully completed, *Hermes* headed back to the Far East.

One of the standard operating procedures on landing a Buccaneer was to open the bomb bay before the engines were shut down to allow the engineers to do the necessary servicing of the bomb bay. It was not the first time, and certainly not the last, when this procedure did not always go to plan. Al, one of our junior pilots, on re-embarking from Butterworth near Penang, where he had been joined by his wife, forgot that he had all her dhobi in the bomb bay as he landed on … Yes, you can guess what happened when an over-filled pusser's grip hit the deck assisted by 35 knots of wind. The sailors had great fun chasing all her smalls across the deck. He never did succeed in convincing them that they were his wife's and not his.

Splash target bombing had its fun moments, especially when we tried to persuade the captain that we wanted to loft bomb the splash target by locking on to *his* ship to resolve the range solution, and fudge the target course and speed to solve the azimuth problem. It took two months to convince him that we were not totally mad, especially when we guaranteed that we could never hit the ship because we would only release the bombs if we were pointing aft of it on the run in. It took another month of successful attacks with practice bombs before he very reluctantly let us loose with some inert 1,000-lb bombs. He balked at high explosives for some unaccountable reason!

On our way home from Hong Kong, via a week's stopover at Fremantle, and another in Cape Town, I could not understand why I had so many moths in my cabin. After a week or so, when the daily numbers I killed had steadily increased from the one or two a day to dozens a day, I tracked the source to a sack of nuts I had bought in HK. When I opened up the sack and was greeted by a great cloud of the wretched things, I ditched the whole lot overboard one dark night. This was done with some trepidation since I wondered whether I might have transgressed some regulation, and hoped that the great splash that the sack made when I ditched it did not excite some vigilant sailor into 'man-overboard' action. Why did I have a large sack of nuts on board? I have no idea, but I suppose it seemed like a good idea at the time with some of the other 'rabbits' I had bought ashore in Hong Kong.

I served under three captains during my time with *Hermes*, and obviously trained them very well because two of them, the then Captains Fieldhouse and Lewin, had benefited so much from exposure to our RAF influence on board, that this broadening of their experience enabled them to each become Chief of the Defence Staff.

After some 25,000 miles of sailing, 100 plus launches and arrested deck landings (DLs) – nine at night (none of us enjoyed night DLs, partly because we never got enough practice, and who in their right mind really wants to put their trust in the mirror landing sight, and a fishtail of three red lights over the stern to assist with line up, in a totally blacked-out ship) – we disembarked at Lossie when we worked up for the 1968 aerobatic display season.

Yours truly, with his previous Hunter display experience, was the one and only obvious choice to do the solo display. It took a little time for their Lordships to accept a 'crab' as the navy's aerobatic display pilot for that year. In fact, the problem was not with them, but with a certain captain at Lossie who just found the idea too hard to stomach – I don't know why – I was quite happy to fly and expose FLY NAVY on the inside of my bomb-bay door. Few people could see it anyway. Their Lordships won – well they would, wouldn't they – and we all had a very good season with me also slotting in as number two in 'Arthur's Five' formation display team. We did displays at Lossiemouth, RNAS Yeovilton, RAF Biggin Hill and took part in Princess Anne's birthday flypast.

Our grand finale was a synchronized, and joint effort with 'Simon's Sircus' of Sea Vixens at Farnborough 1968 – slightly marred by a Bréguet Atlantic spearing in on short finals on one of the days as we were running in. In the 'show must go on' attitude, we were detailed to continue the display through the funeral pyre of black smoke – probably wouldn't happen like that today.

I finished my two-year tour with the Fleet Air Arm with 600 hours of superb flying. I dropped or fired more weaponry in those two years than in any comparable time on any RAF squadron – the navy hated disembarking live weapons at the end of a commission. We had sailed through the Med and the Suez Canal, to the Gulf of Aden, a short detour into the Persian Gulf, and thence to the Far East, Singapore and Hong Kong. A week in Fremantle/Perth was followed by a return to the Indian Ocean and the African coast for two months before finally heading for home for Christmas via Cape Town.

Peter Sturt flies as No. 2 in 'Arthur's Five'.

I have only happy memories of my time on *Hermes* and with the Buccaneer. Like most other Buccaneer aircrew I am sure, I would do it all over again. I was reunited with the aircraft again some 10 years later when 216 Squadron reformed at Honington, but that is another story …

CHAPTER SIX

BUCCANEERS OVER GERMANY

DAVID RAY

The RAF needed the Buccaneer in the overland role to take over from the ageing Canberra on the cold war front line in Germany using both nuclear and conventional weapons. XV Squadron was the second RAF Buccaneer squadron to form, and the first exclusively in the overland role. It re-formed as a Buccaneer squadron at RAF Honington in September 1970 and deployed to RAF Laarbruch in January 1971. Vaughan Morris and I joined the squadron at Honington in December 1970 and were the first 'first-tourist' crew on the squadron. We were also in at the very beginning of the squadron's time in Germany as number 4 in the first formation to deploy to Laarbruch.

The relative proximity (in flying terms) of the front line of the Inner-German Border meant that all our war missions would have been flown at low level, and that is how we trained whenever possible. In the early days Germany had a low-flying system similar to that in the UK. There were a number of low-flying areas joined by one-way link routes, and we could fly down to 250 feet in that system. Elsewhere, apart from various prohibited areas, we could fly down to 500 feet. The ceiling of this system was 1,500 feet above which we were required to have some kind of radar service. The NATO air forces in the region all had fast jets operating at low level, so the low-level airspace was busy, particularly in good weather – good look out was essential.

Of course, weather was always a factor in our operations and every day started with a daily operations brief in the wing operations centre. The first item in the brief was the met forecast for the day, which was usually very comprehensive taking several minutes. However, I remember one met brief when the met man stood up to give his brief, said 'fog', and sat down again. The station commander, obviously somewhat taken aback by

XV Squadron Buccaneers in 1972 in the early camouflage scheme.

the brevity of this, asked the met man to expand on his forecast, whereupon the met man stood up again and said 'thick fog' and sat down. He was spot on – no one flew that day.

Our flying was mostly carried out visually at low level. Our 'official' weather limits were a 1,500-foot cloud base and five kilometres visibility, but in practice we flew around at low level in worse weather than this and others did too – lookout was doubly important and we would quite often pick up another aircraft passing close with only a few seconds warning. When weather precluded low flying in Germany, we would often fly high-low-high sorties to the UK to use the low-flying system and air-to-ground weapons ranges there.

A lot of our low flying was carried out in tactical formations of two or four aircraft training for our 'attack' role with conventional weapons, while singleton sorties usually focused on our 'strike' role with nuclear weapons. Most sorties included dropping practice weapons at one of the air weapons ranges, most often Nordhorn Range in Germany and Vliehors Range on the Dutch coast. The 4-lb practice bomb, which was used to simulate either the 1,000-lb bomb fitted with a 'retard' parachute tail or the BL755 cluster bomb, both delivered from a level 'laydown' attack from 200 feet, or from a shallow dive attack. The 28-lb practice bomb was used to simulate either the 1,000-lb bomb or a nuclear weapon delivered in a 'toss' attack – pulling up from low level, releasing the bomb towards the target in a climb before turning away and diving back to escape at low level. We also had rockets, initially two-inch but later SNEB. These were obviously more expensive than the smaller 'dumb' practice bombs and we didn't get to fire them very often, and then usually single rockets out of the rocket 'pod' which could carry up to 19. Very rarely we would get the opportunity to fire a half or full pod as we would have used in anger.

On one occasion, we flew as number 2 in a formation to Vliehors Range to fire a half pod, which we hadn't done before. For this exercise we flew a pattern around the range at 2,000 feet from which we 'tipped in' to a ten-degree dive towards the target firing the rockets at a set height, hopefully with the aiming mark in the pilot's strike sight on the target. The weather was marginal with broken cloud in the range area. We flew several patterns, but each time we failed to see the target at the tip-in point due to the cloud. Our range time was coming to an end, and we really wanted to fire off the rockets so we flew a final pattern, commenced the dive, picked up the target and got the sight on late, and fired lower than we should. We picked up a ricochet on the windscreen for our trouble, and a one-sided interview with the boss (one of several).

Night flying was an essential part of our training when we would often fly night routes at safety height with the navigators using the aircraft's Blue Parrot radar, optimised for use over the sea to find ships, but modified to give it a somewhat limited overland capability. These routes would usually include a 'target' and a simulated weapon release, which was scored by a radar bomb scoring unit. The heights at which we flew would have made us very vulnerable to enemy defensive systems, and our 'scores' did not give the crews much faith that we had a realistic overland night capability!

As very much the junior crew, at least during our first few months on the squadron, Vaughan and I got a number of tasks, which other crews shied away from. One of these was the requirement to practise quick reaction alert (QRA) procedures: the squadron had to prove that it was ready to take on the nuclear QRA role from 16 Squadron Canberras, which had the task until they were re-equipped with Buccaneers. Part of the task was to demonstrate that the strike crews on the squadron could deliver a practice bomb on target and on time, within certain parameters. Another part was demonstrating that we could launch the aircraft from the guarded QRA site quickly should the need arise, carrying out all the necessary procedures to ensure that the launch had been correctly authorised. This needed a crew to go into the QRA site for an extended period and respond to any alert. A 'hooter' initiated the alert whereupon all the air and ground crews would rush out from the crew building to their aircraft, strap in with the electrics connected and listen for instructions from the operations controller. Invariably, the Canberra crews would be stood down, but we might get the order to launch (if we had no weapon loaded), when we would start engines, the QRA site gate would be opened, and we would taxi out and take off for a practice sortie. From the hooter sounding we were able to take off in about four minutes. To achieve this the aircraft was specially prepared – we had checked and signed the aircraft documentation, carried out the external checks on the aircraft, and pre-set the cockpit switches in accordance with a special check list, and no one else had access to the aircraft thereafter.

The station had a royal visit by HRH the Duke of Edinburgh and this included a visit to the QRA site. All the grass was cut for the visit, but, as usual, the station had not paid the extra to have the cuttings collected up (mistake number one!). We were in QRA for the visit to carry out a demonstration Buccaneer scramble. At this point it is important for the uninitiated reader to understand a little about the Buccaneer engine-start system – there is no internal self-start capability, and an external piece of equipment with a small jet engine (Palouste) is needed to be connected to each engine to run it up to a speed (RPM) at which it becomes self-sustaining, signalled by the pilot giving a 'thumbs up' to the ground crew. In QRA to save time we had a special Palouste with twin hoses, one connected to each engine, so all the ground crew had to do was to switch the output from one hose to the other after the first engine had been started. So, at the appointed hour, HRH arrived at the QRA compound with his entourage, and the hooter sounded as they arrived.

All the crews rushed out and strapped in, we got the message to start and take off for our practice mission, and the Canberra crews were stood down. We gave the start signal to the ground crew, started the port engine successfully, but the ground crew in their enthusiasm for a quick launch disconnected the Palouste from the starboard engine before my thumbs up, and just before self-sustaining RPM had been reached (mistake number two!). Not surprisingly, the engine stagnated and then started to run down. A quick decision was needed in between the expletives from the front cockpit – get the ground crew to reconnect the now-disconnected Palouste and re-start the starboard engine with a significant and unimpressive delay to our launch time, or taxi out on one engine and roar off down the runway on one engine, followed by the inevitable abort. I chose the latter (mistake number three!).

Of course, taxiing the Buccaneer on two engines doesn't need much power, but it's a different story on just one engine. So when we taxied out with the port engine at quite high power and turned left onto the Laarbruch northern taxiway we blew freshly cut grass over the whole royal entourage! When we inevitably aborted well down the runway and out of sight of the royal party, air traffic control asked us the reason for the abort – I said we would phone them. Of course that little episode led to another one-sided discussion in the boss's office.

HQ RAF Germany organised an annual competition between the strike/attack squadrons in the Command for the Salmond Trophy. This comprised each squadron entering a set number of crews for the competition, each of whom normally flew two competition sorties, which included a timed overflight of a simulated target (normally a fairly small visual feature), and a timed and scored weapon delivery at Nordhorn Range. This competition generated great rivalry between the squadrons, and there was considerable pressure on every crew to produce good results on the day. There was also pressure on the organisers to make the competition happen. Thus, there was a planned day for the competition and two reserve days. I remember one year when the weather on both the primary and first reserve days was unfit, and it was little better on the second reserve day, but the competition went ahead, albeit with just one sortie per crew. We had completed our timed simulated attack, and just as we left Nordhorn Range after our timed weapon delivery, we were told to divert to the nearby German air force base at Hopsten as the weather at Laarbruch had deteriorated below limits. So, all the competition crews from both Buccaneer squadrons ended up at Hopsten for an unplanned overnight stay. There had been no flying at Hopsten that day due to the weather, so all the base crews were in the officers' mess consuming

XV Squadron formation seen from the No. 4 box position.

large quantities of beer; we were all invited to join them. All I remember about the flight home the following day was that the weather was again marginal, the boss had asked us to fly a two-hour sortie as the squadron was behind on flying hours that month, but we flew straight back for a radar-controlled approach to land after just 20 minutes, and nursing some rather sore heads!

There was a Buccaneer simulator at Laarbruch and crews were supposed to undertake simulator training on a regular basis. This simulator was pretty old technology – it didn't feel like the aircraft and had very limited 'visual' capability. Indeed the visual comprised a physical model of a fairly limited area of terrain complete with airfields, houses, trees, etc. over which you could 'fly' a CCTV camera. The simulator instructors could be quite touchy about crews 'flying' too low over their model trying to hit something with the camera, breaking something either on the model or the camera. The simulator was quite useful as an emergencies and procedures trainer, but crews didn't really look forward to their simulator training slots. One exception perhaps was the 'wacky' races run in the slots prior to Christmas when there was a prize for the crew that flew the fastest time from brakes off at Laarbruch to a successful touchdown at the airfield on the visual (one of the Danish bases, I think). I remember using all sorts of wheezes to get the best time, like reducing drag on take-off by only selecting flap just before lift-off, and only reducing from high speed at the last minute before selecting the landing configuration. However, we never even got in the running because the visual never caught up with us, so we were unable to make a visual landing which was a competition requirement.

*

My second tour in RAF Germany was as weapons leader on XV Squadron again, when the highlight had to be our inclusion in the first RAF participation in Exercise Red Flag and the associated work-up training. The aim of the exercise was to simulate as realistically as possible operational combat missions, thereby giving Red Flag-trained crews the edge if they ever went into combat for real. Thus in the exercise area we would be permitted to fly down to 100 feet, with every sortie including fighter opposition, live weapon delivery against realistic targets, and a range of electronic warfare challenges, all this in hot temperatures and over terrain that was mostly about 4,500 feet above sea level, with the consequent adverse impact on aircraft performance.

Clearly this was a step up from our routine training which was normally at 250 or 500 feet, and only occasionally with fighter opposition. We therefore devised a package of work-up training focussed on 100 feet low flying: this meant that most of the training was flown in the UK where there were some special low-flying areas in sparsely-populated regions where flight down to 100 feet was permitted. We deployed for short detachment, usually to bases in Scotland fairly close to the 100 feet training areas, and where RAF Leuchars-based Phantoms were usually pleased to provide us with fighter opposition. We also flew a few sorties over the Hardanger Plateau in Norway, which gave us experience of ultra-low flying. All three overland Buccaneer squadrons took part in the Red Flag (208 Squadron from Honington, and XV and 16 Squadrons from Laarbruch) and their capability drew much praise from other participants, very few of whom operated at the heights we flew at. Undoubtedly participation in this exercise was very positive, and a great spur to refinement of our tactics and seeking realistic training at every opportunity.

Of course there is much more I could write about: the regular deployments to Decimomannu in Sardinia for armament practice camps where we flew several short sorties each day on the range at Capo Frasca to hone our weapon delivery skills; the squadron exchanges with other NATO air forces which were a nice mix of flying together and learning from each other in the air and social interaction on the ground; the ranger flights to land away from base and spend the weekend somewhere different; the regular 24-hour periods of duty in QRA; and of course just the whole experience of living and working in Germany, the camaraderie of squadron life, the parties in the mess, and learning to cope with duty-free fuel and booze!

Later, after the Buccaneer had handed over the strike/attack role in RAF Germany to the Tornado in 1984, 237 OCU, the Buccaneer training squadron, then based at RAF Lossiemouth in Scotland, had a war role in Germany. This was using the aircraft's Pave Spike laser designation pod to mark targets for laser-guided bombs (LGBs) delivered by RAF Germany Tornados and Royal Netherlands Air Force F-16s. Because of the inherent co-operation required for these laser-guided bomb deliveries, it was important for both the designators and the bombers to practise together. Therefore, unlike the war roles of some other training units, 237 OCU needed to practise this war role with the relevant 'bomber' units on a regular basis. In my time commanding 237 OCU (1987–1989) we

A 237 OCU Buccaneer with Pave Spike pod,
leads two Sea Harriers of 899 Squadron armed with Paveway 1,000-lb bombs.

sent detachments of two aircraft to RAF Laarbruch to work with the Tornado squadrons, and also flew occasionally with them in the UK. We also used the squadron exchange programme to good effect when we had an exchange with 315 Squadron RNethAF F-16s which offered mutual laser designation training both when we deployed to their base at Twente in the Netherlands, and when they came on the return visit to Lossiemouth.

The training sorties were mostly flown at low level, with the 'bombers' in a lead tactical formation with two Buccaneers in tactical formation behind. The bombers would simulate tossing their LGBs towards the target, which the Buccaneer designators would then acquire visually and designate with their laser pods at the appropriate time to guide the LGBs to their targets. The Pave Spike system had an audio/video recording feature, which proved to be a superb debriefing aid. This training proved to be particularly valuable when the Buccaneer was subsequently called upon to designate for RAF Tornados in the Gulf War in 1990–91, albeit all the LGBs in that conflict were delivered, and designated from high level.

With the effective demise of the 237 OCU war role in 1990, Buccaneers weren't spotted over Germany again, but they had been seen in German skies for nearly two decades, and many of those air and ground crews who had been privileged to fly and service this fine aircraft had done so in RAF Germany on at least one tour.

CHAPTER SEVEN

THREE HECTIC WEEKS ON 12 SQUADRON

Andy Marrs with the individual Gilroy Trophy.

ANDY MARRS

Incident at Karup

In May 1971, 12 Squadron was detached to Ørland in Norway for Exercise Evil Edge. We were to attack fast patrol boats (FPB) off the coast of Jutland as a four-ship before landing at RDAF Karup where 849 Naval Air Squadron (equipped with Gannets) was detached; their ground crew would turn us round. Then we would form two pairs and attack the FPBs under Lepus flares before recovering to Ørland.

'Dutch' Holland and I had done this three times between 4 and 10 May and were scheduled to do the same on 12 May. This was a Friday, and, for obvious reasons, it was necessary to be back at Ørland by 1700 hours. So, the return sortie was to be in daylight as a formation of four. Dutch and I had led on the way down, so, for the return, we reversed the order and we became No. 4.

At this point I must include a reminder about arrestor barriers. The Buccaneer was not cleared to engage a barrier, since it was thought that the in-flight refuelling probe would go above the top cable when it would break off and enter the navigator's cockpit. Karup had a barrier at each end of the runway, and these were to be in the down position for Buccaneer landings and take-offs. If there was any danger of going off the end of the runway, we were to lower the hook and pick up the barrier in the down position.

All four aircraft lined up on the runway for pairs take-offs at 20-second intervals. The wind was from the left so we were in echelon port. All was normal up to about 150 knots,

Andy Marrs' aircraft in the arrestor barrier with 'Dutch' Holland's ejection seat and parachute in the foreground.

when there was a lurch to the right and a nasty rumbling noise. Having previously destroyed a couple of Her Majesty's tyres, one on a flooded runway in a Buccaneer Mark 1, I knew immediately what had happened. The starboard tyre had burst.

So I slammed the throttles closed, aborted the take-off and put the hook down. To keep the aircraft moderately straight, I needed full left brake, full left nosewheel steer, and the control column right back with full nose-up trim to get maximum down force to give maximum brake force to the left brake. We then noticed that the barrier appeared to be in the up position. What we didn't know was the main barrier was down and what we could see was a smaller back-up barrier about 200 yards beyond. Apparently, this second barrier prevented aircraft going down a slope beyond the runway and on to a public road.

Now, of prime importance was the position of the barrier. I made two shouted calls to the tower to get the barrier down. I should have opened the airbrakes and shut down one engine but with my other hand keeping the nosewheel steering engaged, I ran out of hands. The noise level in the cockpit was quite high with the naked wheel skidding along the runway, and the standard warning panel and attention getters sounding off. I never looked down to see what the warning was; it didn't seem important at that moment.

We went off the end of the runway pretty much in the centre at about 100 knots. I was now a passenger. On leaving the runway, the aircraft first slewed through about 30 degrees to the right, presumably as the damaged wheel picked up the lowered main barrier cable. Then, it appeared to hop over the cable, and the hook picked it up and slewed the aircraft back to the left. The over-run consisted of pierced steel planking (PSP). The damaged wheel and the nosewheel dug in, and pieces of PSP were thrown about and punctured the aircraft's skin in places. While all this was happening, I just had to hang on and hope for the best in the time-honoured way.

The aircraft came to rest in the back-up barrier, the nosewheel having dug in so far that the flight-refuelling probe had gone under the top cable. The main barrier had been pulled out to its maximum extent and was, I think, written off.

Once the aircraft stopped, I shut down the engines and jettisoned the canopy in order to make a fast exit if anything started to burn. I stood up and turned round to find an empty back cockpit – Dutch had ejected which, under the circumstances, was exactly the right thing to do. So, I jumped to the ground and ran away, like you do. A crash truck arrived and stopped some distance away. I went over to them and asked if they knew where my navigator was. They pointed across the airfield as I asked if he was OK. They didn't know but had seen the parachute open. Since it was now obvious that nothing was going to burn, I borrowed a ladder and got back in the cockpit to put in the ejection seat safety pins and turned a few items off.

After a short time, a naval officer arrived riding a very small moped, which made a lot of noise while going rather slowly. This was Lt Cdr 'Bodger' Edwards, the air engineering officer (AEO) of 849 Squadron on what he called his 'Bogwheel'. I was very pleased to see someone who showed every sign of being totally competent. He told me that 849 would recover the aircraft, intimating that this was the sort of problem they solved every day in the Royal Navy.

I left the scene to find Dutch who was OK but had been carted off to the local hospital with the usual ejection back injury. Meanwhile, Bodger Edwards and his team recovered the aircraft. Without specialised Buccaneer handling equipment, they lifted up the aircraft with a Gannet jack and removed the damaged wheel. As expected, they did not have a Buccaneer wheel but, for some reason they did have one for a Sea Vixen. This was smaller than a Buccaneer wheel, so it did not fit between the undercarriage forks.

Undaunted, they used a scaffolding pole as an axle, suitably smothered in grease. Then, with a mechanical digger coupled to the aircraft's hook and a towing arm on the nosewheel for steering, very slowly they pulled the aircraft back on to the runway. Flushed with this success they then spent a considerable amount of time towing XV351 round the taxiway to 849's dispersal and left it there with a tape around it with a suitable warning to keep off.

Apart from a bit of skin damage from the flying PSP, the aircraft seemed substantially undamaged except that the starboard undercarriage bay was filled almost completely with a nightmare tangle of bracing wire from the failed tyre.

On the following Monday, an aircraft turned up with a team of engineers and a few spares, including an ejection seat, a canopy and a wheel. Also on the aircraft was Paddy English who was to do the unit inquiry, which he proceeded to conduct in the downstairs bar of the officers' club, which had been built for the Luftwaffe in World War Two, and was still resplendent with its mosaic swastika in the floor.

The next day an Andover arrived to take Dutch, Paddy and myself back to Honington. Nine days after the accident, Bob Kemp and I flew XV351 back to base with the undercarriage down, a very boring one hour forty-minute sortie.

Drama at the Paris Air Show

The task was to overfly Le Bourget plugged into the starboard hose of a Victor tanker with a Lightning on the port hose. We joined with the tanker over the North Sea and refuelled to full on the way south.

Looking at my logbook, the practice was on 27 May 1971. The wind was very strong causing the hoses to flail, so neither the Lightning nor we could plug in, and so we flew over Le Bourget close astern the hoses. Afterwards, we received a snotty signal from the AOC, saying it must be done properly on the day. So no pressure!

The actual day was on 5 June. We were flying XN978 and after we had taken on fuel, the Lightning elected to stay plugged in, while I decided to formate on the Victor's wing for a bit to ease the workload. This was a bad decision, because after a short while we went into cloud, at first it was quite thin, the decaying part of a cumulonimbus, but soon it became much

12 Squadron Buccaneer takes on fuel from a Victor.

thicker and more turbulent. Then I lost contact with the Victor, and so I turned away and descended slightly. Being an excellent operator, my navigator Bob Kemp saw the Victor on radar and guided me back to get behind the hose.

I had never before, nor afterwards, tried in-flight refuelling in a cumulonimbus, and I don't recommend it. The hose was flailing quite wildly and I could see the Victor's wing flexing in the turbulence. So I employed the well-known solution, which I had used successfully before, of closing behind the hose, waiting for it to stabilise, and then stabbing it with the probe. The problem was, it did not stabilise for long enough to get the probe into the refuelling basket.

I have no idea how many times I tried, but I do know it was a very high workload. I knew we were descending because Bob told me, and, quite suddenly, after yet another attempt to make contact with the hose basket, I found that we were a long way below the Victor. I now know that the Victor rolling out of a starboard turn and levelling at the same time caused this.

Clearly, I over-controlled in my effort to get back behind the drogue. Whether we went through the Victor's slipstream, I do not know, but I experienced what felt like an enormous yaw to starboard and I could see nothing outside the cockpit except cloud. I knew I had lost it, and I called, "Eject, eject". We were at 800 feet and I heard Bob go out, and I pulled the seat-pan handle with my right hand. It jammed. It is supposed to be pulled vertically upwards and I had obviously pulled it to the side. I looked down and grabbed it with both hands and gave a mighty pull. The seat fired at 150 feet, but with precious seconds lost.

The Board of Inquiry thought that I had been unconscious for a few seconds due to the clout on the back of my head in breaking through the canopy, but my next impression was of being in free fall. I immediately realised that all was not well, and tried to do a manual separation by pulling the lever on the left-hand side of the seat, but there was no seat there.

I next looked down to see the aircraft burning furiously on the ground. This was a bit depressing, as I thought I was going to land directly into the fire. However, I then felt a small tension on my harness, which was, presumably, the drogue parachute deploying, and shortly afterwards, a huge acceleration upwards as I passed through the fireball.

My next impression was of traversing fast and close to the tops of the oak trees of the Forêt de Compiègne, and I realised that there was soon going to be a big thump. There was, and I found myself sitting on the ground with the parachute hung up in the trees, and with the seat close to my left side with the rocket pack still smoking.

I could feel the heat and hear the noise of the aircraft burning behind me, and so I thought it best to get as far away as possible. So I released the harness and staggered directly away from the fire, until, after a short distance, I came to a road with stationary traffic in both directions. There was a man standing on the verge, and I asked him, in schoolboy French, "Voulez-vous me porter à le gendarmerie?" "Mais oui", so I climbed into his car and he took me to the police station. En route I tried to ask him if he knew anything about Bob, "Mon ami, est-il mort?" "Mais oui". I thought, strewth, what am I going to say to Rosie? They were due to be married in about six weeks.

The gendarme looked at me with Gallic indifference and pointed to a chair. I took off my harness and parked my helmet. I then felt rather unwell with breathing difficulties, so I said, "J'aime un docteur". "Mais oui." So I was loaded back into the car, and taken to a doctor's house. The doctor laid me down and repeatedly took my blood pressure while phoning for an ambulance. Then Bob appeared. I have rarely, if ever, been so pleased to see someone.

We were loaded into the ambulance and carted off to the local hospital. There they cut off my flying suit and slapped an enormous sticking plaster over my broken sternum. I had broken this with my chin during the ejection. The sternum does not break cleanly like ribs, but in a greenstick fracture. The fracture was low down near where the lower ribs join; try getting your chin that low! One of the hospital orderlies offered me a quarter bottle of whiskey if he could have the badges off my flying suit. I readily agreed; well if you are abroad you need to get your duty-free, and anyway neat whiskey is a good painkiller. After a lot of X-rays, which were quite painful when they wanted me to lie on my side, we embarked in another ambulance which took us to Le Bourget at high speed and with blue lights flashing, to catch the Hercules, which had brought a crew to repair a Harrier that had made a heavy landing. So, back to Honington and thence a hospital in Ely.

There I was tended by the orthopaedic surgeon, Dr Bucher (which he liked pronounced as 'Boosher' for obvious reasons). He ordered the plaster on my chest to be removed saying, "We never do that", which was painful, but not the greatest pain I experienced that day. He then said the French X-rays were useless and ordered them to be re-done.

The extent of my injuries was three compression fractures of my thoracic vertebrae (two more were found at a later X-ray), a broken sternum, a lot of bruising, a slight laceration of my left foot where a tree had sliced through my flying boot and a superficially burnt face. That night an attractive red-haired nurse continually bathed my face with saline to stop it scarring. The next day I developed a chest infection due to breathing in hot gasses from the fire. The trouble was I had to lie flat on my back due to the compression fractures, but for the chest infection I needed to sit up and cough, which itself was intensely painful because of the broken sternum. The solution was for a physiotherapist to come every hour, sit me up and hold my chest together while I coughed. Additionally, I was put on the Guinness ration, a bottle a day, to help mend my broken bones. Such was the excellent treatment provided by the RAF medical service.

I'm not sure if it was that day or the next that Ian Henderson and a team from 12 Squadron came with my wife to cheer me up. Unaccountably, they brought, not flowers, but crates of beer, which were eventually put to good use. Unfortunately, I had just been given a shot of morphine for the pain, and I just couldn't stay with it. As my eyes drooped shut, the last thing I saw was my wife dissolving into tears. She was afraid I was going to die. But I didn't. After three weeks I went to Headley Court to do back exercises for another three weeks, and the following September, three months later, I was back on flying after a ticking off by the SASO (noticeably not by the AOC). I didn't have a problem with this; the whole thing was entirely my fault. Afterwards, I was probably a little wiser and a bit less over-confident in my abilities.

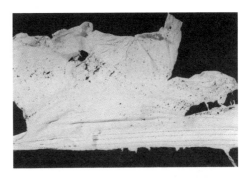

The report on the state of my parachute was interesting. The two anti-squid lines, which are fixed to, but are shorter than the main parachute support lines, had ruptured. They are meant to ensure rapid and symmetrical opening of the para-chute, but are designed to rupture in the case of, for example, a high-speed ejec-tion, to avoid overstressing the parachute. So the upward acceleration I experienced really was hard, presumably caused by the up-rush of hot air from the fire fill-ing the parachute. It was also found that eight of the 24 gores of the parachute had been burnt out making it virtually use-

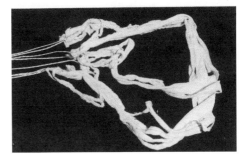

Drogue parachute and section of parachute after passing through the fireball.

less as a parachute, but not too bad for landing in trees. It also showed that, contrary to my thinking that I was descending vertically into the fire I actually passed through it at an angle. So, if it wasn't for those lovely oaks of the forest, I wouldn't be here to relate the story.

Andy Marrs and Bob Kemp receive their SARBE tankard from OC 12 Squadron, Wg Cdr Geoff Davies.

Once the drogue gun had failed to fire, my chances of survival must have been very small.

This all happened 50 years ago, but I can remember the events of that day as if it were yesterday. I have always regarded myself as undeservedly lucky, but I certainly rode my luck that day. Military flying is usually interesting, often exhilarating, but sometimes dangerous. However they used to say 'Any sortie you walk away from is a good one'.

CHAPTER EIGHT

DAWNING OF DETACHMENTS TO DECIMOMANNU

DAVID HERRIOT

Ah! Sardinia! That jewel in the Mediterranean Sea that sits just west of the geographical gamba that forms the Italian mainland and south of Napoleon's homeland, *La Corse*, with its accusing forefinger pointing north towards the heartlands of Europe that he sought to conquer. *Sardegna* and its *Costa Smeralda*, the jet-set jewel in the island's crown.

But no! This tale is not about a jet-setting Buccaneer aircrew, relaxing with the rich and famous, accepting pink gins liberally dispensed by the Aga Khan. This tale takes place and did often during a mud-moving tour in Germany, a considerable distance further south towards the industrial petro-chemical region that adorns much of the coast around the island's capital, Cagliari.

The Italian air force base at Decimomannu was some two hours flying time from RAF Laarbruch and it was there I headed, with my trusty pilot afore me, on my first-ever detachment with an operational squadron, for 14 days in the blazing summer sun and a bit of hard graft on the squadron's annual armament practice camp (APC). It was 3 July 1972; I was 23 years old. But let me start at the beginning.

When I began flying with XV Squadron at Laarbruch in January 1972 the squadron was in the throes of converting to the Buccaneer. Not all of the requisite crews had arrived from 237 OCU and the squadron was very much day, fighter, ground, attack (DFGA) minded! Indeed, to my delight (but probably not his) I had been crewed with an ex-208 Squadron (Bahrain), DFGA, Hunter pilot for the OCU course. He, Iain Ross, and I and Dave Symonds and John Kershaw were posted, as crews, to join the nascent XV (Buccaneer) Squadron in October 1971 from the first first-tourist course to be held on 237 Operational Conversion Unit. DFGA was the only way to go and after a 'Long OCU' course with Iain, I was fully inculcated as a DFGA navigator. It was just as well, because on our arrival, the ethos and training on XV Squadron were very much DFGA! OK, SACEUR did want us to have the

XV Squadron Buccaneers on the flight line at Decimomannu.

capability to deliver 'buckets of sunshine' as well, but in 1972 what was wrong with delivering them visually – we all knew that the Blue Parrot was not designed for, or capable in, the overland role. The soon to be famous epithet 'Blind Tom', our dedicated radar navigation leader, had not even been dreamt of and the young pretender to the radar leadership was known only by his christened name in those early days on XV. Laydown, MDSL, SNEB rockets, five-degree Dive Retard at Nordhorn Range were all routine tasks for the crews working up on XV – all were delivered visually. Initial concentration was on passing the LCR work-up to get you 'strike qualified' and onto QRA and then the CR work-up so that you could go to war but, even better than going to war, you were qualified to go on detachment.

It was here in the bar at Happy Hour that the first germs of the XV Squadron songbook were written. Songs like, 'When XV came to Laarbruch what a happy day! Rocketry and Stripro visual all the way!' (to the tune of *Lily Marlene*) and '2's little boys fly 2's little toys, they call it the Phantom jet' (to the tune of Rolf Harris's *Two Little Boys*) positively flowed from the musical talent of that well known, to us anyway, song-writing duo of Nick Berryman and Colin Tavner. We worked tirelessly to hone our skills in the air and improve our singing voices in the bar. We were, we knew, ultimate DFGA professionals, above average aircrew, exceptional party animals and competent consumers of alcohol who, with further training on detachment, could become well above average in this latter discipline also. We were invincible, or so we thought. It was with this in mind that XV Squadron deployed to Decimomannu for its first-ever detachment. Exactly two years to the day from the first establishment of an RAF presence on Sardinia and a destination that I was bound to return to many more times during my career.

Many years ago, I knew an F4 navigator who used to brag that, over time, he had spent one whole year of his life (365 accumulative days) at Deci. He loved the place. Poor sod, I thought. Well, on second thoughts, I suppose it was in the Mediterranean, it had sun, sea, sand, and Italian ladies (I was a bachelor). But the base was spartan to say the least, was no closer than an hour from the nearest beach and the RAF accommodation lacked the comforts of modern living even by 1970s' standards. The only decent establishment on base was the Italian officers' mess (known as Spaghetti Palace, pronounced palachi, by the Brits) and the only 'place to be' was the Brit pub – 'The Pig and Tapeworm'. Nevertheless, the flying was good, and the weaponry on Capo Frasca Range concentrated, which allowed us all to hone our skills. However, it was Deci and although Sardinia is as beautiful as any Mediterranean island it did not compare with the delights offered by Cyprus or Malta.

For those who flew the Bucc in the 1970s, the word 'Decimomannu' conjures up images to most of rowdy weekends in Sardinia. Of intoxicated soirées at Fortes Hotel Village on the southern coast where golf carts float mysteriously in swimming pools in the early hours of the morning after an evening of strong drink. It wasn't me guv, but I was there, running behind it with a posse of drunks, encouraging its intoxicated crew of two, who had managed to enter its garage, had manufactured a screwdriver into a key and had got it started. Aircrew are more technologically capable than some might give them credit for; certainly, with a belly full of beer.

This, my first introduction to an 'aircrew detachment' and other than the extraordinarily superb flying and concentrated weaponry opportunities, which trust me I will get on to, that the APC provided, was an eye-opener for this young man from Scotland. Gastronomic extravaganzas consisting of barbecued king prawns and 'multo vino rosso' commonly known as 'Deci Red' which, in 1972, cost ridiculously large sums of Italian lire but on conversion was dirt-cheap. Of death-defying journeys, in a ramshackle MT minivan, along tortuous roads that had a sheer drop to the sea on one side, just to get to Capo Carbonara for sand-infested, but compulsory, 'beach barbecues'. Of luxury golfing at Ismolas which, for most then and now, is beyond the pocket of the average golfer – and let's face it Buccaneer aircrew may be red hot in the air, but they are all no better than average golfers. Not to forget the regular funfair in the local towns that, unfortunately for the showmen, was a strong magnet for Buccaneer aircrew and yours truly in particular. All of these activities being social sanctuary for 'bomb-weary' Buccaneer aircrew enjoying their time off from the rigours of weaponry sorties during their annual APC. But a detachment to Decimomannu was more than all that nonsense, and I wouldn't want to give you the wrong impression about Buccaneer aircrew – well, at least none more so than that you have already formed as you venture through this second volume of our derring do.

In those early days, the boss of XV Squadron was the now late and much-lamented Wg Cdr Roy Watson. Roy was renowned as a particularly capable pilot who had flown Thunderjets

Heading for Alpha North at Capo Frasca Range.

during the Korean War. Indeed, one particular story that abounded at the time was that, as a flying officer, on his 100th and final mission he had led a formation of over 40 to bomb bridges over the Yalu River. I was too polite to ask the storyteller if this was for real but in all my 38 years in the RAF, I do not think I have ever seen a flying officer being trusted with himself, let alone 40 plus aircraft! Things were clearly much different in the early post-war years in the RAF. Anyway, Roy's experiences certainly did ensure that he was one of the original 'seat of the pants' pilots. On a memorable occasion at Capo Frasca, Roy and his navigator, Pete Ritchie, were leading a four-ship, which was conducting SNEB rocket attacks on the dive circle. Direct hit (DH) followed DH until after about his fifth pass without a miss, to the surprise of his back-seater, Roy declared to the range safety officer (RSO) that he was 'off dry'. When challenged, "Why dry, boss, the parameters were perfect?" by his navigator, the boss replied: "Sorry, I've just realised that I haven't selected the sight glass up and the BAIs (the first two of whom had recently returned to the squadron from their training) will bollock me rigid at the debrief!" Such it was at Deci!

Buccaneer attack instructors were 'gods' and this was their domain. Sortie debriefs were harsh and often withering encounters, but they had to be. This was not tiddlywinks. We were, on a daily basis, prepared to put our lives on the line for, without wishing to appear too overly dramatic, 'Queen and Country'. At Deci, we would fly two or three times per day to the range, point our aircraft at the target in angles of zero, through five, ten and 20-degree dive at speeds up to 480 kts and hope to get away with it and, in the case of rocket attacks, pull out without receiving a ricochet. We were practising in peace what we hoped we would never have to put into action in war. But for we aircrew based in Germany, the Cold War was very real and, geographically, very close and only some 25 minutes flying time from our base at Laarbruch.

The trouble with Capo Frasca Range, when related to the Buccaneer, was that the bloody targets were not at sea level. It's all very well having a bombing range on the top of a 100-foot cliff, but if the poor back-seater has only a 'strip TAS' and a 'strip altimeter' (fixed to 1013 mb), then placing the targets on top of a cliff is going to do nothing for the accuracy of the weapons. Is it? Moreover, if the peninsula is less than three kilometres wide in the target area on the attack heading then it is not really giving the poor back-seater much of a chance to 'zero' his altimeter directly over the targets. Well, is it? Furthermore, the rear seat of the Buccaneer being offset to provide only a clear view to the right of the pilot's head whilst at the same time trying to etch a 'zero' line on the 'strip altimeter' in your low, left nine o'clock, range three feet, with a blunt chinagraph pencil is less than conducive to bombing accuracy. It's true, isn't it? Finally if the range is split, on the attack heading, into 'left' and 'right' range with either left or right traffic (at the Italian RSO's pleasing) and your pilot is employing you as local interpreter, then it is clearly acceptable that you missed your mark and that you would be eternally grateful if we could do it all again please! Well, of course it is.

Now if you add to that the fact that Capo Frasca is but ten minutes flying time from Deci through Point Golf via Alpha North (R/W 35) there ain't a lot of time to settle to the task before you find yourself hurtling earthwards in a 20-degree dive. However, Iain Ross and I had been crewed together through the OCU and for all of the work-up on the squadron, so we were a team. He understood me and I understood him. On this day in history, we were bound for Capo Frasca as No. 4 to conduct MDSL. For those who have never had the delight of doing manual depressed sight line bombing (or any other DSL for that matter), MDSL was conducted from a pattern height of 4,000 ft and weapon release was initiated by the navigator's 'now' call as the Bucc passed through 2,150 ft on its way to the ground. Highly accurate over a flat calm sea – but on Capo Frasca Range – see above.

Following a very short hold at Point Golf we descended towards the coast to be low level over the sea as we turned onto the attack heading. During the routine 4G turn in arrow my bang seat dropped unexpectedly by about two inches with a quite solid and noticeable 'clunk'. Time waits for no man and, by the time I had panicked, fiddled and failed to ascertain what the problem was with the ejection seat, the four aircraft had joined the range and broken into the circuit, and my height mark had been, to all intents and purposes, non-existent. Now was the time to call it a day! We were now downwind at 4,000 ft for MDSL and I was unable to rectify the problem. However, what I had discovered whilst joining the range was that I could not talk on the intercom or radio and the first panic breath only resulted in my oxygen mask clamping itself firmly to my face. Undeterred and now breathing cabin air, I wrote on a scrap of paper, 'Bang seat dropped two inches; can't breathe, can't speak. Dave!' – I signed it just in case there was any doubt. Then, having stamped my feet to gain attention, I passed it to Iain through the gap above the Blue Jacket where

An exciting beach barbeque with Kellogg's
Rice Krispies on the menu!

the roller map used to be. By now, we were established in the 20-degree dive and my poor pilot was struggling to assess his dive angle without the usual calls from the rear seat; he pulled off dry! Now without the use of dialogue, it is exceedingly difficult to translate one's emotions and a sense of urgency on a scrap of paper and I had clearly failed.

Once downwind, Iain passed the paper back with the message 'Never mind, we'll stay dry!' Now anxious that my bang seat was about to do what it was designed for, I was not so keen on this course of action and using 'curt terminology' advised my friend (in writing) that I was less than happy with this proposal. Of course, the flying of the aircraft and the passing of notes takes time and now two more patterns had passed, and my straps were tightened to breaking point in preparation for the inevitable. However, as all good crews, our sense of airmanship prevailed and we soon departed the range for Deci where, unbeknown to me, as you will recall I had no radio or intercom, Iain had alerted ATC to our predicament. An uneventful straight-in approach with my straps getting ever tighter with an uneventful landing, apart from being chased down the runway by a stream of bright yellow Italian 'blood wagons', followed.

Upon reaching the northern ORP, the canopy motored backwards, and my now frantically gesticulating pilot indicated that it was time for me to depart the aircraft by conventional means – sliding down the starboard UWT on this occasion as no crew ladder was readily available at the ORP. No sooner was I safely on the ground than, without another word, my Buccaneer disappeared back to dispersal. I was stranded. Until, and here is where it pays to socialise in the bar, a familiar Luftwaffe F-104 pilot beamed from his cockpit and gesticulated that I should jump on to his wing and sit astride his drop tank. Five minutes later, back on X-Ray dispersal, I was deposited amongst my fellows and soon, back in the Pig and Tapeworm, regaling all who would listen to my tale of adventure.

Of course, Deci was not all about Capo Frasca Range, there were low levels around and over the island to be conducted and beaches to be revisited from the air rather than by J2 minivan. Every flying day was broken by the delight of one of Enrico's Spanish omelettes or his rather thin but expertly fried steaks smothered with large quantities of dubious salad and chips. The island needed to be explored at weekends (more so after the RAF was banned from Fortes Village following 'that' incident!). Tales had to be accumulated for subsequent transmission down the generations. The extremely tortuous journey across the mountains, past the bullet-ridden road signs, from Cagliari to Arbatax to the hotel that subsequently became known as 'Fifties' (in light of our ban from Fortes) had to be experienced. It was not for the faint-hearted and on this occasion, the experience was compounded by the fact that the whole contingent in the J2 had caught a dose of 'Deci Dog' the day before. Stops en route were many and when we arrived at our destination, the 'heads' beside the Fifties' pool had a roster attached to the door by one of our more considerate brethren. It was hellish – if you missed your five-minute slot you had to wait 50 minutes until your next one. Whether it was high adventure at the funfairs or brushes with gun-toting mafia in local pubs or the gun-wielding Italian orderly officer in the Spaghetti Palachi who took exception to a bread roll fight over dinner one night; whether it was mind-broadening English lessons provided by the ops officer, Master Pilot Wally Cole, when responding to the question why there was no air conditioning in the ops room: "I'm sorry, Sir. The f*****g, f*****'s, f****d!" or the scientific examination of the continuity of the sex life of the female praying mantis, there was never a dull moment at Decimomannu.

For our NATO allies, the Buccaneer was a weird and wonderful aircraft. Predominantly, the Italians and Germans were flying Starfighters and the USAF deployed to Deci in 1972 with F-4s, A-10s, F-111s, etc. All aircraft instantly recognisable in the NATO AOB, but the Buccaneer was new to theatre and unique (in more ways than one). Consequently, as carousing Buccaneer crews, we drew some lively attention in the Spaghetti Palachi from our inquisitive foreign brethren. The Pig and Tapeworm was always the place that USAF crews seemed to discover after the Palachi bar shut or sometimes before it even opened. The prospect of strong English beer was too much for them to refuse an invitation and sufficient to have them soon joining in with the XV Squadron songbook lyrics. Of course, it was all cloaked in the mystery of 'tactical discussions' and ensured that there was always a strong bond between the visiting squadrons at Deci. However, of all, the Italians were perhaps the most reticent. Understandable as they are not renowned for being particularly wild partygoers and the base commander was an Italian with the obvious implications that that had for an Italian officer's career. Nevertheless, on one very memorable occasion and after a particularly enervating day on Capo Frasca Range doing 'divisional MDSL', two Italian G-91 pilots who had, that very day, been at Capo Frasca Range on RSO duties approached us in the bar after a particularly pleasant meal of spaghetti washed down by copious quantities of Deci Red. They explained that they had been intrigued by the Buccaneers conducting 'pairs dive-bombing' and were keen to learn how this was done. Well, of course, in the early 1970s there was no such thing as a QWI, the term BAI was only just establishing itself and the closest AWI to the Spaghetti Palachi was at HMS Fulmar. Anyway, we were all experts and for the price of another 'flaming sambuca' we were all happy to brief the Gino pilots. Picture the scene. Before we could stop ourselves, hands flew, words like 'synergistic effect' and 'No. 2 pickles on leader's release' fell to the carpet. Before you knew it, the Italians had picked them all up, were fully briefed and off to their beds.

The next morning, I was in a four-ship taxiing for take-off bound for one of the early slots on Capo Frasca. Out of the blue, whilst just leaving dispersal, the local controller announced, "London, your mission she ees cancel". "Roger! Reason why?" said London lead. "The range, she isa clos-edd!" replied local. So, with no low level booked and an embargo on take-offs, we taxied back and shut down despondent that our range sortie had been

David Herriot on the left with his pilot and close friend Iain Ross.

cancelled for some yet to be established reason. We did not have to wait long to find out however, as the range had not been closed for those 'early birds' who were prepared to get up at about 0530 hours which, on this day, had included our two intrepid Gino pilots. Eager to emulate their Buccaneer brethren the two G-91s had failed to follow the 'bar room' briefing exactly and had 'clapped hands' overhead the dive circle and both had crashed! One onto the target area and one into the sea. Thankfully, both pilots had survived their ejections and were back in the bar that evening for a bit of remedial instruction.

But all good things have to come to an end and, as the conclusion of that first detachment approached, we were all informed that we would fly home in the aircraft that we had brought down to Deci. It was a cunning plan by the squadron executives who, knowing that our jet, XW531, was unserviceable and needed a double engine change, had decided that Iain and I, the only bachelor crew, would not be concerned about not getting home to enjoy a weekend with our families. First, however, engines had to be airlifted from Laarbruch to Decimomannu, fitted and ground run over the weekend before any thought of getting home could be considered. It all went smoothly from an engineering perspective and on Monday 17 July, 1972, we took off from Deci and climbed to FL300 and headed northwest towards Alghero on the Costa Smeralda and the French FIR boundary. "Do the air test in the climb" the authoriser had said, which seemed logical as we would still have been well within range of Deci if either of the engines had failed to relight after we had shut it down as part of the test. If all went well, we would have covered the first 40 minutes of our flight and be over the Med heading for the French coast once it was complete.

We were well past Ajaccio and settled heading for Nice by the time it was complete. We were looking forward to the home comforts of our own beds in Block 13A and a night far away from the Pig and Tapeworm. Then I remembered it was XW531. The TACAN had not worked on our journey down, but then we had relied on our leader to do the navigation and talk to French air traffic control. I had not snagged it because 'who needs a TACAN on a ten-minute VFR hop to Capo Frasca Range'. So, it had not been fixed. The Blue Parrot radar worked but the latitude and longitude counters on the Blue Jacket Doppler ground position indicator were, as ever, marching themselves steadily eastwards. This was my problem. I had to navigate us home to Laarbruch and I had no nav aids to assist me in the process. The French controller was making all sorts of guttural noises and I could see on the radar that we were homing to a point that appeared to be halfway between Genoa and Toulon but had nothing significant to describe it better on the radar screen. We coasted in and turned for Lyon. What now, I thought. We were GAT over France with not a nav aid to speak of but damned if we were going to give up despite the protestations of *Monsieur Le Controlleur* (MLC) on the ground. The only thing going for us was that it was gin clear and we had good visual contact with the ground below. Then Iain had a brain wave.

"Get the en route supplement out, Dave". "What's Lyon's runway?" He asked.

"18/36," I replied.

"Length?" he responded.

"Eight thousand five hundred feet," I told him.

"Great," he said, as he turned northwards for Dijon, our next reporting point, over an airport with a reasonably long runway that was definitely pointing in a N-S direction. But that was not all. To see the runway and make sure it really was Lyon, Iain had to stand the aircraft on its side so that we could check properly. It was far too hard to see the correct orientation and runway length from straight and level at height. Aerobatics at 30,000 ft or so was not something that the Buccaneer really liked.

Now onwards to Dijon and brimming with confidence we provided MLC with our next estimate; then cloud appeared below us. Luckily, it broke just as our ETA overhead Dijon approached and, following more aerobatics, we dutifully turned for Luxeuil in Dijon's over-head using our now tried and tested method of runway spotting. On the next leg, how-ever, the cloud thickened up to 8/8ths, which prevented any sight of the ground. We were scratching our heads wondering just how reliable the forecast winds would be and whether we were still close enough to our route not to cause a fuss, when we heard a RAF Phantom from Brüggen calling "Luxeuil overhead, Dijon next" and 1,000 ft above us. Excellent! The leg was three minutes long and exactly 90 seconds later an F-4 Phantom passed directly overhead on an opposing heading.

"On track on time," I declared to my man in the front seat.

It was about Zweibrücken that the starboard engine decided to quit but we had had enough of being away from home and although we discussed diverting, we quickly dis-missed the thought and turned left onto 340 degrees. Laarbruch was in sight, well almost in sight, well about 300 kms actually but we nursed it home all the while losing height and wondering whether we would actually make it, but we did for an uneventful single-en-gine landing and a little white lie that the engine had quit at the top of descent – well it had, almost.

Oh! The bang seat? Yes, it had dropped two inches, and, in the process, it had managed to disconnect the lower seat portion of the PEC, which was beyond my sight. Nothing really and, with 20/20 hindsight, easily identifiable had I investigated the problem thoroughly. But hey! Why spoil a good story when it can keep you in beer for a good 24 hours?

And why the golf cart in the swimming pool? And what became of the garage raiders? Well amongst the 'posse of drunks', and in about 15 yards trail, were two of Fortes Village's finest security guards who had been enjoying a quiet cappuccino and sambuca when the balloon went up. Hot-footing it from the comfort of their crew room, they quickly espied the golf cart, the garage raiders and the posse – not difficult, as drunks in full charge tend not to be too discreet. Alerted to this unnecessary attention, the 'raiders' took a sharp left turn into a cul-de-sac that they very quickly recognised as the quiet sunspot where they had been relaxing, and cavorting, the previous afternoon.

Now golf carts do have a fairly good turning circle, when the driver is alert, sober and exercising. However, when under the command of two inebriates in the early hours of a Sunday morning, that is less likely to be so. Faced with a wet end and/or arrest, our two intrepid heroes bailed and left the golf cart to fend for itself. By the time the posse entered the pool area, they were long gone. Rather than attempt to rescue the golf cart, which was now doing the breaststroke across the Fortes' pool, the posse had also scarpered rather than be incarcerated overnight by the now very upset security personnel, whose cappuccino was going cold on their crew room table. The following morning, nursing sore heads, the garage raiders presented themselves to the Fortes' management team and were banned from every Fortes establishment across the globe for the rest of their days.

CHAPTER NINE

SHORT RUNWAYS

Tom Eeles had a long and varied career flying the Buccaneer but he recalls three occasions that provided unusual experiences.

TOM EELES

Detachment to Stornoway – 1972

In 1972 a 12 Squadron Buccaneer caught fire after an uncontained engine failure during take-off from Lossiemouth. The take-off was successfully abandoned, Mike Bush and Pete Locke ran away and the Buccaneer, which was loaded with Lepus, burnt a large Buccaneer-shaped hole in the main runway, putting it out of action for some time. Thus space at Lossiemouth for visitors was very limited, so when the big autumn maritime exercise, Strong Express, was due in September it was decided to deploy 12 Squadron to the NATO forward operating base (FOB) at Stornoway on the Isle of Lewis, something that had never been previously attempted.

Stornoway's facilities were rather primitive. There was a small resident RAF unit, commanded by a flight lieutenant engineer, Martin Palmer, which looked after the radar bomb site used by the V-Force and the few other buildings belonging to the RAF. These consisted of a large Gaydon hangar, home to a huge number of seagulls who used it copiously as an indoor public convenience, and a collection of rudimentary huts which served as sleeping accommodation for junior officers but were unfurnished. The interiors of these huts had dividing breeze-block partitions, enclosing a space for three or four camp beds in each, but they did not extend up to the roof of the hut. Thus, the loud snoring in one bed space (Fg Off Pete Warren) was audible to all the hut's residents. A field kitchen provided messing facilities, and marquees were erected as messes for officers, SNCOs and other ranks. Camp beds and sleeping bags were issued and were essential. All in all it looked like being something of a hard-core camping holiday.

There was a single useable 6,000-ft runway and a radar that could provide a non-precision approach. Given the Buccaneer's propensity to suffer hydraulic failures it was decided

*Stornoway airfield at the time
of the 12 Squadron detachment.*

to install a portable arrestor gear, the RHAG, which was flown in by a Hercules. With Lossie unavailable the nearest diversions were Kinloss or Leuchars, both a fair distance away.

Before deployment we were carefully briefed on the local sensitivities and the political situation at Stornoway. No fast-jet squadron had ever been there to disturb the peace of the Outer Hebrides. We were told that the locals were very God fearing and unused to the high-octane lifestyle enjoyed by the air and ground crews of the Buccaneer community in the 1970s. Sundays were absolutely sacrosanct and nothing happened apart from long church services. Additionally, there was an active peace movement called Keep (or was it Kick?) NATO Out (KNO) who were likely to mount vigorous protests at our presence. There would be no flying on Sundays and all personnel would be confined to camp where there was nothing by way of entertainment facilities. Given these local sensitivities, and 12 Squadron's unfortunate reputation for doing things their own way (and its recent accident record), Honington's station commander Gp Capt Peter Bairsto, aka 'The Bear', decided he would be the detachment commander. He managed to get his staff car, an Austin 1800, a model generally known as a Landcrab, and his own driver, SAC Layton, flown in by Hercules for his personal use. I bet you couldn't get away with that today.

The squadron flew in on 13 September, myself and John Beard as navigator, in Buccaneer S.2B XT276, an aircraft I had flown in the FAA. Despite the islanders' supposed reputation for inhospitality towards irreligious noisy Sassenach incomers, we soon found ourselves downtown in the Cabarfeidh Hotel at a civic reception in our honour, hosted by the great and the good of Stornoway, which included the town's dentist who turned out to be a 'piss artist extraordinaire'. The event went riotously well, I particularly recall the dentist's enthusiasm for whisky and made a mental note never to have toothache on the Isle of Lewis. There was no sign of anyone from the KNO campaign, just the occasional poster stuck on a wall. I note I did not fly the next day, which happened to be my birthday.

It was not long before AOC 1 Group, AVM Peter Horsley, a distinguished Mosquito pilot in World War Two, was flown in by Hunter to visit the detachment and stay overnight. On arrival he was entertained at lunch in the mess tent by those of us not flying. He related a sad story of how, the previous night, his pet cat had wandered out into the main road through Bawtry and had been flattened by a passing truck. We all expressed suitable

A pair of 12 Squadron Buccaneers. Neither have the bomb-door fuel-tank modification.

sympathy. After lunch the AOC and the Bear left to go into town to meet and take a dram with the Procurator Fiscal. Travelling in the Landcrab, driven by SAC Layton, they were led into town by Martin Palmer in his Land Rover. Between the airfield and the town, passing a row of crofts, a cat ran out and was flattened by the Land Rover. "What should I do?" asked Layton. "Drive on," said the Bear. "Stop," cried the AOC, still suffering from the previous night's trauma, "We must find out who the owner is." SAC Layton, holding the corpse by its tail and accompanied by the AOC, knocked on a few doors in an attempt to establish ownership, without success. The cat was then flung over a wall and the convoy continued on its way into town.

As I had a reputation of being a 'yachtie' I had been fingered by the Bear to take him and the AOC out for a sea fishing trip after their visit to the Procurator, using the local RAF unit's motorboat. My passengers arrived in fine spirits, there must have been quite a few drams offered by the Procurator, so off we went full of enthusiasm. Just as we reached the end of the sea loch and the start of the open waters of the Minch the engine spluttered and stopped. I tinkered with it for a while but was unable to revive it. So, without a radio or life jackets, there was no other option than for the Bear and me to man the oars and row the heavy motorboat back, with the rapidly sobering-up AOC sitting unhappily in the stern. He never offered to help and no fish were caught that day.

At some point during the same day one of our officers, who fulfilled the role of squadron adjutant, but must remain nameless as he is still a regular attendee at our reunion events, was detailed off to make sure that the squadron's silver and special table mats were available at a Dining-In Night for the AOC. The subsequent turn of events is a bit hazy after almost 50 years, but there are different versions of what happened next. The adjutant still

A Soviet navy Kashin destroyer shadows a NATO exercise.

claims that he purchased some fresh lobsters for his personal use, only to have the Bear offer them to the AOC. Others claim that the adjutant himself offered to get some fresh lobsters for the AOC. That evening the event for the AOC was held in the mess tent at which, not unsurprisingly, alcohol flowed. The AOC was due to leave by Hunter next morning. Again, there are two versions of what happened that morning. The adjutant claims he handed over the lobsters to the AOC (already strapped into the Hunter), standing on the pan in the keen Hebridean wind, clad in a flying suit worn over his natty pyjamas, with smart red leather slippers on his feet. The other variation has the aforesaid officer, standing by the Hunter, clad in pyjamas, a Paisley-pattern dressing gown and smart red leather slippers, explaining to the AOC that there were no lobsters because he had overslept. We may never know the truth of what happened, the AOC is dead and the adjutant is unlikely to tell us.

What of the flying? There was a lot of it going, mainly long-range sorties with AAR and Nimrod support, many down into the South West Approaches, which raised the question of why we had not been deployed to St Mawgan, a much more comfortable FOB closer to the action. But it would not have been so much fun. This was before the days of the great eight-aircraft co-ordinated attack profiles so the sorties were generally pairs or four-ships. I note from my logbook that I flew 13 sorties out of Stornoway, the longest being three hours 40 minutes, a total of 28 hours. Add to that another two hours Hunter flying at Honington and my monthly total was 30 hours despite 12 days leave at the start of the month. Not bad for three weeks and unlikely to be matched by today's front-line squadrons.

Not all the flying, however, was in support of Exercise Strong Express. Bob Kemp provided this memory, which I quote in full.

"The Bear and I took a montage of the Stornoway Golf Course with the photo crate. I spent about three hours cutting and pasting and then framing the final product after we landed. We then presented the framed photo montage (about four feet by six feet) of the whole course to the club captain that evening who in turn presented the Bear with a bottle of malt. I got nothing. What was rather humorous, as we taxied back to the pan after the sortie (and we had broken a few rules to get pictures of every fairway and green in the right direction), was that there was a posse of about ten police with a couple of police dogs waiting at the chocks. The Bear thought his end had come. He said to me (in that rather high-pitched voice he could muster on the Tannoy during Taceval) 'Bob, I need to brief you. At no time during this sortie did we deviate from the flight plan, (what flight plan? I thought to myself) neither did we, at any stage, fly over land below 250 ft nor over any populated area below 1,000 feet. Got that?' 'Yes, sir'.

"I was first down the ladder (the Bear still trying to silence the last engine and no doubt jazzing his worry beads). Flt Lt Martin Palmer (station commander no less) said, 'Bob, we are delighted that the Lewis police force are visiting the station today and would love to be shown over the jet.' At that point the Bear came down the ladder looking like death warmed up, but quickly ascended into air marshal mode when he realised the local bobbies were on a day out. 'We've had a most wonderful sortie today over your delightful country. Bob and I just love Harris.' I interjected, 'Lewis, boss, Lewis'."

Off duty, the Cabarfeidh Hotel proved to be a welcome watering hole and the Bear generously allowed his driver to run us around the island in the Landcrab on sightseeing expeditions. I also have a recollection of a swimming competition held on the beach adjoining the airfield on one of the no-flying Sundays. All I can remember is that the waters of the Minch were very cold in September. We all flew back to Honington on 28 September and, as far as I am aware, 12 Squadron never deployed to Stornoway again.

One benefit to the islanders was that now Stornoway had been established as a viable fast jet FOB, any buildings within two miles of the airfield qualified for free double glazing. The canny islanders built a lot more houses and opened businesses within this footprint. Looking at Stornoway airport on Google Earth today, it does not appear to have changed much. The coastguard SAR helicopters still there use the Gaydon hangar. The huts have disappeared and there is a smart new terminal building and car park. The road where the cat met its end has a lot more modern houses beside it. The Cabarfeidh Hotel is still in business but I doubt the drunken dentist is still in this world. Bob tells me he is still remembered in Stornoway today with great affection. Happy days!

The Sunderland Incident
Amongst the many airfields I visited during my tour on 12 Squadron in the early 1970s, the most unusual one was the old wartime airfield of Usworth on the edge of Sunderland

and home to a local flying club. Sadly it no longer exists having been swallowed up by the huge Nissan car factory.

On 28 August 1974 a pair of 12 Squadron aircraft were tasked with carrying out simulated attacks on a German warship in the North Sea some 100 miles east of Newcastle. The lead aircraft was flown by Rob Williams and the No. 2, Buccaneer XN977, by Captain Bill Petersen, the USAF exchange pilot on 12 Squadron. His navigator that day was Graham Pitchfork, who took up the offer of a trip at short notice, as he was on the newly formed 208 Squadron that was waiting to receive its first aircraft.

During the attack profile at 100 feet and 540 kts, Peterson's aircraft suffered a serious bird strike which destroyed most of the front half of the canopy. Large chunks of Perspex swept over the fuselage spine, removing the radio aerials and puncturing some of the fuel tanks. Fortuitously, Graham had his head down peering into the radar visor; he was hit by a combination of seagull and large pieces of Perspex travelling at high speed, which stunned him, covering him in blood and left a stiletto of Perspex embedded in his sternum. He also found himself buffeted by a 540kt gale as the canopy above him was left intact, although the blast screen between the front and rear cockpits had been destroyed and the visor of his bone dome had disappeared.

Petersen pulled up, turned west and put out a Mayday call on the standby UHF, which used the lower pair of aerials. His garbled call was answered by the distress and diversion emergency service, manned that day by one of the last Polish air traffic controllers in the RAF. Thus a combination of open-top Buccaneer, agitated American accent and guttural Polish controller did not make for good communications.

The controller's intention was to direct Petersen to Newcastle Airport where the full range of safety services were on standby. However, as he approached the coast, Petersen saw a town with a harbour (Sunderland) and, thinking it was Newcastle, saw just beyond it a runway, which he headed for. You can imagine the surprise and astonishment of the members of the Sunderland Flying Club as a Buccaneer suddenly appeared and landed on the very short runway and, amazingly, stopped just beyond the end of it, just avoiding falling into a derelict open-cast mine. The club's Land Rover fire tender arrived, and the driver was physically sick when he saw the state of the navigator. Meanwhile, Rob Williams was scouring all the local airfields for a Buccaneer and confirmed it had landed at Sunderland. The airborne SAR helicopter was informed, and it arrived to take Graham to Sunderland Royal Hospital where he was cared for.

A ground crew party was sent to Sunderland to restore XN977 to a 'one flight only' return to base condition. They replaced the canopy, the navigator's ejection seat, patched up the holes in the fuel tanks and jagged edges of the blast screen.

I was detailed to collect the aircraft and return it to Honington so along with my nav, 'Ratty' Adams, we were delivered to Sunderland by a Devon, clutching our helmets, life-saving jackets and harness and an ODM (operation data manual). The runway was indeed very short, just over 3,000 ft, but at a light weight with a blown take-off, I calculated we would make it if we took off downhill on the easterly runway. Luckily the wind, such as it was, favoured this. Virtually everyone in the local area had come to the airfield to witness

Tom Eeles lands XN977 on Victorious *and loses his Bullpup missile.*

this unique event, so 'Ratty' and I, assisted by our ground crew, decided to milk it for what it was worth. We decided to emphasise that the runway length was barely sufficient, and advised that a tower block just beyond the airfield boundary should be evacuated, and the A19 trunk road closed. Thus a great sense of occasion was rapidly generated just as the press arrived.

We strapped ourselves into the aircraft, which still stank of dead and grilled seagull, so 100 per cent oxygen was needed. Unsurprisingly, the take-off worked out perfectly, but I did keep XN977 very low over the A19 just for added drama. The flight back to base lasted 35 minutes.

This was not the first excitement I had experienced in XN977. The aircraft had been on 801 Naval Air Squadron embarked in HMS *Victorious* when I was an exchange pilot on the squadron. On 2 April 1967 I was flying the aircraft on an exercise to fire a Bullpup anti-shipping missile at an atoll in the South China Sea but the range was full of fishing boats and the firing had to be aborted. As I landed back on board *Victorious* and engaged an arrestor wire, the Bullpup broke loose, careered down the deck, bounced over parked Sea Vixens and deck handlers and fell into the sea with a mighty splash. For a time I stood accused of firing it by mistake, but the deck-landing film showed no smoke trail and I was exonerated.

CHAPTER TEN

FOXY TALES OF THE BUCCANEER AND GIBRALTAR

MAL GROSSE

How on earth did I end up as a maritime strike/attack pilot on a two-seat aircraft after 12 years' service as a day-fighter/ground-attack pilot on the Hunter?

After four years of flying instructional duties at RAF Valley on the Hunter, I was looking forward to a return to single-seat operational flying, preferably on the Jaguar. My wish was granted when, in December 1975, I was posted to RAF Lossiemouth for a Jaguar conversion. The following month I was promoted to squadron leader and my posting was cancelled. By April, after hopping between Valley and Brawdy to maintain flying currency, I had still not heard of my next appointment. Then in May, I was told to return to Brawdy for a short weapons refresher en route to Honington as training officer on 12 Squadron. Imagine my dismay, even being regaled with the prowess of the Buccaneer by one Tom Eeles – then with 79 Squadron at the TWU. Not the Jaguar, not single-seat, but three years of flying over the oggin with a navigator for company! My nine-year association with the Buccaneer was about to begin, and little did I foresee the pleasures that awaited.

Following a surprisingly enjoyable time, and very hot summer on 55 Course at 237 OCU, I joined 12 Squadron in November 1976. In my role as training officer, and subsequently as squadron exec, some six weeks of my tour would be spent on the Rock of Gibraltar, and coming up next are some recollections of those activities, and one or two others.

I was introduced to the complexities of maritime strike and attack operations and life with a navigator by the squadron's naval exchange officer, Ken Mackenzie; a man of both high professional ability and social charm. In no time at all the entire squadron was detached to RAF Gibraltar for Exercise Locked Gate. In January 1977, after a lengthy trip to Gibraltar involving AAR, and accompanied by a young and inexperienced navigator, we let down through heavy weather, breaking cloud at around 800 feet on final approach. Imagine my reaction on hearing the words from behind me, "Christ sir, I always thought it was an island!"

After landing, and keeping my mirth concealed, we joined the other crews for a rapid departure to the officers' mess at North Front. A quick change and spruce-up, and I was dragged off across the runway into town, where the delights of the 'Wig 'n Gown' and 'Penelope's' awaited; the former a very small hostelry once the haunt of local legal chaps, the latter a nightclub. I was to become very familiar with both over the next three years. The sounds of Gerry Rafferty still ring in my ears, selected endlessly by the crews crammed into the Wig.

Aside from a demanding, and very enjoyable time operating against RN and other NATO ships with the unflappable Ken at my helm, a certain social occurrence stands out. That was when the squadron decided to throw a cocktail party in the mess for the resident officers, visiting Nimrod crews and, of course, the schoolteacher fraternity. Early in the proceedings our squadron commander, immaculately dressed in a cream-coloured safari suit, decided to address the assembled guests. Stood next to him was the famed navigator David Herriot, clutching a very full glass of red wine. Clearly unbalanced, David wobbled, and in the process emptied the entire contents over the boss's new suit – giving some meaning to the term Smarty Pants!

A few days later, I accompanied the boss on a visit to one of his civilian pals who was resident on the Rock. After quaffing copious amounts of brandy, midnight struck, and we decided to stagger back to the mess, bemoaning the fact that the two of us were programmed to fly the first sorties of that day with a 0700 hours pre-flight briefing. Thus, after about five hours kip, our two-ship headed off way out into the Atlantic, tasked with locating a naval taskforce and lobbing practice bombs into their wakes. After a very long straight and level transit, the ships were sighted; and for some reason (for which I was very grateful) the boss elected to abandon the bombing, instead carrying out a lazy orbit, followed by another sedate transit back to Gib. All of this was flown at the unusually high altitude of 500 feet. I well recall the silence from the rear seats that accompanied all of this, and the sighs of relief from our navigators once we were safely back on terra firma. No post-flight breathalysers in those days.

My next trip to Gib was for Exercise Open Gate in April 1978. A relatively low-key exercise involving co-operation with the USS *Nimitz* carrier and her aircrews. But the more memorable activity was shooting sequences for the MoD publicity film '12 Squadron Buccaneers'. The *Chariots of Fire* director, Hugh Hudson, accompanied by a very pretty continuity girl, and an equally attractive MoD PR lady, headed the friendly production crew. No further mention of their activities. Filming included several sortie briefings, wrestling with aircrew equipment, take-offs and landings, and a simulated engine fire emergency featuring myself

Mal Grosse (right) with Phil Leckenby and Jock Frizzell 'host' Kit Williams,
production manager of the MoD publicity film made at Gibraltar.

and my one-eyed navigator Phil Leckenby; who, in his previous life had been a pilot on Vulcans and Jet Provosts before a car accident at Cranwell had unfortunately removed his left eye. More of this to come.

One storyline of the film would be Phil and myself recovering to Gib with a simulated engine fire. This was demonstrated for the cameras by pulling the fuel jettison lever and dumping Avtur, giving the impression of a trail of white smoke from the affected engine. After landing, we were taken to the engineering office where the analysis of our exploits was shot at length. We were both very sweaty and fairly knackered which added to the realism of things. Also, as was the norm, Phil wore his eye patch throughout. Whilst we all thought this would confer a unique input to the script, when the draft was sent to London for approval, those at MoD took a different view, insisting that the scene should be re-shot with the absence of Phil's patch. PC was alive in those days! After our return to the UK, the scene had to be re-enacted in the 12 Squadron line hut. But just prior to filming, we both had to be splashed with water whilst running on the spot, thus creating a semblance of our demeanour in Gib. Fortunately we possessed reasonable acting skills.

After some great flying with the Yanks around the Med, some jolly times with Hudson and his team, and of course the locals from Town Range, the film and the rest of us were well-canned! And then it was back to Honington for some further film sequences. One of these sorties called for the recording of the launch of a TV Martel missile over the Irish Sea, which was part of the regularly held Mistico trials programme. After a decidedly dodgy descent over Wales in foul weather, we located the firing Buccaneer and closed up to witness the event. Only at the last moment, upon looking in my rear-view mirror, did I realise that in order to get the best shots of the missile launch, Phil had completely unstrapped himself from the ejection seat, crouching with large camera in hand. For this and his other exploits behind the lens, Phil was subsequently made an honorary member of the Institute of UK Film Cameramen (or some such). What a star!

Four months after the Mistico firings, I took three aircraft to the French base at Cazaux on the west coast of France close to Bordeaux for the AR (anti-radar) Mistico trial. There, over three weeks, we carried out firings of our AR Martel missile. Each one was aimed at an active radar antenna sited on the coast at Cazaux, fired from a range of 20 miles at 200 feet. Our little Scotsman, Jock Frizzel, lined up our missile from the rear seat, and as I pulled the trigger I had this vision of a huge grey log leaving the port wing, trailing a bright exhaust as it climbed towards 20,000 feet, locking onto its target and zooming down to its radar target, scoring a direct hit. Impressive piece of Anglo-French kit.

A couple of months or so prior to Open Gate, John Beard and myself were operating out of Honington at night as a singleton maritime probe, searching for targets in the North Sea. We had just taken on fuel from a Victor tanker, before descending to low level some halfway between Scotland and Denmark when there was a loud explosion and flash of light. Looking around, it was not clear which engine was affected – until the port engine instruments revealed a gradual loss of RPM and increasing jet pipe temperature. Shutting the thing down, we crawled back to the coast on the surviving engine, landing at RAF Marham – where the mess bar inhabitants ensured our composure. A main bearing had disintegrated.

In September 1978, Phil and I gave ourselves a treat and set off for a four-day break to the Rock. Now, the route from the UK to Gibraltar is very straightforward. Leave Land's End and head across the Bay of Biscay to the north-west tip of Spain, turn left and then left again at the south-west tip of Portugal. That day however, there was total cloud cover, so more than a Mark 1 pilot eyeball was needed. As we left Land's End, Phil tuned in to BBC music and tucked into a sandwich. That was the last I heard from him for about an hour. Loudly rousing him from his snores, I exclaimed that perhaps we should have turned left by now. "Oh Christ, do it now," was the alarmed response. Ah well, that little detour into the Atlantic was an extremely rare pig! Aside from spending the next few days whiling away most of the time in the Wig 'n Gown (and a glance at Penelope's), we wandered up and down the Spanish coast before coming across HMS *Ark Royal*, sailing close to Gib. After a quick call to Flyco (flying control), we carried out a long-landing approach to the deck, overshooting at about 50 feet. Phil had previously completed an exchange tour on the carrier and was unperturbed. But I was a 'crab' at heart.

In June 1979, I made my final visit to Gib whilst serving with 12 Squadron. Princess Alexandra was visiting the Rock and Honington was asked to provide a flypast during her time there. So, along with that jovial Irishman Kyle Morrow, off we went. A simple task, quick night-stop and back to base. Or so we thought. The display format was straightforward; departure, burn off fuel over the Med, return for a low overshoot and flypast, turn downwind and land. All went OK, until we were downwind when the hydraulics failed.

*Mal Grosse and Phil Leckenby
entertain Miss Gibraltar.*

The CHAG (chain arresting gear) was set up for our arrested landing (no brakes). Unlike the RHAGs in the UK and elsewhere, the CHAG was a basic affair comprising a cross-runway wire attached at each end to a long set of very heavy chains. On landing we took the wire and were slowed down by the unravelling of the chains down both sides of the runway, accompanied by a loud clattering noise, and large clouds of dirt, dust, sand and gravel.

Towed back to dispersal, we quickly retired to the officers' mess where the princess was awaiting our arrival on the patio looking out over the runway, from where she had seen the escapade. She was, she said, delighted with our display – especially the spectacular show on landing. The next week was spent carrying out repeated taxi tests with the ground crew trying to resolve a binding-brake problem. Kyle especially enjoyed a couple of these as I replaced him in the rear seat with the then Miss Gibraltar. His job was to assist her ascent up the ladder with a gentle push from behind, followed by strapping her into the seat. Eventually we gave up on the lame aircraft, returning to the UK by civil air. So ended around six weeks' worth of detachments to Gibraltar with 12 Squadron.

Including my time on the Rock, my tour on 12 Squadron comprised a total of 24 weeks away on detachment throughout Europe on various joint NATO maritime exercises. These were very operationally realistic, involving day and night simulated war operations over the Arctic, Atlantic, North Sea, Skagerrak, Kattegat, Baltic and Mediterranean. One of the more demanding, and less enjoyable, of these was performing simulated rocket attacks on surface vessels in the Skagerrak, conducted under the glare of our own Lepus flares, which we had tossed shortly beforehand. One such sortie was executed over an unsuspecting cruise liner, where the passengers and crew were no doubt somewhat alarmed at the antics going on around them.

Most of these exercises were preceded by one of our crews visiting the host operating base to agree our forthcoming activities. For Exercise Furbelow at Aalborg in Denmark, Phil and I undertook this duty; and in so doing we got to know each other somewhat better. Our Danish host had kindly arranged our two-day accommodation in a nice four-star hotel – with a huge double bed, in a single room. Needless to say, the bolster was put to good use on both nights!

There were better experiences. Courtesy of Exercise Bright Horizon, we came to know

12 Squadron at Schleswig with German F-104G pilots.

quite well the German F-104 Starfighter operators based at Schleswig and Eggebek in northern Germany. Our first visit started with four days off in order to acclimatise ourselves with the hosts and their local haunts. This, of course, involved much familiarization with the refreshments in the mess bar and various hostelries. Our boss, Peter Harding, began the proceedings by appearing holding his tipple, dressed, out of character, in a long shabby raincoat and cap – looking for all the world like the comedian Peter Cook. However, the squadron engineering officer managed to upstage him by disappearing completely for the next seven days – befriended by some German family and friends, he spent the entire time consuming copious quantities of German beer, eventually turning up looking worse for wear. When I eventually left the squadron, I next came across him some eight years later lying on a bench in a park adjacent to the MoD Main Building. A lovely guy and excellent engineer – sad sight to discover.

One less stressful detachment was a two-week spell in Italy, dropping practice bombs at the range at Decimomannu. That said, my flight down to Deci did involve a certain degree of angst. Halfway across France, my navigator, Dave Cleland-Smith, noticed that my speech was becoming somewhat slurred. Between us we discovered that my oxygen hose had become disconnected and I was becoming anoxic. A rapid descent and diversion to the French base Istres ensued. On landing, I was ambulanced to the medical centre, where I quickly recovered and was assessed as fit to fly on to Italy. Thus, I was taken to the mess where I met up with C-S. There I found him tucking into a fine lunch accompanied by a half-consumed bottle of red. I had no option but to join him and polish off the other half. We then took off for an uneventful low-level transit over the Med to Sardinia. A few days later Dave sought revenge. He was a scuba diver and had brought his kit with him. On a beach to the south of Deci he offered to introduce me to his hobby, fitting me with all the gear, including body weights, and throwing me into the deep water which he had carefully chosen. Almost instantly, and well submerged, I found myself in a panic, struggling for air. Of which there was none, as he had ensured that my air-tank was empty. Fortunately, people like Tim Aaron were there for my rescue. Beers were on C-S for the weekend!

In June 1979, HM the Queen visited Honington and I had the privilege of leading a 13-aircraft formation flypast in her honour. We carried out four rehearsals for the event, which began with a form-up over the North Norfolk coast followed by a southerly transit, culminating in a pull-up from 500 feet at the airfield boundary, overflying her dais at 800 feet. To herald our arrival, I decided that the rear five formation aircraft would operate their fuel jettison handles so that a stream of what appeared to be white smoke was emitted in Red Arrows fashion, as we had done in Gibraltar. It was on our last rehearsal when the person pretending to be the Queen, and sitting in her place on the dais, was showered with our paraffin – no surprise that we were forbidden from using this ploy. Almost 12 months later, when receiving my AFC at Buckingham Palace, Her Majesty recalled (well-briefed) her visit and the flyby. Thank goodness she didn't have to recount me soaking her.

In October my tour with 12 Squadron came to an end with a four-day squadron exchange visit to the German base at Nörvenich, along with my last navigator 'Sparky' Powell. He eventually joined me in a different role in the Buccaneer office at HQ 1 Group, RAF Bawtry. RIP Sparky.

The remaining 10 years of my RAF career included attendance at the RAAF Staff College in Canberra, two tours at HQ 1 Group, and a final tour at the MoD. I was also appointed to command 54 Jaguar Squadron and 27 Tornado Squadron. These unfortunately did not come to fruition – but that's another story.

After the RAF, I spent 12 years with BAE Systems trying to sell the Eurofighter Typhoon. The last four of these saw me back in Canberra heading up the sales campaign trying to persuade the Australians to acquire the aircraft. I failed – majestically!

CHAPTER ELEVEN
ALWAYS VIGILANT

DAVE AINGE

After four tours on the Hunter, I joined 208 Squadron in November 1977 as the squadron weapons leader. Fritz Davidson, a very experienced Buccaneer back-seater, was my navigator for my first flight and proved more than capable of encouraging me along the right path, but others also shared the task of bringing the 'new guy' up to speed, the strain proving too much for one individual.

I soon found that at anything other than circuit speeds, the Buccaneer handled like a big Hunter, and much of the weaponry and tactics were similar. One of the main differences however was the 'time line'. With the Hunter we had a means of mutual defence with our guns so maintained battle formation of between 2–3,000 yards abreast between pairs of aircraft but the Bucc had nothing. Low-level formation was flown much wider, three–six miles, sometimes even out of sight to each other and when a threat was detected, the defence was to split to the four winds thus leaving the enemy with only one target out of the four or more aircraft. After continuing independently, we later re-joined on the 'time line', a procedure about which I initially had severe doubts, but was soon converted after seeing it work with all aircraft almost miraculously sliding back into position.

After my initial flying, I paired up as a constituted crew with Roger Carr who was on his second Bucc tour and was, in my opinion, one of the finest navigators on Buccaneers. With his experience we became a good team and 1978 was a busy year.

In May we deployed to RAF Leuchars in Scotland for the Tactical Fighter Meet (TFM), which provided the opportunity for tactical low flying with attacks on the weapons ranges and with fighter opposition in the form of both Phantoms and Lightnings. The exercise culminated with an attack on the Otterburn Weapons Range with a full war load of six 1,000-lb HE bombs.

At low level over Labrador.

It also led to some interesting situations, one when we were returning to Leuchars in fairly murky weather and spotted a Lightning converging from the gloom to the right. He obviously hadn't seen us so the tactical thing would have been to creep away and disappear back into the murk, but I couldn't resist the temptation of turning in and 'attacking' him. This led to an upward 'scissors' combat in which we were soon out-powered so we broke off at around 6,000 feet and plunged back into the murk at low level running flat out. The next we saw of him was in the Leuchars circuit with the Lightning calling for priority landing short of fuel. We finished the TFM by leading a mixed formation of six Buccaneers and five Lightnings back to Honington via Leeming and Binbrook where the Lightnings left us.

In July, and after a lot of hard work by the ground crew preparing the aircraft, we deployed to RAF Lossiemouth for the Tactical Bombing Competition (TBC). Also taking part were our sister Buccaneer squadrons, XV and 16 from Germany, teams of Jaguars, Harriers and A-7s of the USAF. The format was similar to the TFM, but with more emphasis on weapons.

There followed another exhilarating week of tactical flying and by some good luck with the weapons on my part, and Roger's excellent navigation, we finished in overall second place in the Leader's Trophy. Unfortunately, the week highlighted the obsolescence of the aircraft's weapons delivery system in comparison to the other, more modern aircraft with their laser ranging and more sophisticated weapons systems. It was only later, after we were equipped with the Paveway LGB (laser-guided bomb) system, that the Buccaneer entered the same league in the overland role. We finished the week leading nine aircraft on an airfield attack at Finningley to show off the Buccaneer to the budding navigators training there before forming up as a Diamond Nine back at Honington.

By this time Mike Bush had retired to join Monarch Airlines, a path I was later to follow, and I was appointed to replace him as B Flight commander. In July we deployed, with Victor tanker support, to Goose Bay in Labrador on the east coast of Canada to give us experience flying over terrain similar to that we would encounter if the Cold War turned hot. Labrador is extremely flat, interspersed with a myriad of lakes and the occasional river, and with pine trees stretching from horizon to horizon. Signs of man are virtually non-existent with only the occasional line of power cables and cluster of houses near the coast to denote his presence. We were cleared to fly down to 100 feet above ground level, and at that height navigation, with the lack of distinct features, was very different and far more difficult than in Europe. We normally flew as a four-aircraft formation with a single aircraft deployed as 'bounce' to simulate an enemy air threat.

One of the more interesting aspects was the occasional dead tree in the endless carpet of evergreen pines, just thin, sun-bleached poles sticking well up above the others and very difficult to see until the last minute. After landing from one sortie, when I thought I might have come a bit close when turning hard, the ground crew came up the ladder to inform me that I had hit a bird, there was a dent near the wingtip. He also informed me that it must have been nesting as it had a twig in its beak at which point I called for the squadron engineering officer. Sure enough there was a bit of sun-bleached tree in the wing, which the engineers were able to fix without recourse to spares. The trees in Labrador are exceptionally tall, and this was all part of my personal learning curve, fortunately with no serious results or repercussions.

In October 1978 the squadron deployed to Nellis AFB near Las Vegas in Nevada for Exercise Red Flag, which has been so well covered by Dave Wilby in *Buccaneer Boys*. For those who haven't read it, Red Flag was a regular exercise devised by the Americans to better prepare their squadrons and crews for war, Vietnam having shown up major deficiencies in their training leading to very high casualty rates. A large part of Nevada was declared 'enemy' territory, a training area where all forms of flying, including delivery of live weapons, could be practised. Each day a 'Blue' Force of some 160 aircraft would be briefed to attack realistic, full-size targets in the area with live war loads whilst 'Red' Force, some 80 air defence aircraft plus surface-to-air missiles (SAMs) and guns, tried to stop them. A mass debrief with all crews attending was then held using telemetry and film to assess the results from both sides.

On one sortie leading a strike against an airfield target we were approaching the final run in at 550 knots when an engine low-pressure warning illuminated. The procedure was to throttle back and return to base but, not wishing to land back at Nellis with a full load of live HE 1,000-lb bombs, I decided to continue. With radio silence in force I hoped the others would cope with the inevitable reduction in speed. Of course they did, and Ricky 'Ramjet' Pierson with Al Vincent, having stayed in formation to avoid inflicting fragmentation damage on me, claims that we were both credited with direct hits, seaman's eye obviously still worked.

After the attack I handed over the lead so that we could make our own way back independently to declare a precautionary landing. Meanwhile Rick, whilst evading an F-106 fighter which circled overhead, became a bit too enthusiastic with his low flying and hit a telegraph line later measured at 38 feet above the ground. Having declared an emergency, he returned to Nellis minus the radar nose cone and with an engine damaged by debris. The coordination of the recovery to Nellis of well over 150 aircraft before Rick landed was a master class in air traffic control. Fortunately, the aircraft was soon flying again, but such things do not go unnoticed by higher authority, and it led to the convening of a Board of Inquiry to investigate the incident with some intense scrutiny of the minimum height rules.

Shortly after Rick's incident we were leading a pair of aircraft as part of an airfield attack when our route took us fairly close to an SA6 (SAM) site. The SAM sites were able to 'lock on' to us down to our minimum height, and the only defence was to weave and fly straight at them to try and break any missile lock achieved. Sure enough, this particular site 'locked on' and we started a high 'G' jinking weave while releasing 'chaff' from our airbrakes.

Immediately after landing we were met by the detachment commander, the formidable Gp Capt 'Whisky' Walker. He had already seen the preview from the SAM site when my manoeuvring led to the American operator exclaiming about us 'kicking up the dust' before we roared overhead, and he questioned us very closely about our minimum height, a hot topic at the time. I pointed out that it was not dust but the 'chaff' we carried to break the radar lock, which looked remarkably like a dust cloud when released and Rog, who had watched the radio altimeter (Rad Alt) like a hawk, was able to assure him that we had not flown below 100 feet. However it certainly made for an interesting talking point when shown at the mass debrief and was later featured on Anglia TV.

As part of the overall war training at Nellis there was a section which dealt with escape and evasion in the event of being shot down in enemy territory. At the end of the squadron's involvement in Red Flag, and to ensure our allowances continued while we waited to ferry the aircraft back, Stu Ager, our escape and evasion training officer, asked if we could be given a special course even though we were not scheduled.

The survival training consisted of a couple of days of classroom work followed by three days in the wilds of Nevada 'surviving'. Our instructors were a couple of sergeants, a Texan and a Kentuckian, both of whom displayed a less than favourable reaction to being lumbered with a bunch of limey greenhorns. After the classroom bit, we set off into the wild. However there is survival, and there is survival, and we had no intention of suffering unduly so we had taken the precaution of carrying a number of cold boxes stacked with beer and steaks so that we wouldn't die of thirst or starvation. Having arrived at the site chosen, we were given a parachute and told to build a shelter for the night, our two sergeants departing, convinced that they would return to a scene of chaos with these limeys clueless as to what to do. Relationships improved remarkably when they came back to find us well established with shelters built, fire going, beers to hand and steaks ready. Several hours later, well fed and watered, we slept like logs, helped even more by the bottle of bourbon, which our instructors magically produced.

The next day after breaking camp the Texan produced a 0.22 rifle with which he shot a jack rabbit, a form of mountain hare. Not to be outdone, Dick Pringle asked if he could

Red Flag 'survivors'. Back from left to right: Al Smith, Stu Ager,
Simon Deacon-Elliott and Dave Ainge. Front: Ron Trinder and Joe Hellyer.

try and, much to their surprise, came back with another. I couldn't resist having a go and returned with a rabbit, a cotton tail, with a hole through the head – I didn't let on how close I had been. By this time any reservations our two sergeants may have still held finally disappeared, and the evening progressed with steak and rabbit on the menu washed down with more beer and bourbon, and the two instructors leading the singing with an accordion and a ukulele. After a very late start the following morning, we returned to Nellis our allowances well earned.

In June 1979, as training for our deployed role, we detached to RDAF Aalborg in Denmark for a NATO exercise. I had already carried out a pre-detachment review of the base, one of the most important requirements being to ensure a copious supply of duty-free alcohol, the Scandinavian countries being notoriously expensive. Our squadron GLO, Maj Gavin Anderson, was given responsibility for this and decided we hadn't ordered anywhere near enough and he would take care of it. He did. As we came to the end of the detachment we realised we still had far more duty-free than we could take home, so the store was opened to the Danes and the queue stretched around the hangar! We had still saved sufficient to host a final party in the mess and the sight of already well-inebriated Danes repeatedly asking for their glasses to be filled to the top before downing in one is an abiding memory.

Dave Ainge's suitcase bombing memento.

The trip back to Honington was also memorable. We crossed the North Sea at low level and evaded a Phantom patrol before carrying out a practice attack on the Cowden Range target. We were leading and I briefed the flight to remember not to open the bomb bay – our baggage was secured in there. However Roger arrived too late to put his bag in our Bucc, so had to send it back in the Hercules, was this a premonition?

During the attack at Cowden the inevitable happened – I opened the bomb bay! The routine was automatic, it has to be in wartime, and although my call of "bomb bay open" was greeted by an immediate cry of "No" from Rog, it was too late. Back at Honington I opened the bay so that the ground crew could retrieve my bag, still hoping that I had closed it quickly enough. After what seemed like an eternity, the airman re-appeared holding up the remnants of the straps, no bag and a quizzical expression on his face; my bag was in the sea at Cowden.

Needless to say I became the laughing stock, not just of the squadron and the assembled wives, but soon the whole station; it was an embarrassing debrief. Several weeks later at our regular weekly aircrew meeting, Rob Wright, who had recently arrived as OC A Flight, handed me a brown paper parcel. I opened it and out fell my uniform jacket, rather dishevelled and still adorned with seaweed! It had been handed in to the local constabulary at Cowden who found my identity card in the pocket and tracked me down.

Graham Pitchfork, 'the Fork', a very experienced Bucc navigator, having served tours with the navy as well as the RAF, had recently replaced Phil Pinney and after this introduction to the squadron, he must have thought his time as CO could be very short indeed.

A sequel to my incident came a couple of years later. Rob, who had been the cheerleader, was flying up to Lossie with Graham for the annual tactical bombing competition. On the way he did exactly the same as I had, and on the same range, but this time it was not only their personal luggage in the bomb bay but also Graham's briefcase with all the squadron aircrews' annual confidential reports – including Rob's. He who laughs last etc., but it didn't have any lasting effect on Rob's career as he was finally to retire as AM Sir Robert Wright.

With Roger approaching the end of his tour, I needed a good act to follow him. Al Vincent was a first tourist on the Bucc after a tour on Canberras, and he had already made a good impression, so I poached him. It was a good choice and together we soon built up a rapport that stood us in good stead in the future; I was very lucky to have flown with both Rog and Al.

1979 finished with a detachment to Decimomannu in Sardinia for an armament practice camp. The format was familiar with weapons training on Capo Frasca Range and low-level sorties around Sardinia en route. Al and I managed to win the squadron bombing competition.

We socialised in the IAF officers' mess with the famous flaming sambucas, and played some golf. During one round at the magnificent Is Molas golf club the afore mentioned Rob, having won the last hole, struck a magnificent drive whilst the rest of us watched on in amusement; he had teed up pointing the opposite way to the fairway! What the Italians thought I have no idea, but our laughter must have carried a very long way.

As a change one Sunday, the squadron hierarchy hired a minivan and headed for the south coast to play beach golf followed by a meal at a local taverna. We agreed that we would not leave until the bill came to 100,000 lira; it sounds a lot but there were a lot of lira to the pound at that time so it was reasonable, honest. It did, however, subsequently lead to a request from the local priest, who was trying to conduct his evening service in the church across the road, to quieten down. Apparently, his flock was more interested in our goings on than they were with his sermon, and had taken to leaving the church to peer in through the windows.

Having judged that we had passed our target, we asked for the bill only to find that 10% had been deducted for our good custom so, much to the owner's astonishment, "more wine" was called for. When the final bill was presented, 'the Fork' was taking a comfort break and we hid from him. The look on his face to find the room deserted, and the thought that we had left him to pick up the tab was priceless. Finally we left with John Babraff, the most junior member, being appointed driver, after all it was his birthday. I have to say there were one or two scary moments as we negotiated the narrow, winding coastal road back towards Cagliari, so much so that we felt it necessary to stop there for further refreshment before continuing back to Deci. Work hard and play hard was the norm, but the thought did crop up afterwards that the event could have led to everyone moving up a rank on the squadron!

In February 1980 we travelled to Nellis AFB where the two Germany squadrons had already started their Red Flag exercise. We were programmed to take over their aircraft so we deployed by VC10.

Then tragedy struck on the day we arrived; one of the German crews crashed in the exercise area and all Buccaneer flying ceased as we waited for the Air Accident Board to investigate the accident and establish the cause. With the publication of their interim findings, we were shocked to learn that a whole wing had detached while the crew had been turning hard at low level; they never stood a chance. The Buccaneer force was immediately grounded until the cause, and a solution if there was one, was found.

A sombre party arrived back at Honington to wait to find out if this was the end of the

208 Squadron back to being a Hunter squadron …
this time with a navigator boss!
Dave Ainge second row on the right.

Buccaneer force. The cause was finally traced to hairline fatigue cracks in what was known as the 'spectacle' frame, so called because it is in the shape of a pair of spectacles traversing the centre of the aircraft, and to which the wings were attached. This was in an area normally impossible to access because fatigue there was never thought possible; after all the aircraft was built for carrier operations, and the frame was milled from solid metal.

A solution was found in the form of grinding out any fatigue cracks, but it involved checking all aircraft to find those affected and deciding which could be saved. With the foreseen reduction in the fleet, Graham Pitchfork became embroiled in a battle to prevent 208 being disbanded immediately. Fortunately, his arguments prevailed and we settled down to a long wait.

In the meantime, the squadron was able to carry on flying with the Hunter T.8s, but this was severely limited, and so a request was put in for some single-seat Hunter F.6As that were in storage. Happily, this coincided with my return to flying (I had dislocated my shoulder skiing), and Rob Wright, Terry Heyes and myself, 'the Fork's Hunter Mafia', came up with the cracking solution that the F.6As should only be flown by pilots who had flown a tour on Hunters, thus narrowing the field down to we three. My logbook shows three months of purely Hunter flying. This may sound a bit harsh on the others, but we also acquired four two-seaters allowing everyone to stay in practice. Although 1 Group turned down our request to carry out weapons' training, with three former Hunters PAIs we were allowed to carry out tailchases. This somehow evolved into full-bloodied combat and – since we hadn't requested this activity – it hadn't been refused.

Finally, we received the all clear to start flying the Buccaneer. After a refamiliarisation trip, Al and I flew over to Wales and racked it round the hills, not without a little trepidation I have to admit, but the Buccaneer was a fine aircraft and I never really doubted that it would look after us. I then flew with Graham to get him back in the air, and that was my final Buccaneer sortie before posting; the Buccaneer was back in service with 208 just as I was about to leave.

208 Squadron's Hunter Mafia. Terry Heyes, Graham Pitchfork (honorary member), Dave Ainge and Rob Wright.

A final gift that I still have in front of me as I write, was a cartoon sketch drawn by Corporal Law [see page 94], the GLO's driver, and a talented artist. It is titled 'DA about to demonstrate his revolutionary new concept in weapons delivery!' It shows me standing in my flying kit leaning on a suitcase bomb – I was never to be allowed to forget the Cowden incident. All the aircrew, and many of the leading lights of the ground crew signed it. It still brings back many happy memories of a wonderful tour and a fine aircraft and is something I treasure. So I left 208 to move to a desk just a couple of hundred yards away as the wing weapons officer.

Having arrived in my new job, the station commander, Gp Capt Mike Shaw, obtained authority for me to continue flying the Hunter. The final highlight of my time in the RAF, and with 208, was an invitation from Graham Pitchfork to join the squadron on its detachment to Lossiemouth for the work-up for Maple Flag, the Canadian equivalent of Red Flag. I was given the role of flying the Hunter to simulate an enemy air threat, and so I spent the next two weeks hurtling around the glens and highlands making life as difficult for them as possible, and having the time of my life. At the same time Graham, a navigator, had amassed 100 hours in the Hunter and Rob Wright, Terry Heyes and myself, his Hunter 'mafia', presented him with a 100-hour scarf. That detachment was the icing on top of the cake, and a great way finally to end my time in the RAF. Thank you, Mike Shaw and Graham.

CHAPTER TWELVE

HAIRY MOMENTS

Flying high-performance combat aircraft is not without its hazards and the aircrew are trained to deal with the unexpected. Outlined in the following paragraphs are four examples typical of the situations that a crew might have to face and resolve safely.

A Tale from the High Seas – Mick Whybro RAF

The carrier, HMS *Hermes*, had just left the vicinity of Gan in the Indian Ocean and was heading for Singapore. Someone decided that it would be a good idea to send two Buccaneers of 801 Squadron on a long-range strike against a military target on the island, thereby demonstrating the aircraft's range and its ability to hit a target and remain undetected in the process. The crews would enjoy a night 'downtown' – a pre-emptive soirée before the rest of the team disembarked to RAF Changi a couple of weeks later.

And so it was that two specially selected crews, CO/SOBs and AWI/AWI Obs (there's a surprise), launched on 16 August 1968. As a crab navigator [Author: Mick was the AWI observer], I thought it prudent to calculate a point of no return (PNR) on such a long leg, especially one without diversions between ship and Butterworth near Penang. We had just reached the PNR when one of the general service hydraulic pumps failed. The drill in the emergency procedures was clear. It stated that the undercarriage and hook should be lowered immediately. This was all very well, but did we have enough fuel to reach Butterworth in that configuration?

Mick Whybro's arrival at Butterworth.

In those days there were no fuel figures for such a situation. So, after a short discussion we agreed an empirically derived figure. Based on this it was too soon to lower the gear. (I should add at this juncture that our gallant CO and SOBs assumed we had everything under control and hotfooted it to Changi leaving us to make our own arrangements.)

When we lowered the gear and hook, we got four greens promptly followed by the failure of the other hydraulic pump. We were now committed to landing without airbrake, flaps and with limited wheel brakes – and the hook was redundant since there was no arrestor gear at RAAF Butterworth.

However, this proved to be the least of our worries since we were clearly using fuel at a faster rate than we had anticipated. My continuous calculations indicated that we would run out near to coasting in at Penang. I was able to raise Butterworth on HF and alert them to our situation. In the event, the wind became more favourable and we found ourselves with a few pounds remaining as we crossed the coast in North Penang for a straight-in approach to Butterworth's Runway 18. Having been exposed to a cold soak at altitude for so long, and then having to make a very high-speed touchdown, it was too much for the tyres and they both burst. The aircraft left the runway and came to a rapid halt on the soft surface. The Australian crash crew informed us that the starboard wheel was burning well until it buried itself in the soft mud. So ended our steely attack on Singapore.

A Farnborough Frolic – David Scott

In September 1970, 12 Squadron was tasked to provide a Buccaneer at the Farnborough Air Show for a week to demonstrate air-to-air refuelling. With a Phantom 'plugged in' to the Victor's starboard pod, I was to plug in on the port side and the combination would fly over the air show at low level.

It was a very simple and straightforward mission that required an RV over the Bristol Channel followed by a long let down to Farnborough, plugging in prior to a low-level flypast west to east over the airfield before unplugging in the climb to return to base.

On 8 September the weather left a bit to be desired, with extensive cloud cover in the south from 800 feet to about 10,000 feet with squally showers beneath, i.e. bumpy. The RV was uneventful and we let down in close formation through the cloud with the intention of plugging in on the final run in at low level. I blessed the steadiness of the Buccaneer, but was unprepared for the flexing of the Victor wing and consequent antics of the drogue/basket. With the airfield appearing in peripheral vision there was an urgency to succeed. However, there was no way the Phantom could make contact and the Buccaneer fail. It was more by luck than good judgement that a successful contact was made in time.

Dave Scott plugged into the Victor tanker over the Farnborough Air Show.

The plan was to unplug immediately after the flypast prior to the climb through cloud. I saw the Phantom disengage so I throttled back to do likewise but soon realised that we were a long way back and still connected. I saw the hose unravel in the pod and had to apply power to rewind some of it back on to the spool in the Victor's refuelling pod. My intrepid nav, John Beard, suddenly started to take an interest in an otherwise normally routine manoeuvre. We were forced to climb and I had to hang in while we sorted out the problem. The tanker confirmed that he had no control of the pod brake system, it being entirely automatic.

The Phantom remained in attendance, I suspect with a certain amount of amusement at our predicament. As we headed for the Bristol Channel we reviewed the options, which appeared depressingly few. To let the hose unravel would risk it whipping back over our aircraft and flail with the basket still attached. It could wrap around the canopy hindering any attempt to eject had we needed to or it could have struck the tailplane.

I remembered somebody saying the refuelling nozzle incorporated shear bolts, so I tried every manoeuvre within the limits of the proximity of the tanker and the need to stay close to avoid the hose unravelling completely. It didn't work. At this point the tanker captain said he was getting short of fuel. In desperation I had closed under the Victor's wing in the hope the bolts might work. This proved too much for the hose, which snaked out of the pod, hit our tailplane, at which point the hose became disconnected at the join with the basket and disappeared into the Bristol Channel leaving the basket stuck on the end of our probe.

Having been connected to the tanker for 50 minutes it was a relief to turn for home. The Phantom crew did a visual inspection and confirmed that there was a dent in the tailplane but no hydraulic leak. All cockpit indications were normal so we headed for Honington, adding the statuary 10 knots for a landing in an unusual configuration. We taxied into dispersal with our decoration on the probe where we created a deal of mirth and, subsequently, it continued in the bar.

Ejection XW525 – Peter Hill

On 208 Squadron in the mid-1970s, those heady days for the Buccaneer overland force, most of England, Wales and Scotland were our stomping ground. We spent most of our time at 250 feet in four-ship formations, attacking simulated targets, dropping bombs on a variety of coastal ranges, avoiding marauding fighters and occasionally topping up our fuel from Victors or our Buccaneer 'buddy-buddy' tankers.

On 4 April 1977, I was flying a conversion sortie in XW525 with Terry Summers who had recently joined the squadron and was working up to be combat ready. With a strong westerly wind and lumps of scudding cumulus at around 2,000 feet, we got airborne from Honington and set off at 250 feet for Holbeach Range for a first-run attack (FRA) before heading west through the tactical link routes to mid-Wales to make simulated attacks on a couple of targets before winding north at low level for the weapons range at Jurby on the Isle of Man.

We approached the IP for our first target then pulled up for a bunt-retard shallow-dive attack against the dam at the end of the Claerwen Reservoir. The climb topped out around 1,300 feet before we tipped in to the dive at 500 knots for a simulated bomb release around 500 feet. It was my job to call out the heights as we dived and then at the release point.

All went according to plan until we saw two Hunters some 2,000 yards in our one o'clock, just before we entered the dive. Their close formation positioning indicated that they were probably part of a four-ship. I called the spot to Terry, who was now concentrating on lining up his aiming mark on the target. I then had a quick look in the area where I expected to see the other pair of Hunters before getting my head down to call out the heights. Seconds later, in the dive, I experienced a violent onset of positive G coupled with a shout from the

FIRST SIGHTING

Hunters
420 k

Scale

0   1   2

Nautical Miles

Buccaneer
500 k

Line of sight

Intended Attack Track

POINT OF CONFLICT

Buccaneer
IMPACT
POSITION

Pull-up
point

Track of the aircraft involved in Peter Hill's accident.

front seat. I blacked out but was still acutely aware of the loud and rather disconcerting deepening tones of the airflow direction detector (ADD), which I had only previously heard in the simulator. There was a wing rock to the right, some heavy buffet and a couple of loud thuds immediately followed.

I lost no time in surmising that it was no longer safe to remain where I was and reached for the nearest ejection-seat handle. I was probably gone within a couple of seconds of it all turning to worms. Terry, meanwhile, with two Hunters flashing across our nose some 50 yards ahead, had pulled hard back on the control column and boldly reached 9G. That proved a bit too much for our tailplane!

Terry immediately pushed the control column forward and the aircraft bunted. Initially he assumed this was as a result of his input, but it more likely resulted from the aircraft being tailless. Quickly realising he was no longer in charge of this rolling and pitching machine, and possibly hearing a loud bang from my seat, he decided to join me outside.

My own arrival in the fresh air at some 480 knots broke both visors on my helmet. My arms flailed wildly breaking my left arm, and my ribs with it. As I recovered consciousness, hanging in my parachute after what seemed like a long sleep, but was only a few seconds, I felt euphoric. I was still in this world! I offered up a prayer to my maker.

Unfortunately, I could not breathe, a sensation overshadowed by the realisation that I was fast approaching terra firma but unable to see it. I therefore adopted a position vaguely remembered from mogul skiing, rather than parachute instruction, awaiting the worst. I had no idea whether I was attempting a front, right or rear-left approach. As I pulled my knees up, almost blind, I just made out our stricken jet, tailless and upside down – well that is how it looked to me – plunging towards its final resting place in the reservoir.

Terry now wisely elected for a wet landing beside the Buccaneer from where he inflated his dinghy, thus qualifying for the Goldfish Club in addition to the Caterpillar Club and

The tail of XW525 by Claerwen Reservoir.

getting his free Martin-Baker tie. I had to settle for the latter two.

I was less fortunate, hitting the ground in some 25 knots of wind, which kept my parachute inflated dragging me along on my back as I tried to release the two Koch fasteners. Unfastening the right one with a broken arm was not easy and I kept sliding on my back until it dawned on me that undoing the easy one would collapse the canopy and stop my ever-faster sleigh ride.

With vision to one eye improving I gave a friendly wave to one of the Hunter pilots who stayed to cover the action. It occurred to me that I might fire a flare to indicate my well-being, but as the RAF had recently produced blunt dinghy knives, I found it impossible to open the plastic wrapping. So, instead I sat on my dinghy and monitored the approach of a man in a brown raincoat. This Welsh shepherd stopped some 10 yards away as if I was an invading German storm trooper. Eventually he inquired if I needed anything "boyo" to which I responded by asking for a cigarette. Although I smoked a pipe, a fag seemed more appropriate in the circumstances.

He felt in his pockets, produced a yellow packet of some rare make and held it out. I couldn't get up, and he was not going to get any closer. The moment of frustration passed when he announced that he hadn't got a light. Searching for matches in my dinghy pack was not an option, so I waited for the arrival of a helicopter from the SAR Flight at Valley. I was not disappointed. They saved me from the antics of some local firemen who fitted me with a leaking rubber splint, and then nearly dropped me off the stretcher as they stumbled down the hillside.

Delivered to the nearby hospital at Aberystwyth, Terry and I were both rewarded by a multitude of medical staff who had been briefed about an air disaster with many injured passengers. They seemed rather let down with just the two of us.

The highlight of my stay in that hospital was waking from an operation to find a Catholic padre beside my bed. Expecting the worst, I began examining myself, but he opened his cassock to reveal four cans of Guinness – I became a Catholic at once.

I managed to call my mother to pacify her as we had been mentioned on the news. She immediately called my sister and said, "It's Peter, but don't worry, he's all right, he's just ejaculated over Wales."

I thanked Martin-Baker, spent three months recuperating at Headley Court, got my tie and tried to avoid 9G thereafter.

Nick Berryman and his navigator,
Colin 'Kabong' Tavner.

Lightning Strike – Nick Berryman

It was 13 December 1973 – my 28th birthday. My navigator, Flt Lt Colin 'Kabong' Tavner, and I were tasked for a night cross-country flight in Buccaneer XW531. Being mid-winter, it got dark very early in Germany, so it was an early evening take-off from Laarbruch, which would get us back in plenty of time for the special roast pheasant birthday dinner that my wife was preparing for when I got home.

The forecast weather for the route over the North German Plain and North Sea was not great – very windy (over 50 mph), cold, and cloudy, but as Colin was going to navigate using the radar throughout the flight, it wasn't vital for us to remain in sight of the ground.

Certainly, it turned out to be a pretty turbulent and bumpy flight, and as we flew close to the island of Heligoland, we could see the 'white caps' on the sea, with big green seas breaking over a ship just below us. I recall discussing with Colin that it would not be a good idea to eject into that sea – we were both wearing bulky waterproof 'immersion suits', and it would be really difficult to inflate and board our dinghies; even if we survived a parachute descent into the sea, would a rescue helicopter be able to locate and winch us up in those awful conditions? Not to worry though, I'd been flying for eight years without recourse to a 'Martin-Baker Let-Down', and Colin for much longer, so why would that night be any different?

We were flying at 2,000 ft at 450 knots when, with absolutely no warning, the aircraft was struck by a tremendous bolt of lightning on the windscreen. It was fortunate that Colin was 'heads-down' looking at the radar screen at the moment the lightning struck, *because I was not.* Immediately, everything seemed to go bright red, then black – I was completely blinded (hopefully temporarily) and couldn't see the instruments in order to keep the aircraft flying straight and level.

Apart from the blinding flash, it sounded as if there had been a massive explosion in the aircraft, and despite our discussion only a few minutes earlier, Colin's first instinct was to eject from the aircraft. Fortunately, he delayed just long enough for me to convince him that the aircraft was still in one piece and responding to the controls, so he stayed where he was.

Although there were no flight controls in the rear cockpit of a Buccaneer, Colin was able to tell from his altimeter that we were climbing, and as his compass was on a steady heading, that I had the wings more or less level. As I could see nothing, the important thing for me to do was not to over-control, and as I pulled back gently on the control column to gain altitude, Colin was able to give me corrections to keep flying straight, and speed information to help me control the engine power and climbing attitude.

Once we had crossed inland from the German coast, if my sight didn't return, at least we stood a slightly better chance of surviving if we had to eject. At around 14,000 feet, my sight slowly returned, although my arms and shoulders ached badly, and I had quite a headache to go with it. I was also still pretty shocked (excuse the pun) and shaken, and as we had no idea what damage the aircraft had sustained, we decided to land at the nearby German air force airfield at Jever, rather than fly all the way back to Laarbruch.

After a safe landing, we contacted XV Squadron operations, and the duty flight commander assured us that he would let our wives know what had happened (no mobile phones in those days). Hopefully, it would be possible to reheat my birthday dinner the following evening! Naturally, we had no spare clothes to change into, and had only the uncomfortable and sweaty immersion suits we stood up in, but our German hosts insisted that we join them for a 'few' beers in the officers' mess, and provided us with beds and blankets once the bar closed.

Very early the following morning, a NATO exercise was initiated at RAF Laarbruch, and the squadron wanted us to fly the aircraft back as soon as possible. After a *number* of beers, with little sleep, it was therefore fortunate that our German allies refused to disturb us until we were fully recovered from our traumatic experience (in the aircraft, not the bar).

When we finally managed to rise, we ventured out to the aircraft to examine it for damage. Having entered through the nose of the aircraft, the lightning had exited via a static wick on the starboard wing, and although the wingtip and navigation light had been frazzled, we decided it would be safe to fly back to Laarbruch (being also under some pressure from the squadron to get back in time to take part in the station exercise). Although we returned to base without further mishap, we discovered that the magnetic compass had been badly affected – challenging Colin's navigational skills to the utmost.

Apart from the wingtip and compass, it transpired that the main damage was to the brace of pheasants that had burned to a crisp in the oven at home. The flight commander had forgotten to tell our wives what had happened, so my wife had assumed that Colin and I had decided to celebrate my birthday in the officers' mess bar instead of going home (we did have a bit of previous in this respect, so I couldn't entirely blame her!).

Without doubt, it was our close friendship and absolute trust in each other that got us out of trouble and safely on the ground, so I was absolutely delighted when Colin was later awarded the Queen's Commendation for Valuable Service in the Air for his part in the drama. Forty-seven years later, he is still my best friend.

CHAPTER THIRTEEN

A NAVAL OFFICER ON EXCHANGE SERVICE WITH THE RAF

KEN MACKENZIE

I have a very clear memory of climbing up the six steps to strap in for my first Buccaneer flight in March 1974. For reasons I will explain below, it was the first time I had been animated about a flight in an aircraft, and it was a daunting experience. Ground school and simulator training on 237 OCU had been intense and, for the first time in my naval career, I experienced a serious personal challenge. Bob Newell gave me the perfect introduction to the aircraft during Nav Fam 1, explaining all his front-seat actions and patiently prompting all of mine. Seventy minutes later, we walked back across the Honington dispersal and I was utterly hooked. But I clearly needed to up my game. And this is why …

It had been a long ten-year journey. I had joined the Royal Navy in 1964 because, well, I came from Plockton, a seafaring village in the Scottish highlands. My father had a distinguished, albeit irregular, wartime career as a sub lieutenant RNVR commanding a Greek caique in the occupied Aegean. He won a DSO. He was a schoolmaster in my local school, and so he had holiday times free to encourage us to sail. I applied for Dartmouth to be a seaman officer in 1963 and was accepted. Impressed by the articulate and confident public schoolboys at my interview board, I was surprised not to see them at Dartmouth one year later. John Winton's semi-fictional novel *We Joined the Navy* offers an explanation. The schoolmaster on the board observes that the candidate does not seem to be very bright. "That's not a problem," says the admiral president: "We want half-wits and the navy will provide the other half!"

A career in aviation was not initially on my horizon. I recall a helicopter winching exercise from an elderly Sycamore in a field above Dartmouth. Not fun. We were then bussed to Roborough near Plymouth for air experience in the Tiger Moth. It was the middle of winter, the ground was frozen, and as soon as I got into the two-piece rubber goon suit I needed a pee, but there was no time to go. The brief flight was cold, noisy and bumpy. I was unimpressed.

Seaman officer training for those on the general list was a protracted business in those days. Short service commission officers, like Tony Ogilvy, Frank Cox, Robin Kent and my other contemporaries at Dartmouth who joined to fly, disappeared to air stations after a few months at college while we stayed behind to study naval lore, drill and 'stuff'.

Almost all the contributors to this book dreamt of a career in aviation from a young age. Not I. In my second year in the navy, I went to sea as a midshipman. HMS *Invermoriston* was an open-bridged minesweeper in Singapore. The Britannia flight took two sweaty weeks. It was during 'Confrontation', a shooting war in the Singapore Straits and Borneo, which nobody knew about back home. I told my gunnery officer captain that we had expended 400% of our annual ordnance allowance in our first quarter. He said, "submit". I did. No response from on high.

Our minesweeping squadrons didn't sweep any mines but it was 'buccaneering' fun, especially in Sarawak. A family friend from Plockton, George Glasgow, was a Javelin pilot based at RAF Tengah. I had a back-seat ride over Borneo with him, but couldn't see much, and was more impressed crewing his Snipe dinghy to success in the 'Round the Singapore Island' New Year race.

In 1968 I went back to sea in HMS *Kirkliston*, Singapore based again, but rotating duties in Hong Kong. My inspirational CO was the Buccaneer observer Mike Cole, whose passion for precise ship handling, all forms of navigation, and mental DR, I eagerly absorbed. Our entry through the HMS *Tamar* breakwater was timed on the Queen's Pier clock. He expected me to be within ten seconds; if not I had to buy the wardroom a drink.

On Mike's recommendation I elected to specialise in aviation. RAF Church Fenton in the winter of 1969 was an odd experience. I enjoyed the comfort of the enclosed Chipmunk cockpit. My first solo crashed through two snow walls as ATC changed the duty runway on my final circuit, and failed to notice the blocked intersection. But I sensed no natural affinity with the front seat and so observer training at Lossiemouth offered a happier option. RNAS Lossiemouth enjoyed the roar of three Buccaneer squadrons and a riotous mess life, but we were the Sea Prince trainee observers destined for helicopters under the watchful, quiet, sober and conscientious eye of our course officer, the irrepressible Neil Law, another 'Buccaneer Boy'.

ASW helicopter training at Portland failed to inspire but, on qualifying, I was quirkily appointed as the staff and operations officer of a commando helicopter squadron, No. 848 embarked in HMS *Albion* on a 12-month Far East deployment. This was fun. As a highly paid Wessex aircrewman, I set up jungle camps, ran detached exercises, inserted and recovered Royal Marine troops from remote jungle clearances, and loved the camaraderie of the Junglie/Royal Marine/Carrier environment. The deployment was a terrific social success, but not remotely professionally demanding, and so the time eventually came for me to exercise my ASW skills on the front line. This was 820 Squadron embarked in HMS *Blake*, an impressive six-inch gun cruiser grotesquely modified to carry four Wessex helicopters in a smoke-filled hangar welded on to the back end. I don't recall detecting a submarine, friend or foe, throughout this appointment. Fuel was the main preoccupation. We enjoyed some great runs ashore, however, and the squadron hierarchy boasted two illustrious Buccaneer Mark 1 heroes: Maurice Fitzgerald as senior pilot and Mike Maddox the senior observer.

In early 1973 I chanced upon the DCI outlining the 'RAF Fixed Wing Integration Loan Scheme' (RAFFWILS), which aimed to maintain a basic level of fixed-wing aviation expertise in our predominantly rotary navy following the demise of fixed-wing naval training. I eagerly applied and was accepted. The other observer was Keith Tatman who went on to a Phantom squadron in Germany. The RAF didn't know what an observer was, but we persuaded Finningley to spare us the Varsity experience. We did, however, complete the full Jet Provost and Dominie courses (with three RAF *ab initios* including a young Alan Vincent – another destined for the Buccaneer) and qualify as RAF navigators. I have the certificate and a brevet. The periscope sextant is a wonderful instrument, but thankfully it still won't fit on the Buccaneer canopy.

Honington in March 1974 saw the start of my Buccaneer experience on 237 OCU. It wasn't an easy transition. I was a laid-back Scottish west-coaster with a rotary 90-knot brain, so the experience of seven or eight miles-a-minute navigation, with the added requirement to understand all the aircraft control and weapons systems, was novel and extremely daunting. The RAF/RN OCU staffs were supportive and encouraging, and their professionalism and enthusiasm in the crew room, classroom and cockpit were so infectious that I gradually got up to speed. I reserve, however, my special gratitude for my successful OCU course completion to the two pilots with whom I then flew predominantly during my subsequent front-line Buccaneer career: the late, lovely Norman Crow (299 sorties on 12 Squadron) and my best man, Rick Phillips (163 Sorties on 809 Squadron). Thanks so much for everything guys.

Norman and I moved across the dispersal to 12 Squadron in August 1974. Flying with Norman was a delight. As a 'creamed-off' QFI, his handling was safe, confident, smooth and accurate (unlike some!) and, although only Bruce Chapple more completely obscured my forward field of view, we perfected some great contour-following low-nav sorties through the Scottish glens. Norman was a bit of a sartorial shambles on the ground, and his casual debriefs reduced the QWIs to tears, but in the air he was the consummate professional as we progressed to six-ship lead. Did I mention that we won the Gilroy Trophy? He knew we'd nailed it, with no time faults and great bombs, so we barrel-rolled most of the way back to base.

12 Squadron's primary task was maritime ship strike and it was fascinating to see our anti-ship tactics being developed and refined over this period. It was clear that the opposition's ability to detect and respond was ever improving, but we were stuck with iron bombs, and so was born the 12-ship co-ordinated saturated ship strike using toss and laydown bombing deliveries. This evolution was not only an exercise in strategic and tactical flying

*Ken Mackenzie and his pilot Norman Crow
received the Gilroy Trophy from Honington's
station commander, Gp Capt Martin Chandler.*

skills and practice (we had to locate and identify our target in radio silence), but also logistically daunting as SEngO (senior engineer officer) had to get 12 appropriately armed jets on to the line – with spares.

From my naval perspective the success of our maritime attack depended on an undetected approach, and I sometimes felt that electronic warfare (EW) voices on 12 Squadron had to shout to be heard. That should all have changed when AR Martel, with its programmable detector head, gave us a fabulous game changer. Graham Smart (the boss) and Dave Wilby used 'under the lobe' radar range advantage, and 'doubling the angle on the bow' ranging techniques to completely surprise a Soviet Kara guided-missile destroyer off Iceland.

As a squadron new boy, I apparently needed a demanding secondary duty. Having narrowly missed out on gardens officer, I was awarded the coveted 'First Day Cover' officer role by the boss. Sticking 1,000 stamps on to 1,000 envelopes within a two-month deadline was a challenge that very few of my new squadron 'mates' wished to share, so I ended up with the bulk of this exciting project myself. Once franked, Andy Carolan and Stu Stringer completed the task by flying my precious postbag (or perhaps a spoof one?) in the bomb bay. I note that there is still one of these highly desirable items left on eBay. Any takers??

Others have had fun elsewhere commenting on Norman's and my rogue TV Martel incident. Mick Whybro comprehensively, and most sensitively, covered in *Buccaneer Boys* the technical aspects of my debacle, but at the time it was quite a serious issue. How could the RAF have allocated one of its rare live firings to a left-handed naval officer? The controller was hard-wired on the right-hand side of the office and its control inputs were the opposite of the similarly placed radar joystick. Was it foul play or incompetence? But wait, I had completed the 'thousands' of hours in the TV trainer box and flown many TVAT sorties so I was technically qualified. Eventually the missile fault was identified and honour restored. I just remember the spectacular roar and mighty flash as this huge missile left

A TV Martel on the inboard pylon with a Westinghouse ALQ-101-8 ECM pod.

the rails, Norman's immaculate low-level escape manoeuvre, and the blurred video of the unsuspecting Phantom as my wayward missile emerged vertically from the clouds heading for him. Thankfully only pride was hurt.

Squadron detachments were always fun. The crate load of duty-free booze delivered by Hercules resulted in momentous Norwegian drinking bouts in the Bodø mess and with the Tromsø-based FPB squadron. The 'cafe cognac' return hospitality from the resident F-5 squadron was even more lethal as it was, of course, home-made. The flying in the four-hour daylight window was, however, utterly spectacular.

I knew Gibraltar and Malta well from previous RN visits, but our squadron detachments were a great mix of social and professional excitement. An early Gibraltar visit was particularly piquant as I met a lovely WRAF air traffic controller. We played Scrabble (honestly) in the control tower during her long boring night watches and enjoyed a day trip to Tangier on the Mons Calpe. Ten years later, after her Hunter/Harrier pilot marriage, Jane and I married. A long story but another great result.

Our weekend Lone Rangers to the Mediterranean were also a welcome sunny break from the interminably foggy Suffolk winters. Apparently they were intended to familiarise us with overseas ATC procedures. Who knew? I also remember a 'black flag' Honington weather brief on a Monday morning. Clearly no flying was possible for at least a week, so the boss phoned HQ 1 Group and posed the question, "How about a four-ship detachment to Gib?" Lunchtime saw us making an R/V on the Victor tanker towline off the Scillies, and sundowners in Gibraltar. Ah, the flexibility of airpower!

*Norman Crow and Ken Mackenzie
with a TV Martel-armed Buccaneer.*

Life on 12 Squadron was busy and never dull. Some of us back-seaters were lent to 208 Squadron, across the hangar, to convert them to the dark arts of AAR. The tanking went fine, and their over-land role flying was a challenging break for me. I recall a night AAR sortie to the Victor towline off Flamborough Head. The weather was fine, I established radar trail and got confirmation from the front seat that he was visual the light. After a while we didn't seem to be closing. He was heading for the planet Venus!

The Buccaneer Blitz is now a key event in our social calendar, but I recall its initial concept in 1975. Those of us in 12 Squadron excluded (happily) from the annual 1 Group cocktail party decided to hit London for a few drinks and a meal. My recollections of the evening are vague, but we eventually shared a riotous supper in a Greek restaurant with the starlets of the newly formed London Weekend Television.

Less exciting was the two-week sojourn in the Lossiemouth Strike Force Dispersal (SFD), (a bunch of caravans, folks) awaiting instructions to launch JMC exercise Orange strikes against Blue. We watched an awful lot of dire television in those days and ate rather badly.

After two years on 12 Squadron I got a unique request to be lent back to the RN as 809 Squadron had run out of RN observers. This was duly granted, and I thoroughly enjoyed a three-month embarked deployment to HMS *Ark Royal* on exercise in the Med. My pilot was the irrepressible Bob Joy who modestly accepted my grateful thanks and appreciation for my first-ever arrested landing (a Blue, of course) and who, unlike Norman, obliged me with a splendid forward view as he always had his seat wound fully down. My introduction to embarked carrier aviation was another steep learning curve. Pre-launch tailplane trim and all-up-weight calculations. Both vital for the hands-off launch. This was a welcome, and an invaluable, return to embarked naval Buccaneer business as I later learned that, contrary to the RN master plan which had me returning to general service, I was to be appointed to 809 Squadron permanently on completion of my 12 Squadron tour, resulting in a further two and a half years on the Buccaneer for another great result for my unplanned career path.

My final five months on 12 Squadron were interesting but exposed the pitfalls that are always ready to trip the unwary and over-confident. Norman was re-appointed and I was considered sufficiently competent to fly with some new squadron pilots. Pete John was the first, then Mike Perry who was the first naval pilot to qualify on the Buccaneer in the RAF fixed-wing loan scheme. Scott Lidbetter was the second helicopter pilot to qualify through the programme, but he bypassed the RAF squadron appointment and went directly to 809 Squadron.

Two 12 Squadron incidents spring to mind during this period, neither of which show me in a good light but they were amusing at the time. We were cruising at low level; again, through my favourite Scottish glens when No. 2 came up alongside with Mike Hall waving his chart board writing 'You're transmitting'. Apparently, he and Pete John, and the entire congregation on Highland Radar, had been entertained by my navigation patter, interspersed with some comment from the previous night's run ashore, and irreverent views of the squadron hierarchy. My foot had stuck on the 'press to transmit' button.

I was then issued a newly converted single-seat Hunter punter pilot, Mal Grosse. Our first trip was to show him the local maritime environment; the North Sea oil rigs and light vessels followed by a leisurely cruise down to the English Channel and back home through the London TCA. It all went horribly wrong. None of my courses worked and we blundered. I'd picked up somebody's beautifully prepared quarter-mil map with all his headings in magnetic! Mal and I later had some lively social adventures in Gibraltar and I am happy to say I prepared him adequately for his subsequent star 'Vangellis' BBC film roles on the Rock with Phil Leckenby.

My final years of embarked Buccaneer aviation in *Ark Royal* were 'business as usual', exercising the entire spectrum of our varied roles in UK waters, the Western Atlantic and the Mediterranean, but with the depressing knowledge that the fun and challenge would soon be over. The TV programme 'Sailor', with Rod Stewart's singing, added to the nostalgia but there was still unfinished business. Our RAF first-tourists wanted to be fully qualified carrier aviators, and so it was that, while the wardroom and ship's mess decks were regaled with the chorus of 'Sailing', some of us observers were flying 'duskers' sorties followed by

A pair of 12 Squadron Buccaneers inspect a North Sea oil rig.

black night approaches and landings. I was very proud to be associated with this initiative, as I truly believe that the RAF appointed some of their best pilots to exchange service with the RN, and they richly deserved this ultimate qualification. On 3 November 1978, I had my first night trip with a pilot who'd never done it before. Rick Phillips, of course, cracked it with some aplomb then, three weeks later, on 27 November, Rick and I disembarked from the Mediterranean to RAF St Athan in the last Buccaneer ever to be catapult-launched from a British aircraft carrier.

My five years, and 1,500 hours on the Buccaneer, amounted to only a tenth of my total naval service, but they totally defined my life and career. A unique period of raised awareness, challenging and varied experiences, great and enduring friendships, constructive inter-service liaison, and the camaraderie of a joint enterprise on a wonderfully iconic aircraft. I still bask in this reflected glory.

CHAPTER FOURTEEN

LIFE ON THE LINE

PETER BROWNING

I learned fairly early on in my time on Buccaneers that the aircraft could be pretty reliable given the right amount of tender loving care from aircrew and ground crew plus a little sunshine on its back to keep the avionics functioning. I was fortunate to be detached to 12 Squadron in November 1970 to take part in Exercise Lime Jug 70 in Malta. We had eight aircraft and on the Press Day launched all eight, the only outfit to launch 100 per cent of its aircraft. 43 Squadron (F-4 Phantoms), who were operating from the adjacent hard-standing to us taxied six, but a fuel tank fell off one as it entered the taxiway, so they were down to five. The nav from that aircraft did not appreciate one of our corporals serenading him with the Sinatra classic 'Tanks for the memory'. He actually swung his 'bone dome' at him.

During my time on 12 Squadron, the ground crew, when on detachment, were in the habit of rewarding the aircrew with sweets, if they brought back a serviceable jet. There was often disappointment when one crew member was denied a sweet, having snagged his bit of the jet. On a detachment to Schleswig in northern Germany in the spring of 1977, we had managed to acquire packets of 'Space Dust', which was all the rage at the time. If you put a few granules on your tongue it would pop and fizz in a quite pleasant and enjoyable manner. During an evening beer call at the line hut, we persuaded Jock Frizzel that some of his fellow aircrew should try it. We told him that a good handful was absolutely required to appreciate it fully and off he went. His two victims did as instructed and mayhem followed as the good handfuls exploded. Jock was out of the crew room door like a greyhound out of the traps! I recall that he had a fair turn of speed for a guy with short legs and was at least 100 yards down the flight line before his victims caught him.

In June 1978 I was lucky enough to be selected to go on a squadron exchange with 3/3 Ardennes Squadron of the French air force based at Nancy-Ochey. They were a Jaguar squadron equipped with Martel. I clearly remember the detachment commander, Sqn Ldr Erskine-Crum, stating that this was somewhat of a misnomer, as it was only the natural curvature of the earth that allowed a Jaguar aircraft to get airborne when armed with two Martel missiles.

The French appeared to have a relaxed attitude to alcohol, as there was actually a bar, open during the day, in the squadron hangar. Flt Sgt Jack Fisher almost had kittens when he discovered it and the troops were left in no doubt what their fate would be if caught consuming alcohol while on duty.

At the weekend we were bussed over to the hangar for a game of football and a barbeque. I remember that slide tackles were a rarity during the game, as the station flock of sheep had been seen grazing on the pitch just a couple of days before! The barbeque was a pleasant and sociable event, but by late afternoon the bus arrived to take us back to the domestic site. Noting that there were several of our hosts still around, and being keen to continue socialising, Bernie Thorne and I contrived to miss the bus by taking a call of nature and watching it sail past the window. Fortune favoured our ruse as a kindly French officer offered us a lift back to the domestic site. During the drive back he asked how things were for us. We told him that our only difficulty was that the SNCOs had nowhere to socialise as the only facility available was the conscripts' mess. We duly arrived at the officers' mess and thanked him for the lift, then made to leave. He asked us in for a drink. We said that we did not want to upset anyone, but he stated firmly that it was his mess and he could invite who he liked. So we followed his lead. We were then greeted by several of our aircrew and on repeating our story about the conscripts' mess were invited to join them. About 30 minutes later a breathless Jack Fisher arrived with several other SNCOs in tow. Apparently Jock Frizzel had phoned the accommodation block and told Jack to get to the officers' mess as soon as he could and to bring as many SNCOs as he could find with him, then promptly put the phone down. Jack was most relieved to be offered a beer and a seat rather than as he put it "quell a riot from our troops". Needless to say, a most convivial evening followed.

Also, during the weekend our hosts laid on a sightseeing coach trip, which took us through the Vosges Mountains and ended up in the pleasant and picturesque village of Riquewihr in the wine-growing region of Haut Rhin. We were wandering through the narrow streets and past quaint buildings when the 12 Squadron trophy to top all trophies was spotted. Outside a vintners on a wine barrel stood a leaping fox with a wine bottle clasped between its front paws. Jack Fisher's first words when it was pointed out to him were something like "oh shit"! His instructions were rapidly passed around the coach party that, under no circumstances was the fox to find its way onto the bus, as it would probably set off an international incident. Jack was held with such high esteem by the troops that despite the potential trophy being greatly admired, no one let him down.

Later in 1978 the squadron had been on a detachment to Gibraltar and the word came down that a small party of us would be going to Malta for about a week to support six aircraft. We duly arrived in Malta and flew regular sorties with the aircraft again proving highly reliable. After a couple of days operating, our two armourers were forced to go on the scrounge to a Phantom squadron operating nearby. Our guys were asked: "How many

The XV Squadron Standard Party
with Peter Browning the escort on the right.

of you are there here"? The answer was "nineteen". The response from the F-4 armourers was "oh, the same as us. We have nine on each shift and a chiefy on days". To which our guys answered, "No, you misunderstand, there are 19 ground crew all told. A flight sergeant in charge, six SNCOs and 12 airmen!" I have to say that trip is probably the one I get the biggest buzz out of remembering.

My last tour on Buccaneers was on XV Squadron at Laarbruch and during that time Ken Tait and 'Rusty' Ruston sadly lost their lives in an accident on Exercise Red Flag (Nellis USA) in February 1980. I was not on the detachment but can confirm that their loss was keenly felt back at Laarbruch too. Some weeks after the event, it was decided that a planned squadron exchange to Lechfeld in Bavaria would actually go ahead as a morale builder, despite the Buccaneers still being grounded. So, one Sunday morning a small detachment of ground crew set off from Laarbruch by RAF coach, not designed with comfort in mind, to provide support for two Hunter T.7 aircraft. A gruelling journey was ended with a superb welcome by our German hosts, as we were marched straight off the bus on arrival and into the officers' mess for a couple of cold beers. There followed a fairly liquid period, working half a day every other day and being royally entertained by our hosts every evening. I recall going in to work one morning and arriving at breakfast in the flight-line canteen to be greeted by a jolly lady with "Guten morgen, wie geht es Ihnen?" (Good morning, how are you?). My response was "ich habe eine kleine Kopfschmerzen, aber kein Problem". (I have a small headache, but no problem). She smiled. As part of the festivities our hosts laid on a games evening which included a squadron commander's cycle race on bikes with no tyres, and a tug of war. Our hosts confessed that they were impressed with the way we cheated and stated that they would be employing some of our tactics at their next inter-squadron games evening. For instance, a crowd formed around the host squadron commander when he mounted his steed for the cycle race and while patting him on the back someone pushed the cycle lock back into the back wheel. He finished second of course and missing several spokes. We also won the tug of war as our hosts found our team immoveable, which was no surprise, as immediately behind our anchor-man was a 1960s Mercedes which had the rope tied to its front bumper.

Our hosts also laid on a coach trip to Neuschwanstein, which finally ended up at Kloster

Andechs where they brew some of the strongest beer in Germany. If our host brief was to help rebuild morale on the squadron, they certainly knew how to go about it. It was a rowdy journey home. Our noisy arrival back on base was suddenly interrupted by two of the guys shouting: "Stop! Stop the bus!" They rushed to the front and ran back the way we had come. Most of us on the bus probably thought, call of nature. However, several minutes later they clambered back on board with a black and white street sign, complete with metal post and a concrete lump on the end. It turned out to be a brilliant trophy and that is how Richthofen Strasse came to adorn a wall in the Golden Hind (crew room) on the XV Squadron site at Laarbruch.

Lineys at work on the flight line.

PAUL SMART

October 1978 saw me heading for Germany, to RAF Laarbruch – destination 16 Squadron.

My trade was LMech AC (Air Communications) but on 16 I was to be used more like a flight-line mechanic as the 'Recs Team' was already manned with a corporal and J/T on both shifts. My allotted tasks, along with other mechs, were to carry out before flight (BFs), and after flight (AFs) servicing together with marshalling duties, seeing off and seeing in the Buccs on their various sorties.

One of the first things I noticed about the Buccaneer was how high off the ground it was. I had just finished three years on Canberra PR9s, which while not a small aircraft, were a lot lower to the ground than the behemoth before me. It was, and still is, an awesome sight up close.

We were working from hardened aircraft shelters (HASs), which were concrete buildings, reported to be bomb-proof. This was never tested I'm glad to say. They were big enough to house two Buccs with wings folded, or one with its wings down, which was the general norm. The HASs were arranged in pairs away from the squadron office, and if you were very unlucky you got the one furthest away, which meant a decent walk. But we managed to take short cuts through the woods surrounding each HAS so it wasn't as long as it could have been.

For me, the worst part of the AF/BF was changing the LOX (liquid oxygen) bottle. This was located at the rear of the aircraft, accessed through a small hatch close to the arrestor hook. It was a case of having to manoeuvre the heavy bottle above your head to rest it on a ledge so you could actually get yourself through the hatch to put the bottle in place,

A Buccaneer parked by a HAS at Laarbruch.

and then lock-wire the studs so they didn't come loose in flight. Good job I was young and fit in those days.

There were characters in all parts of the squadron. The ground staff crew room was full of them and there was always some mirth happening between sorties, like a raucous game of Uckers, which was based on Ludo but more aggressive. The aircrew had their own characters too. One such was a pilot, whose name I do remember but will not divulge for reasons of possible libel. Those involved will remember the incident I am about to relate.

Two of us were assigned to one of the further HASs to see off a sortie. We got there in good time to make sure the Bucc was ready. Squadron transport arrived and the navigator got out, and the transport departed. Seeing our quizzical looks the nav said: "Pilot was answering the call of nature just as transport arrived. He'll be along shortly." Not long after, we heard the sound of a two-stroke motorcycle being ridden along the track through the woods and onto the HAS apron. The pilot, helmet already in place, got off, threw the keys of his Yamaha DT175 to my colleague and said: "Take this back, there's a good fellow." He knew the bikers on the squadron and we were both in that brigade. He then proceeded to do the walk-round as if nothing out of the ordinary had happened, and he still made his take-off time!

There were some non-flying days. If the weather got too bad, and there were some harsh winters at that time in Germany, the aircraft were grounded. At these times other jobs were found for the 'erks' such as hangar cleaning. This involved a line of 'lineys' with brooms walking from one end of the hangar to the other sweeping up anything that got in their path such as leftover chicken s**t that was used to mop up oil spills, or nuts and bolts that had been dropped while trying to fit a new system in awkward places – and there were plenty of those on our beloved Bucc. One particular winter a team of us were told to go and clear the squadron entrance of snow … in a snowstorm.

There were some high jinks at times too. For events such as Families Day, when the camp was open for families of all airmen, with displays from each unit on the station, or the visit of a dignitary, the aircraft had to look their best. This usually involved the cleaning of an aircraft to be used for static display. So, a team of the ground crew was tasked to get one looking nice and shiny using cleaning solution and fire hoses. One bright summer day we were employed on this very task and I was in charge of the hose, when I inadvertently directed it over the back of the Bucc onto the team on the other side of the aircraft. One rather large member of the team took umbrage, walked round the back straight into the full force from the hose, but somehow managed to keep going and turned the hose round on me. Great days, great fun.

Then there was the serious side of things. Every so often we were tasked to spend time in QRA (quick readiness alert). There would be two ground crew plus an NCO, together with two aircrew spending 24 hours locked in a compound surrounded by barbed wire whose perimeter was patrolled by an armed policeman and his dog. This was a two-week duty with working alternate days.

There would be one aircraft in a single HAS which was loaded with the ultimate weapon of choice at the time of the Cold War. The idea was, should the worst happen, to get the aircraft out and airborne within two minutes. We had one call out during my time on the squadron, which was only an exercise, thank goodness. We managed to get the kite out and on the runway in the specified time, then it had to taxi the whole way down the runway to return to the QRA compound where we had to AF it as if it had completed its mission. It was good to know we could actually complete the task QRA was designed for.

It really was a case of 'work hard, play hard' in Germany. There were many times when the night shifts had to work all through the night to get aircraft ready for the next day's flying programme. I remember helping the airframes (riggers) guys fit fairings in the bomb bays. This was done by a couple of us lying on our backs on the HAS floor and literally kicking the fairings into place so the rigger could line the bolt holes up.

Unfortunately, there were a couple of tragedies during my time there. We lost two aircraft in separate incidents when one of the wings folded in flight [see Chapter Eleven]. This was due to the 'lynch pin' that locked them into place failing with the stress of the G forces the aircraft was subject to when manoeuvring. All the squadron felt the loss of the aircrew that went down. For some time, the Bucc was grounded so we were flying Hunter trainers to keep the aircrew current, and that meant learning a whole new set of procedures for us ground crew too for the BFs/AFs.

These were the days before health and safety went OTT. There wouldn't be a hi-vis vest in sight, ear defenders used when marshalling were painted in whatever colour or design you wanted them, issued 'cold/wet gear' lived up to their name and an assortment of headgear of personal choice was worn while on the line.

All in all, my time on 16 Squadron was one of the happiest I spent in the RAF and I feel very privileged to have worked with some excellent members, both ground crew and aircrew. It is a time in my life that I would not have missed for the world, and the Buccaneer, despite its idiosyncrasies, will always have a place in my heart.

CHAPTER FIFTEEN

A LIFE AT SEA WITH THE BUCCANEER

FRANK COX

During the summer of 1952, aged eight, at a Yeovilton Air Day, I cajoled my mother into giving me a ten-shilling note for a flight around the local area in an Anson that was giving 'joy rides'. After queuing for a couple of hours, I was ushered up front into the right-hand seat. The rest, as people say, is history. So, via gliding, flying grading in Tiger Moths, basic and advanced flying training with the Fleet Air Arm, two of us from the six that remained from a course of 11 proceeded to Lossiemouth, and our choice of the Buccaneer; Mark 1s in those days.

And so it came to pass a few days after my 22nd birthday on 13 January 1965, after four Hunter T8B sorties, I flew Buccaneer Fam 1 with Carl Davis perched in the rear seat, he being on the short side. My lasting memories of this trip were that it was in a pre-production, all over white, aircraft where switch placement bore little resemblance to that which I had become accustomed to in the simulator. At this stage, I was teamed up with my observer, Noel Rawbone, a Sea Vixen convertee. I notice from my logbook that the course was somewhat stop/start with periods of concentrated flying with up to four sorties a day interspersed with periods of inactivity. Such was the serviceability of the Mark 1 in those early days.

It was in one of these slack periods that my fellow course pilot and I were kicking our heels when we thought a trip in a Sea Vampire might add a little spice to the quiet day. So, on enquiring of the senior pilot whether that was a possibility, he thought it was indeed a good idea, and having phoned the CO of Station Flight on our behalf, sent us on our way. On arrival in pipe-puffing Monty Mellor's office we expected a full briefing. However, he handed us the Pilot's Notes – the scruffy little blue book variety associated with aircraft of a certain age – pointed to the aircraft on the line, and said; "there it is, enjoy it", or words to that effect. After leafing through this somewhat dog-eared publication to determine the relevant speeds and settings, we signed the Form 700 in the line office, where nobody

An 800 Squadron Buccaneer S.1 tensioned
on the waist catapult of HMS Eagle, *October 1965.*

turned a hair at two young unknowns passing through; we enjoyed 50 minutes of fun. Can you imagine such freedom these days, not that station flights exist anymore?

In June 1965, together with Noel, I joined 800 Squadron under the leadership of David Mather with Dave Howard as his senior pilot. The squadron embarked in late August in HMS *Eagle* where I was to experience my first catapult launch whilst she was in Lyme Bay. This was a new and exhilarating experience, which was probably less traumatic, due to the wind generated over the deck, than that offered by the Bedford Catapult, which was out of service. Also, Noel, being an ex-Sea Vixen looker, was actually able to see what was going on outside.

Domestically, I found that I was to share a cabin on four deck, just a couple of steps from the quarterdeck on the port side, with Graham Pitchfork an RAF exchange officer from the Canberra world. We survived a year without any arguments or grumpiness despite my loud music at times. A fine cabin mate indeed.

In October, I teamed up with David Thompson after Noel, with his past experience, was to be crewed with a pilot having some difficulty with deck landings. We were crewed together for the remainder of my time on 800. The same month we transited the Suez Canal. Some memories of that still remain with me; firstly, the ship had to defuel into an RFA tanker to reduce the draft before entering at Port Said, and later meeting another in the Red Sea to top up once more. Also the 'canal effect' effectively reduced the depth of water under the ship, which was magnified when forced to increase speed in order to maintain steerage way in the cross wind – all good interesting 'fish head' stuff. Of course, there was the obligatory Gully-Gully man trading his dubious wares, who came aboard to keep us entertained.

Having transited the Red Sea, flying got under way in the Indian Ocean to the south of Aden with much weaponry against the ship's splash target; two-inch RP, dive-bombing and

A Scimitar of 800B Flight tanks a bomb-laden Buccaneer S.1 of 800 Squadron.

close air support inland all interspersed with low-level navigation and photo-reconnais-sance sorties. I well remember coasting in on one particular sortie when I was surprised to see trees just inland from the shoreline, and so adjusted my height to just clear them when I happened to spy the radio altimeter which was indicating around 20 feet – they grow dwarf trees in Aden and keep herds of camels in 'nests' of thorn bushes! I also learned about the performance of the Mark 1, or more especially that of the Gyron Junior, in hot and high conditions. Approaching a distant mountain at low level one day at the usual 420 knots, we initiated a climb only to find that the mountain was getting closer with the engines running out of puff, the speed reducing at a somewhat alarming rate and to find the top was close to 8,000 feet. A lesson learned.

Many other lessons were learned whilst operating off Aden, notably that Gyron Juniors did not appreciate starting or accelerating in the prevailing high temperatures. Starting the 'downwind' engine when ranged aft required taxiing forward to face into wind to give the Palouste a helping hand in order to keep the turbine temperature somewhere below the limit.

The next excitement was when tensioned for launch with the nose in the air and the FDO's green flag waving gaily above his head. As the engines accelerated, there would reg-ularly be one that decided it did not want to play ball and went into a noisy compressor stall. Meanwhile, its mate on the other side was well behaved and effortlessly reached full power thereby slewing the aircraft off centre. The FDO continued to wave his flag with gusto with us hoping his arm would not tire. The only way to get the recalcitrant engine to accelerate was throttle to idle, switch on the blow to unload the compressor, and gin-gerly open the throttle whilst carefully monitoring the temperature. This procedure was against SOP, but the only way to salvage the sortie. Having coaxed the engine to behave and achieve full power, the aircraft straightened itself and all was well for the remainder of the sortie. Another quirk of the Gyron was to suffer corrosion in the compressor blade roots which resulted in the blades becoming slightly 'off centre' causing the compressor to become out of balance and vibrate, the after effect of which caused the mechanical fuel control unit to play up, which inevitably led to further excitement and increased heart rates. The solution to preventing this was found to be to dose the engines with a pint of WD40 via the intake on every shutdown. The follow-on effect was that a strong smell of burnt custard emanated from the air conditioning on the next start-up; 100 per cent oxygen for a few minutes was in order.

At this time, the junior crews started night deck qualification when I learned two salutary lessons. First, bolting (failing to catch the arrestor wire) at night was not a particularly pleasant experience, and a diversion ashore was mandatory on reaching 'chicken' fuel state. On one occasion after a night bolter, the ship gave its position 30 miles closer to the diversion than planned; hence another circuit was in order. David, ever on top of things, was unhappy about the situation. However, three 'command stripes' versus one 'minor stripe' prevailed and, to add further insult to injury, I bolted again so we set off on our diversion. It was only then that we discovered that the ship was 30 miles further from Aden. With fuel way below that required for an orderly arrival, and with gauges on zero for the last few minutes, combined with a glide approach from 6,000 feet to clear the Aden Crater, the situation made for an interesting, although firm, arrival that culminated with the port engine flaming out as we turned off the runway. Having refuelled, we returned to *Eagle* and hooked on safely around 0100 hours the same night. Second lesson: never allow anyone to override your better judgement regardless of rank. Discussion post the event is preferable to putting oneself, and aircraft, in jeopardy. There was another lesson learned when ashore in Aden, and this was always to watch one's goodies being packed in front of you. Those packed in the back room, out of sight, magically transformed themselves into bricks.

Post Aden, we proceeded east for a disembarkation period at RAF Changi, arriving on 11 February 1966 where such necessities as QFI checks and IRTs took place in the resident Hunter T.8B, and the obligatory shoes and suits were ordered for collection the following day. Our accommodation was in the salubrious setting of the Straits View Hotel on the sea front. Aircrew were allocated a 2CV pick-up, which, I must say, was just very slightly abused and almost always overloaded. Bedok Corner was the stopping-off point of choice for our post night-flying meal of the most wonderful street food, all served from bicycles.

In early March 1966 we again disembarked to Changi for a planned three-week stay while *Eagle* was in the dockyard for essential maintenance. However, in the meantime *Ark Royal* managed to catch fire off Mozambique during the Beira blockade and, as a consequence, *Eagle* and her air group were scrambled the day after arriving ashore. Needless to say, this was not a popular move. After a fast passage across the Indian Ocean, we fell into a daily routine of ship searches, some long range with refuelling from our resident Scimitar tankers. It was whilst at low level at the extremity of one such sortie that the

Frank Cox and David Thompson release eight 1,000-lb bombs from a medium-toss profile against a wreck on Scarborough Shoal off the Philippines.

warning bells chimed; not exactly an unusual occurrence in a Mark 1 Buccaneer. I was not unduly concerned as I hit the cancel button, but when I peered down, I saw 'fuel bay fire' which, according to the book, required ejection if the warning did not extinguish within ten seconds. However, being some 400 miles from 'Mother' at low level over shark-infested water, and 'scratchy' HF contact with the ship, together with an otherwise fully serviceable aeroplane, we decided it was a better option to stick with it and return home with the warning still shining brightly for 50 minutes. Subsequently, five other aircraft were found to have the same chafed fire wire. As a result of the Beira deployment we flew non-diversion for over 70 days. A record I believe.

After a return to Singapore and Changi for a fortnight's leave, we re-embarked for a period of operations around the Philippines. A memorable sortie for me was to be entrusted with eight 1,000-lb inert bombs for a medium-toss trial on a shipwreck target on Scarborough Shoal to the west of the Philippines in the South China Sea. Now one may imagine a Mark1 Buccaneer with a full bomb load, and temperatures in the mid-30s, and little natural wind is only able to launch with limited fuel. So it was planned for us to refuel immediately after launch and, as the target was so remote, dispense with checking if the range was clear of shipping and to proceed with a first-run attack followed by a return to the ship, conserving as much fuel as possible.

All went exactly as planned. David mentioned that his radar showed two targets and that he would lock onto the left-hand one. All eight bombs departed the aircraft in good order, and we rolled over to follow them on their way. It was at this time we noted a potentially serious problem over which we had no control; a junk was alongside the other section of the wreck. Powerless to do anything about it, we watched the progress of our bombs with a degree of trepidation as to the outcome. As it turned out, we achieved a perfect straddle on the section we were aiming at. Great happiness all round, the engineers because their weapons system tweaking had proven successful, and the crew of the junk for the gift of 8,000 lbs of scrap metal from heaven.

Following further exercises off the west coast of Malaya, *Eagle* made her way home via the Suez Canal and the Med. The squadron disembarked off Marseilles to Lossie with a stop at Yeovilton. After a relatively quiet three months at Lossiemouth, when the squadron converted to the Mark 2, I departed to become a tactical instructor in 738 Squadron followed by the AWI course in 764 Squadron.

Bullpup firing.

*

I became re-acquainted with the Buccaneer in August 1969 with a short refresher course with 736 Squadron prior to moving on to 809 Squadron as the AWI. At this time, the RN had a stockpile of Bullpup missiles, which were rapidly becoming obsolete. This first generation 'stand-off' weapon was designed for launching in a dive. The missile had a flare, which the pilot tracked using a button under his left thumb. However, as the firing aircraft had to follow the missile until it impacted the target, this made the aircraft extremely vulnerable, as it could not manoeuvre during the weapon's flight. We therefore developed a 'buddy-buddy' system from a low-level launch by one aircraft with a second some two miles behind to control the missile. This worked well but there were many difficulties to overcome to make this viable, not least the use of two aircraft to deliver just 250 lbs of warhead. However, we had great fun 'shooting' at Gralis Sgier Island off the north Scottish coast.

Two incidents come to mind. The first was when I was leading three aircraft to fire four missiles between us. The trip, by then routine, was proceeding normally; we had let down into the range area, broken cloud around 3,000 ft, checked the area for shipping and set ourselves up for the first attack. The run-in went well, the photo aircraft was correctly positioned, and the missile was fired at the optimum range. Within two seconds we were all taken aback as the missile took it upon itself to emulate a Saturn V moon rocket, and it disappeared vertically into the overcast. As can be imagined, there was some consternation among the team as to where this errant bird was going to come down. Needless to say, we neither saw nor heard of it again.

The second incident occurred towards the end of the trial during a take-off. I was crewed, as usual, with Brian Jackson-Dooley, and we set off down Lossiemouth's Runway 23 with

809 Squadron embarked in HMS Ark Royal. *Frank Cox in second row on the right.*

full fuel and two live missiles in murky weather with a 200-foot cloud base. As we rotated, Mr Rolls' starboard engine decided to quit in the most spectacular fashion. There was a very loud explosion on the starboard side, accompanied by flames shooting forward beyond the nose. Having assured Brian that the single-engine performance was proving adequate to propel the whole mass into the air and, indeed, climb sufficiently well to clear the, by now unseen, high ground, we settled back to climb to a safe height, dump fuel and return for an uneventful landing.

In June 1971, after a further three months embarked on *Ark Royal*, I was appointed to 764 Squadron, the AWI school, flying Hunters where I remained as an instructor until August 1972 when it was back to the Buccaneer, albeit one of a different colour at 237 OCU at Honington as a staff AWI. My main memory was of the great camaraderie that developed between the light and dark blue, and the special characters who 'performed' at Friday Happy Hours. Messrs Mulinder and Crone immediately spring to mind and there were several others that the ageing memory has lost.

Following two splendid years with the US Navy teaching students to attack and, more importantly, hit targets in the visual mode, as most Brits had to do, without the use of a very clever computer in the A-6 Intruder, it was back for a short Hunter UK reorientation course, followed by a Buccaneer refresher, before I joined 809, this time as senior pilot in August 1977. After a short period embarked in *Ark Royal*, with exercises off Norway and in the Med, we returned to Honington to continue with all the usual front-line Buccaneer maritime activities including, for the first time, Martel, which pilots found a somewhat boring exercise, although those who sat in the back undoubtedly had their hands full with the TV version. At this time, due to the imminent demise of fixed-wing carriers, and the associated reduction of fixed-wing flying training, we had an infusion of light blue aircrew to make up the numbers. Despite the occasional clash of culture, we settled into becoming a well-oiled machine under our boss, Tony Morton.

Embarked once again in April 1978 and over to the States with eight weeks of exercises and heavy weaponry, much of it live, on the Atlantic Weapons Ranges off Puerto Rico. Particularly good sport was the demolition of the highly manoeuvrable 'Septar' speedboats with two-inch rockets, much to the chagrin of the USN range officers. Even when limited to single shot we managed to keep their salvage and repair teams busy. Then followed a five-week period disembarked to NAS Cecil Field prior to re-embarking and heading east to operate in UK waters for a short time, which included a flypast for the Queen Mother who was visiting the ship for the final time before *Ark* decommissioned.

The final swan song for *Ark Royal* and 809 was to spend six weeks in the Med before we finally flew off from south of Marseilles to St Athan. I ferried two aircraft, the second of which was memorable due to flying with the main gear down with ground locks in and with the nose gear up to reduce the drag a little. The reason for this unusual configuration was that the frame holding one of the starboard gear trunnions was seriously cracked and required minimal stress, so wheel braking was not permitted except in emergency. Towing onto the catapult and an arrested landing satisfied the requirement. Not the greatest final sortie with which to end my Buccaneering career.

There followed a two-year appointment as senior naval officer with the Tactical Weapons Unit at Brawdy mentoring the last of the naval fixed-wing pilots destined for the Sea Harrier, followed by 18 months with Naval Flying Standards Flight as the AWI introducing helicopter pilots, also destined for Sea Harrier, to the joys of high-speed flight, tactics, combat and weaponry. A side-line of displaying the Fairy Firefly and the Sea Fury for the Historic Flight was, for me, the icing on the cake prior to leaving Her Majesty's Senior Service in January 1983 for FRADU and onward to 5,800 hours in corporate aviation.

In my mind, the Buccaneer was a masterful design optimised, as it was, for a single role with a weapons system, although by modern standards antique, which worked relatively well. The Mark 1 was underpowered, but the Gyron Junior was the only engine of that period able to provide sufficient bleed air for the boundary layer control whilst maintaining sufficient thrust during the approach. The introduction of the Spey in the Mark 2 overcame this and, of course, increased the operating range. A total electronic upgrade rather than piecemeal add-ons during the early life of the Mark 2 would have undoubtedly improved the capabilities to match those of the slower US Navy A-6 Intruder. The next generation multi-role Tornado overshadowed any further development. However, the mighty Buccaneer was a great aircraft of its era and I felt privileged to fly it amongst so many outstanding colleagues.

CHAPTER SIXTEEN

THE FINE RED LINE

(BETWEEN A HONORIS CRUX AND A COURT MARTIAL)

DRIES MARAIS

Cassinga in Angola was one little square on communist Cuba's chessboard for the planned full-scale conflict afterwards where the battlefield dynamics regarding intensity and numbers of enemy ground assets – including ground-to-air assets – compared to well-known conflict theatres in World War Two. Regarding force levels not many people know that in the final battles 3,500 South African soldiers went in and knowingly faced 52,000 enemy troops.

Russia poured advanced weapons into Angola in volumes and at a rate which was truly staggering because they saw the opportunity for real-time testing of a number of modern, advanced weapons systems.

The first principle of war is 'Selection and Maintenance of the Objective'. Had it not been for a leader like Colonel Jan Breytenbach, the assault force commander who inspired his men to adhere to this principle throughout that battle, the results would have been tragically different.

The Dawn Bombing Attack

After a number of tactical postponements, the Battle of Cassinga was finally planned to start with a bombing attack on a South West Africa People's Organization (SWAPO) camp at 0800 hours on 4 May 1978. The pitch-dark take-off of four Canberras, and later our five Buccaneers, over Pretoria must have woken up a few couples in the pleasant apartment blocks of Sunnyside with hopefully the comforting thought that 'at least that noise is from our own combat aircraft and not Russian MiGs attacking us'. They could not know that every thundering heavy jet that went over them at a quite uncomfortably low height carried eight HE bombs, each weighing 460 kg. Climbing was out of the question for a minute or so – getting the heavily laden aircraft up to speed was the main concern. 2,000 kilometres north of Pretoria my target at Cassinga was the admin headquarters – a

Top: Buccaneer S.1 XN956 of
801 Squadron near the Moray
Firth – May 1963.
Above: Buccaneer S.1 XN970
of 800 Squadron overshoots –
September 1965.
Right: An 801 Squadron
Buccaneer S.1 prepares to taxi
on HMS *Victorious* in 1965.

Above: Buccaneer S.2 of 809 Squadron arrives on HMS *Hermes*, 1970.

Above: 237 OCU Buccaneer S.2As on the Honington ASP.
Left: A 12 Squadron Buccaneer S.2 fires a full pod of two-inch rockets.
Below: A brand new Buccaneer S.2 of XV Squadron on a Laarbruch dispersal.

Top: Officers of XV Squadron (OC Wg Cdr R. Watson) in 1972.
Below: A 237 OCU Buccaneer S.2 ready to launch from the
Bedford catapult.

Above: A 16 Squadron aircraft at readiness in a hardened aircraft shelter.
Left: Picketed to the deck of HMS *Ark Royal* at Naval Station Mayport, Florida.
Below: 16 Squadron on the flight line at Nellis AFB for Exercise Red Flag.

Above: A 16 Squadron aircraft over Germany displaying the crown having taken part in the Queen's Silver Jubilee flypast earlier.

Right: Three 24 Squadron Buccaneer S.50s over South Africa.

Below: The 'survivors' wonder what John Deane has done to the steaks! L to R: Ron Trinder, Stu Ager, Al Smith, Rog Carr, Dick Pringle, Simon Deacon-Elliott, Bob McLellan.

Above: 208 Squadron ground crew monitor a very cold start-up at Goose Bay in 1982.
Left: 208 Squadron en route Goose Bay – Cold Lake for Exercise Maple Flag in April 1981.
Below: Armourers load 1,000-lb bombs during a tactical bombing competition.

Above: A pair from 237 OCU over the Western Isles.
Below: 237 OCU trial with a Sidewinder.

Above: Approaching the westerly runway at Gibraltar.
Below: Crossing the main road after landing at Gibraltar.

Above: XN976 displays 208 Squadron's 75th anniversary scheme as it taxis at Abingdon in April 1991. (Adrian Balch Archive)
Below: Hunter T.7s were a crucial element of the Buccaneer force. These two are in latter day schemes.

Top: The Lossiemouth Wing lined up prior to a 30th anniversary flypast in 1988. *Above:* Armed with Sea Eagle. *Right:* The Pave Spike pod and Paveway 1,000-lb LGB destined for an Iraqi target.

Above: Manning up for a Gulf War mission.
Left: Cpl Mark Hewitt and Sgt 'Taff' Muzyloowski of 12 Squadron manage to commemorate 'Red Nose' day with XX901 whilst deployed to Bahrain.
Below: En route to a target in Iraq. (MoD)

Above: Wg Cdr Nigel Huckins leads the final formation with each RAF unit and 809 Squadron represented – March 1994.

Right: A 12 Squadron aircraft, in the all-grey colour scheme, prepares to land at Lossiemouth.

Below: 208 Squadron shadow a Sovremenny-class guided-missile destroyer.

Above: Early arrivals. The first Buccaneer Aircrew Association reunion at RNAS Yeovilton – April 1996.
Left: XX901 prepares to leave Kemble for the Yorkshire Air Museum.
Below: 24 Squadron's Buccaneer 412 positioned at the main gate of AFB Waterkloof.

Above: Tom Eeles, ex-OC 237 OCU (kneeling), gathers strong support on the occasion of the presentation of the unit badge to the RAF Club.

Right: An exceedingly cold day at Bruntingthorpe for a fast taxi run – April 2019.

Below: The BAA's XX901 rolled out for a night shot at the Yorkshire Air Museum.

A 24 Squadron Buccaneer S.50 at low level over the South African veld.

farmhouse amongst tall trees some 800 metres – or so the scale marked on the photo maps indicated – distant from the very visible parade ground where the main attack by Canberras and the other Buccaneers was going to take place.

A little more than two hours later we were there and in the dive exactly as the sun rose over the horizon. Within the few seconds one has to find, identify and track the impact point for the bombs, I failed to see the HQ building amongst the trees where it should have been, so I just aimed and put my bombs at the proper place 800 metres from the parade ground. Photographs taken by one navigator showed afterwards that the smoke of my bombs was an unacceptable distance away from the required point of impact. We much later learned that our target photo maps were made and presented with the wrong scale – the same reason why a full complement of paratroopers missed their landing zone by the same scaled margin.

After the attack we headed south to our temporary base at Grootfontein in south-west Africa and on landing congratulated one another on a successful outcome – the airborne assault by the paratroopers would be a walkover, we firmly believed. How wrong we all were. The veteran SWAPO soldiers were not killed en masse and neither were they shocked out of their wits by the terrible explosions of our big bombs as had been so staunchly advocated by air force commanding and staff officers.

A tense briefing at AFB Grootfontein. From left to right: Maj Koos Botha, Dries Marais, Capt J. Strydom, Capt Crow Stannard (partly hidden) and Lt Leon Burger.

Later testing showed the huge craters these old, heavy World War Two munitions created in the ground, simply flinging a few large, wide strips of shrapnel upwards at a 45-degree angle, and these fell 500–600 metres away with not sufficient personnel fatalities near the impact point. Soon after Cassinga we decided that we needed to carry more bombs of about quarter the size of these old 'thousand-pounders', and which needed to burst 15–25 metres above a target with pre-fragmented casings to create much more shrapnel of much smaller size – going downwards and not upwards. That requirement did not go unheeded and later in that war the South African Air Force would have the best unguided munitions in the world, bar none. First there were the super-quick, and then super-super quick fuses, and eventually the radio-altimeter-triggered air-burst fuses. What a difference these made, combined with low-drag, pre-fragmented bombs.

Anti-aircraft Artillery, Tanks, and Tracers

After landing at Grootfontein, and having gulped down a quick breakfast, navigator Ernie and I hastened back to Cassinga to assist the assault force with close air support should they need air power, using 68-mm HE rockets from four canisters under the wings, each carrying 18 of these optically aimed, little ballistic missiles.

When we again arrived at the target the fighting on the ground was evidently very fierce and we had a few opportunities to take out some machine-gun positions, and on request of the assault commander, I attacked a white Toyota Land Cruiser with a big red star on the doors which was fleeing the scene, but to my embarrassment I was not altogether successful with my three rockets at a time. The driver was aware of me and was taking good evasive actions, driving the vehicle into dense vegetation. I shall never know whether I was able to kill the fleeing, no doubt high-ranking officer. The Bucc needed a high-capacity, multi-barrel cannon system like the 30-mm DEFA on the Mirage, were my thoughts at the time.

After our rockets were expended, Lt Dick Warncke and his navigator Lt Riaan Mouton arrived in another Buccaneer to take over from us and we went back to Grootfontein to prepare for a support attack west, at Chetequera where Major Frank Bestbier and his mechanised column would do an assault on an enemy infantry base. I knew Frank from the air force-army combined-attack courses I did with him. A sunburnt, focused leader if I ever saw one. We had done many tasks together on those courses. I was looking forward to being of assistance to Frank, doing the real thing.

Like with the previous sortie I found my aircraft loaded with 72 rockets with high-explosive heads. No armoured resistance was expected at Chetequera, so the anti-personnel, high explosive grenade-like terminal ballistics were quite correct. BUT … some nagging little voice inside me wanted a change. For a totally inexplicable reason I asked the armourer, Flt Sgt Reg Rivers, to remove every third HE rocket and replace it with one that had a hollow-charge head for armour piercing. These rockets did not explode like an outsize hand grenade, but their shaped charge caused a forward jet of directionally focused molten metal at 7,000 ft/sec to simply burn a neat hole through the armour of a tank after which the intense heat and secondary explosive caused its own damage. There was no need for this when attacking lightly protected gun positions, vehicles or personnel on the ground. To this day I remember the armourer's perplexed expression. He showed me his orders for HE rockets – meaning: "No sir, can't comply."

I curtly ordered him to implement the change immediately. He shrugged, noted my request in his log and replaced the rockets, as I wanted. Ernie of course also criticised me and asked whatever had come over me to weaken our explosive load by 33 per cent as it were. I was in a strange way totally detached from his concerns, as I could not even explain my unfounded, if not silly decision to myself, so I simply ignored his questions and opinions. I started the engines; we did our pre-take-off checks and then enjoyed the impressive acceleration of the Buccaneer unencumbered by the 8,000-lb bomb load of the morning.

After settling at our cruise altitude of 14,000 feet above sea level and on track to our target near Chetequera I checked in with operational headquarters, and soon after crossing the 'cut line' border into Angola, I heard Dick Warncke call up as he and his navigator Riaan Mouton were leaving Cassinga. There was a distinct note of concern in his brief but pointed commentary. He was out of ammunition and reported that a substantial armoured column consisting of BTR 152 troop carriers, led by a number of T-34 tanks, was approaching Cassinga, having set off from their Cuban base to the south. He also informed TAC HQ that the assault force was virtually out of ammunition. The fight had extended now for seven hours where the planning was for a two-hour walkover. The enemy was thick and angry and ready when the battle started.

I heard two Mirage III fighters being scrambled from Ondangua, and then I heard the leader, Commandant 'Ollie' Holmes, calling that they were airborne and informing Major Gert Havenga, the operations officer, that they carried only HE ammunition for their 30-mm DEFA cannons. The Mirages had been on high alert for air intercept should there have been any reaction by Russian MiG-21 aircraft to our flaunted enjoyment of air superiority in Angolan air space. Ollie told TAC HQ that their 30-mm cannon would have no effect on the tanks.

Then suddenly I knew why I had the compulsive impulse to request that every third HE rocket on my aircraft be replaced with an armour-piercing one. The news of the armoured intervention meant a crisis of big proportions for the assault group at Cassinga, as well as for what then must have numbered about the full complement of helicopters on the SAAF inventory. The implication for massive losses of men and materiel was acute.

The tactical radio frequency was by now cluttered with animated chatter and there was not a moment's chance in which I could ask permission to divert from our track to Chetequera and head out to Cassinga to attack the tanks. I asked Ernie if he still had the morning's maps with him – which he did not – but he had Cassinga's latitude and longitude coordinates programmed into our navigation computer. I asked him to display the info on my horizontal situation indicator and suddenly I had a heading and time-to-fly to Cassinga. Without further ado or discussion I opened the throttles and turned on track for that hotspot, accelerating to maximum speed.

This un-discussed action solicited a long paragraph of rather astonished discontent from Ernie and I think I simply responded by saying: "We're going to get those tanks that the Mirages won't be able to stop."

We were less than a minute away from Cassinga when, for the first time, there was a break in the transmissions on the operational frequency. Being a thinking man, I dared only say to tactical headquarters that I carried armour-piercing rockets to stop the tanks – certainly not informing them that we were in fact about to attack the tanks. The operations officer Gert Havenga immediately made the decision to divert me from my mission to Chetequera, saying: "Yes, Dries, you are cleared to go, and I'll back you up." (Meaning that later there likely would be repercussions – which indeed there were.)

When I was about to roll into my dive towards the armoured column, I heard the two Mirage pilots talk to one another, and I recognised the number two as Major Gerrie Radloff, a friend of long standing. The Mirages were on a converging track to Cassinga, likely having been flying at our own speed of almost 600 knots. By some turn of good fate (although I do not at all believe in fate) we achieved two of the most important requirements of any attack, namely surprise and concentration of force: in my dive towards the tanks I saw the two Mirages evenly spaced out ahead of me as if the attack had been planned that way. (Maybe it had, who knows) …

Before I could speak I saw the ineffective flashes of Ollie Holmes's 30-mm HE bullets exploding on the outside of the front tank and I informed him I had proper rockets for the tanks. He simply lifted the nose of the Mirage and I could see the dust of his exploding shells running into the front troop carriers that obligingly travelled in a closely spaced convoy; then Gerrie Radloff's twin DEFA cannons spat death at 6,000 rounds a minute into the second group.

"*Dit is hoe die boere skiet, julle bliksems*" (sorry, not translatable into English) were my exact thoughts and then my first 12-rocket salvo went out to the front tank and I had to break hard left and up to avoid the explosion and debris of the rockets. Earlier I had asked Ernie to select three rockets from each launcher. You cannot see the impact as the aircraft's own speed takes you towards the target at about 280 metres per second and you have to break out hard the very moment you pulled the trigger to avoid being hit by your own shrapnel. I strained my leg and stomach muscles to assist the G-suit against the 7G force caused by the tight turn, trying to prevent the blood from being pulled into the lower body, not wanting to black out but at the same time needing to get around as quickly as possible for another attack, while trying to look back over my shoulder to keep the target area in sight.

Then I saw the T-34 burning like a fanned furnace, red hot flames and metal bursting out from inside. During the dive onto the second tank I again saw the Mirages creating havoc amongst the BTR 152 troop carriers. The second tank also succumbed to immediate immobility in similar fashion after our second salvo of 12 rockets.

We had no knowledge of the position of our own forces but, later in 2013, I met one of the assault force soldiers who at the time was leading a stopper group sent out to mine the approaches into Cassinga. He was very close to the tanks when my rockets hit. He described to me how some rockets passed right through the tank (no doubt the armour-piercing type) and exploded underneath it, causing the whole vehicle to jump up into the air before bursting into flames.

I turned in again to get the third tank but there were none on the road – the remaining two or three had moved off into the dense bush and were nowhere to be seen. Then the assault commander, Colonel Jan Breytenbach, called and asked me to take out a heavy machine-gun position, which was pinning them down. We took care of that with the aid of excellent directions from the forward air controller on the ground, Major Frans Botes; another soldier I had known for 20 years and completed a forward air controller's course with. Oh, by the way, we always used first names during operational radio transmissions and not aircraft call signs.

Ernie complained about an anti-aircraft gun that had been firing tracer in our direction for some time, but my attention was focused on the priority of finding the tanks and killing them: "Ignore that gun, they do not have a snowball's hope in hell to hit us at this speed," was my rather arrogant reply. We were flying at about 600 knots ground speed; doing one kilometre every four seconds and I felt almost invincible in the Buccaneer. (To his later chagrin and the ire of the squadron commander, Commandant Simon van Garderen, after we landed a rather unpleasant sight of quite a number of large projectile holes from all angles into and through the aircraft greeted our eyes during the post-flight inspection. That put an end to the speed theory I had.)

The constant stream of visible tracers annoyed me too – and of course 10 times more lead – heading towards us from that one particular anti-aircraft position. It was diverting my attention from searching for the tanks hiding in the dense bushveld vegetation below us so I decided to take it out. Ernie was seeing a few more AA positions, which my tunnel vision on this one had blocked out. I turned in towards my target and in the dive saw a whole band of troops gathering around the gun and all were firing their assault rifles at us. Then I recognised a BTR 152 close by. I think it had been towing the gun I had destroyed.

This clustered group of Cubans created an ideal target for our HE rockets. As I pulled the trigger my front windscreen outer laminate cracked and spider-webbed as one of the 14.5-mm bullets from the AA gun hit. The reinforced windscreen prevented me from taking the fire between the eyes.

Out of Ammunition

Pulling out from the dive I saw the gaggle of helicopters landing in the extraction zone and my fear for them and the troops grew; that mood morphed into a firm resolution when I saw one tank emerging from cover, racing towards the helicopters and firing its main weapon. Thinking we still had 12 rockets left I asked Ernie to give me six – for two final attacks – and dived onto the tank from the rear, being quite sure of an easy kill while the tank commander's attention was focused on the targets ahead. When I pulled the trigger there were no rockets and in the heat of the moment I snapped at Ernie that he had the rocket switches wrong. I did a tight turn to repeat the attack. Again we were lined up but when I pulled the trigger all was quiet – no rockets. What now? The tanks simply *had* to be stopped.

Without consciously thinking it through, I pushed both Rolls-Royce Spey engines to full power and kept the aircraft in the dive, levelling out at the very last moment and flew as low as I dared over the tank at possibly in excess of Mach 1. We flashed low over the tank and I turned around hard and ran back at him from full head on. In retrospect I have often wondered where the most unpleasant viewpoint was – from poor Ernie's seat in the rear cockpit looking into the tank's gun muzzle from about ground level, or from the tank commander's position seeing the pilot at eye level.

The tank's main gun belched flame; actually firing at us head on and I remember laughing at his valiant effort at the time. Later in life I contemplated my would-be embarrassment at the possibility of having gone down in history as the only attack aircraft ever to be shot down by the main gun of a tank.

A few times I repeated this ploy on the two remaining tanks and, as it turned out, this indeed caused the tanks, as well as the Cuban troops in the few remaining BTR 152s, to halt their attacks on the helicopters. The extraction was more hectic than had been planned but it was successful – Puma pilot John Church even returning and checking that there were no men left on the ground. Had there been, I know he would have landed despite being under fire. We stayed around until Norman Bruton arrived with a Mirage III and shortly after that the late Neil McGibbon with another Buccaneer. I believe Matthew Morton, who had served in the Fleet Air Arm, was the last Bucc pilot to see the sun set over Cassinga and its smoking skeletons.

Capt Dries Marias and Lt Ernie Harvey with Buccaneer 416 at Grootfontein after their heroic deed.

*A rare newspaper photograph of Dries Marais and his navigator Ernie Harvey
taken immediately after landing from their heroic mission.*

Landing back at Grootfontein we were shocked to see the amount of damage to my Buccaneer; both engines had ingested bullets, there was a 76-mm AAA hole through the left-wing root and small-arms damage to the tail near the electronics bay. Not a single important system or component had suffered damage.

I was severely criticised for having been reckless in having subjected 'the aircraft and the navigator to danger', and back at Waterkloof a 'D.D. 101' (start of a court martial) was opened against me. When I eventually submitted my answering affidavit it was only one sentence: 'I shall plead not guilty to the charge as nobody had informed me that war had become dangerous.'

That ended the court martial proceedings and some time later I was informed that I had been awarded the Honoris Crux Decoration.

Author's Note: The Honoris Crux Decoration is one of South Africa's highest awards for gallantry. It was awarded 201 times between 1976 and 2003 when it was replaced. Only three members of 24 Squadron received the award, Dries Marais being the first.

CHAPTER SEVENTEEN
FRONT-LINE JEngO

MALCOLM WARD

Towards the end of engineer officer training our post-ings were announced and mine was to be the junior engineer officer (JEngO) on 208 Squadron, operating the Buccaneer in the overland strike/attack role from RAF Honington. I was cock-a-hoop to be posted to a front-line fast-jet squadron

When I arrived at Honington in the autumn of 1981 as a lowly flying officer, I was interviewed by the squadron boss, Graham Pitchfork, who as a wing commander was so far above me in the pecking order that the thought of meeting him frightened the life out of me, but he soon put me at ease with his warm welcome. He warned me that the experienced airmen and NCOs could run rings round me but that they would refrain from doing so, not out of any respect for me, but because they knew that I was here to gain experience. It was sound advice and I soon learned to ask the SNCOs for their views, before airing mine.

My first task was to get to know the ground crew and the aircraft, which was not easy since my arrival coincided with the departure of most of the squadron to Cold Lake in northern Canada for Trial Tropical, the evaluation of the Pave Spike laser-designator pod and the Paveway guided bomb. This marked the beginning of the RAF's precision-attack capability and was a huge leap forward in the development of UK air power. But to me, it just meant that I was notionally in charge of a rear party at Honington, with few aircraft running a small daily flying programme.

The training of engineer officers was not good in those days and the 'essential' pre-employ-ment training was seldom possible before actually arriving in post. The only thing I learned from the two-week Buccaneer engineering management course was that the aircraft's brakes were very, very good. There was a set of wheels in the ground school, which had been removed from an aircraft, which had landed with the parking brake on, thus producing a beautifully cross-sectioned training aid, with a large segment of the wheel hubs just ground away. The marks in the runway were still there for all to see.

208 Squadron's ground crew busy during a turn round at Honington.

Although the ground crew were very professional, they would mercilessly tease each other, and me. This was long before political correctness was invented and some of the ribbing could be very sharp, with language unsuitable for repetition in this tome. But it kept us on our toes and contributed in no small way to the spirit of the squadron, where everyone would go the extra mile in order not to let down their mates or the squadron. I once foolishly 'crinkled' when a pilot, Jules Flood, inadvertently called me Jerry (my predecessor's name) – thereafter I was 'Jerry the JEngO'. The exuberant attitude extended into the social life of the squadron, especially on detachment away from prying eyes and station rules. The boys could put away enough beer to float an aircraft carrier, but still turn up for work the next day bright eyed and bushy tailed. I practised hard, but never could keep up. I recall, vaguely, my first-ever dining-in night in the mess, when one of the navs encouraged me to fill the silver bowl on the table with port from the decanter on its passage round the lower reaches of the table, thus allowing us to top up our glasses whenever we wanted. I made it through the loyal toast and the opening lines of the speeches, but I must have dozed off, as the next thing I remember is the self-same nav shaking me and saying: "wake up JEngO, we're going to the bar."

The Buccaneer was a big, oily beast. The undercarriage bays and the bomb-bay door were invariably streaked with OM-15, the dark red hydraulic oil that powered almost everything on the aircraft. The jet efflux from the twin Rolls-Royce Spey engines left a trail of soot all the way down the fuselage, from the titanium 'pen nib' fairings to the huge clamshell airbrakes at the back. The Spey was a very reliable engine and I had been on the squadron for over a year before I witnessed an engine change. But there was airframe work aplenty. The Bucc was a rigger's aircraft and the airframe tradesmen made up by far the largest group on the squadron. After the fatal accident at Red Flag in 1980, the programme to restore the airworthiness of the Buccaneer had introduced a huge range of 'servicing instructions' or SIs, which had to be carried out at regular intervals, based on fatigue consumption. Most of these involved removing components that were never designed to be removed in service, such as the fin spar bolts, for intrusive X-ray or dye-penetrant inspections that took hours and hours of work.

The ground crew worked a two-shift system, with the day shift running from 07:30 to 16:30 and the night shift coming in at 16:30 and staying until the work was done. Often, this meant going home at 08:00 the next day, after handing over to the day shift, but they never complained. That was squadron life. However, the support services from the station worked strictly Monday to Friday, 08:00–17:00. I recall one period, when yet another new SI had been published, after cracks had been found or suspected in the tailplane attachment bolts. This required the whole tailplane to be removed and new bolts to be fitted, before the next flight. A crane was needed to lift the tailplane and the civilian crane driver would not, or could not, work overtime, so the squadron could manage no more than one inspection each day. I was surprised to see the night-shift rigger SNCO, Sgt Ray Burdaky, on a tractor, inching a Bucc back and forwards in the hangar. He had realised that it was possible – just – to park an aircraft directly underneath the chain-operated block and tackle in the hangar rafters and to use that to suspend the tailplane, whilst the bolts were changed. He and his crew worked all night and there were two more serviceable Buccaneers on the line the next morning. Enterprise!

The Bucc had no auxiliary power unit (APU) and no autonomous start capability. So every engine start required two huge pieces of ground equipment; a Palouste low-pressure air starting trolley (LPAST) and a Houchin diesel-driven ground power unit (GPU) to run the electrics. The LPAST was a miniature jet engine, which provided air pressure to spin the Bucc's engines up to speed. The crew plugged the air hose into one side of the aircraft, then waited for the hand signal from the pilot to start the engine. After the first engine was running at self-sustaining speed, the ground crew unplugged the hose and connected it to the other engine, where the procedure was repeated. One set of ground equipment was positioned between two cabs, but although the Houchins were very reliable, the poor old Paloustes would be gasping after two engine starts, so it was quite common for the lineys to have to drag another LPAST into place to get the last aircraft started. The sound of the Palouste pop-surging was often heard and was always followed by frenetic activity to get a replacement in position.

The aircraft had an ingenious rotating bomb bay, incorporating a large fuel tank. Instead of having doors, to allow the weapons to be dropped, the whole bomb bay, bombs, fuel tank and all, rotated 180 degrees when selected to open or close. This was powered by the aircraft's high-pressure hydraulic system and when it moved, it moved very quickly. There were lots of electrical and hydraulic components on the ceiling of the bay; to get at these for servicing it was necessary to depressurise the hydraulics and crank open the bomb bay by hand. It was a long process, but the ground crew were an inventive lot. I was walking through the hangar one day, when a group of electrical tradesmen were working on an aircraft. In response to a muffled call of "open", the technician in the cockpit selected the bomb bay to open; it did so and an electrician with a torch rolled out. I think that he was checking the fire wire in the bomb-bay roof and, by doing so from inside the bomb bay, had saved a couple of hours of preparation. I should have given the whole team a thorough dressing down for ignoring the proper procedure, but I was too impressed by their can-do attitude.

This was tested every 18 months or so by NATO's Tactical Evaluation (TACEVAL), a three-and-a-half-day exercise to check every aspect of a unit's war role. This came in two parts, the first being a no-notice alert, which required the squadron to 'generate' loaded aircraft, ready to go to war. This phase ended when 80 per cent of the squadron's aircraft were ready. If this was not achieved within half a day, it was a 'fail'. Part two was a longer affair, with lots of flying and lots of air raids and incidents, which we had to react to as if it was the real thing. This part was programmed into the calendar and usually lasted three days. The only time I took part in TACEVAL on the Buccaneer force, the hooter went at the civilised hour of 06:00. I dashed from the officers' mess to the squadron HQ, to find that the night-shift team leader, Chief Technician John Hehir, had just finished the paperwork, signing off the repair of a tricky snag on the last aircraft. The ground crew had already started towing the other aircraft onto the flight line for the armourers to load with a war load of 1,000-lb bombs. We had no aircraft in the hangar at that time, so we reached 100 per cent serviceability, with all aircraft loaded and ready to go within a couple of hours of the alarm sounding. It does not get any better than that.

*

As I gained experience, I was gradually entrusted with more responsibility. One of our aircraft had flown though a flock of birds in northern Norway and had diverted into Andøya with a shattered canopy and a punctured fuel tank. I was tasked to assemble a small team to recover it, and a Hercules arrived and was loaded with a replacement canopy, tank and ejection seat, which had also been struck by the remains of the seagulls coming through the canopy. We left Honington early on a Monday morning, too early for the station accounts staff to get any foreign currency for us, so I was issued with a 'letter of authority', which I was assured would enable me to walk into any bank in Norway and walk out with as much of Her Majesty's money as I liked. No passport, no bankcard, just my RAF ID card and a letter from the accounting officer. To my surprise, it worked and we had plenty of beer chits to spend in the hotel that night. The Norwegian bar staff had a unique way of declaring last orders. They pulled back the curtains at 11 p.m. and sunlight streamed into the bar – it was midsummer's day and we were over 100 miles inside the Arctic Circle.

The next day, the ground crew finished the final checks on the explosive cartridges in the seat, the canopy and the tank ejector units. I insisted on sitting in the back cockpit, to make sure that all was well. I saw nothing amiss and was happy to declare the cab serviceable. When we got home, the navigator of the crew that brought the aircraft back to Honington handed me a large piece of Perspex, complete with seagull feathers stuck to it, that he had found in the cockpit. So obviously, I did not look hard enough and it was another step up the steep learning curve.

The 'strike' part of the squadron's strike/attack role was a euphemism for the use of

Armourers of 208 Squadron position 1,000-lb bombs for aircraft loading.

tactical nuclear weapons, which we practised loading at the end of every station exercise and TACEVAL. The training weapons had, obviously, no warhead, but were treated exactly the same as the real thing, with armed guards and meticulously observed procedures for loading and unloading. This was an open secret but was never spoken about. After leaving the squadron, I kept schtumm about my small part in the nuclear deterrent until, decades

Buccaneer S.2 XT270 fitted with the bomb bay fairing and a CBLS mounted on one of the two bomb-bay pylons.

later, when I took my son to the Imperial War Museum at Duxford. There was one of 'my' aircraft, resplendent in 208 Squadron markings, albeit the cleanest, shiniest Bucc I had ever seen. It looked like a big Airfix model, with not a trace of OM-15 or jet efflux. And there, on a trolley next to it, were two 'shapes' – training versions of the tactical nukes. So I guess it is not a secret anymore.

The Buccaneer's bomb bay could hold four 1,000-lb bombs, but only two nukes. In order to ensure a clean separation from the aircraft, special fairings had to be fitted into the bomb bay, before the weapons were winched into place. Unlike the RAF Germany squadrons, 208 did not hold QRA, so it was only a couple of times each year that the fairings were fitted. The first exercise I took part in, it took a long time to get the fairings to fit, as they had not been used for some time. This slowed down the end of the war and, more importantly, delayed the subsequent push to the officers' mess bar. So after that, we used to assemble kits of the fairings and pre-position them where we knew the aircraft would be at the end of the exercise.

Apart from the strike fairings, we seldom had to carry out role changes on 208. We also did not conduct much night flying from Honington, as the aircrew were often deployed to northern Norway, where they got more than enough night hours to stay current. The standard fit for our aircraft was to have the under-wing tanks permanently fitted on the inboard wing stations, with a practice bomb carrier, carrier-bomb light store (CBLS) on each of the outboard stations. These could be loaded with up to four 28-lb or 3-kg practice bombs. The streamlined 28-pounders had the same ballistics as a 1,000-lb bomb, whereas the 3-kgs were ugly little blue tubes, designed to mimic the flight characteristics of a 'retard' weapon. I was walking along the flight line one morning, when the armourers were struggling to get a 28-lb bomb onto the rack in the CBLS. This involved crouching awkwardly under the wing and lifting the bomb into position, before giving it a shove and a twist, to engage the crutch on the suspension mechanism. I foolishly offered to have a go and to my surprise the bomb went home at the first attempt. I tried not to look smug as the shout went up: "JEngO got the bomb on!"

The Buccaneer was also equipped with the Westinghouse AN/ALQ-101-10 electronic countermeasures (ECM) jamming pod. However, they were not routinely fitted, as a fully loaded CBLS was of greater training value than an ECM pod, which could only be switched on within the confines of a dedicated ECM range, such as Spadeadam. The pods were programmed against specific 'threats' for exercises and were fitted on the outer-wing station. The AN/ALQ-101-10 was not designed to be tilted, but the Bucc always folded its wings for parking, meaning that the coolant would dribble out of the pod and have to be replenished immediately before every flight by a liney using the sort of backpack hand pump more often seen by council workmen spraying the weeds. For a six-ship wave, the liney would be lathered after running from aircraft to aircraft, as they unfolded their wings.

When the Falklands War broke out in 1982 we were ordered to measure engine oil consumption meticulously, to see if it would be possible for a Buccaneer to reach the Falklands with extended air-to-air refuelling. It wasn't. The morning after the *Belgrano* was sunk, the squadron intelligence officer, Flt Lt John Plumb, placed *Janes' All the World's Ships* on the crew room table, with a big black line through the entry for *Belgrano*, with a neatly written 'AL1' in the margin. But other than that, the Falklands War passed us by.

Towards the end of my time on the squadron, we started to practise operations from the hardened aircraft shelters (HASs), which had been built on the far side of the airfield for the shiny new Tornado. These were phase-two HASs, much bigger than the RAF Germany phase-one shelters. It was possible to park four Buccaneers, wings folded and airbrakes open, in one shelter, but we would normally put two in one HAS, with the front

208 Squadron at CFB Cold Lake for Exercise Maple Flag 1983.

one being towed outside before engine start. Starting a Buccaneer inside a HAS was unbelievably loud and is probably the reason why I now wear hearing aids. The noise from the engine itself was not too bad, as the jet efflux could escape out of the ducts at the back of the HAS. But the normal whine of the Palouste became a banshee inside the HAS, because the exhaust pointed straight upwards: the curved roof of the HAS would act like a sound lens, sending a barrage of extremely loud, high-frequency noise back down at the ground crew. The first few times we did it, molten putty would drop from the roof of the HAS. Although I do not think that we actually set anything on fire, it was not a procedure that would pass health & safety rules nowadays.

In the spring of 1983, 208 Squadron deployed to Cold Lake again, this time for Maple Flag, the Canadian version of Red Flag. And this time, as an experienced engineer officer, I was part of the team. We flew in the cargo hold of a Hercules, together with the vast amounts of ground equipment and spares that we took everywhere. After a brief night stop at Goose Bay, we followed the Buccaneers to Cold Lake, Alberta. At the end of our training period the aircraft were to be used by 16 Squadron arriving from RAF Laarbruch, to take part in the second half of Maple Flag. They brought their own ground crew, but whilst most of our team went home after the first three weeks, a sweeper party was left behind, to bring the aircraft home, once the second phase of Maple Flag was over and I was delegated to take charge of the sweeper party.

The recovery from Cold Lake was delayed. One aircraft had a problem with an electrical generator, which kept tripping off line. The biggest delay, however, was yet to come as our Hercules suffered an undercarriage malfunction on the way to Keflavik in Iceland. The snag could not be fixed, so the Herc flew home with the gear locked down – and home meant Lyneham, not Honington – so we had to arrange for surface transport to bring the sweeper party and our tons of Paloustes, Houchins and spares from Wiltshire to Suffolk. It was Friday by the time I got back and I was due at Cranwell on Monday morning for yet another course prior to my next posting. The new JEngO already had his feet under my desk, so I introduced him to Jules Flood as 'Jerry' and set off for Cranwell.

I left the Buccaneer force, but it never left me. My time on 208 Squadron shaped me and taught me lessons that stood me in good stead for the rest of my career and, like so many others, my first squadron was the one I have the most affection for. And it has not changed – all these years later I am still the editor of the 208 Squadron Association's annual newsletter.

CHAPTER EIGHTEEN

FAR FLUNG TALES

MIKE BICKLEY

Prelude

When I joined 801 Naval Air Squadron as senior observer in September 1967 at RNAS Lossiemouth, the squadron was due to embark in HMS *Victorious* for service in the Far East. Sadly, two months later the ship suffered a minor fire while in Portsmouth, which provided the government with an excuse to have her withdrawn from service. Almost symbolically, Lt Cdr Johnny Johnston flew his last sortie as CO 801 with me in the back seat on 13 March 1968, leading a small flypast at sunset on the day the ship was decommissioned.

By this time, 801 had been rescheduled to embark in HMS *Hermes* at the end of May 1968 with seven Buccaneer S.2s, eight crews and Lt Cdr Mike Hornblower in command. But first we deployed in mid-April to RAF El Adem, with RAF Victor AAR support, for three weeks' intensive flying in a large-scale tri-service exercise. High-low attacks on RAF Akrotiri defended by 893 Squadron Sea Vixens, close air support on a desert range, revisiting World War Two sites, much jollity in the bar, and the boss reclaiming his identity card from the station commander were all good for squadron cohesion. The return flight to Lossiemouth, again with Victor AAR, was uneventful apart from the boss testing the emergency cockpit depressurisation without warning at high level while I was munching a sandwich. Back at base there was ample time for MADDLS (mirror-assisted dummy deck landings) before two days of deck-landing practice (DLP) sorties with Lt 'Bush' Skrodzki before embarking in *Hermes* at the end of May for a work-up programme in the English Channel and Moray Firth.

The 801 Squadron military lament. From left to right:
Peter Bucke RAF, Mike Bickley RN, Tony Francis RN and Mick Whybro RAF.

Deployment

The Far East leg of HMS *Hermes*' fourth commission lasted from mid-July 1968, on completion of work-up, to the ship's return to Portsmouth at the beginning of April 1969. As a result of the Six Day War in June 1967, the Suez Canal was still closed, so the ship would have to deploy to the Far East via the Cape of Good Hope. This in turn meant that the opportunities for flying on passage with suitable diversion airfields for inexperienced pilots would be severely limited. Pilots on their first operational tour, therefore, disembarked to Lossiemouth for continuation flying; they re-joined the ship in Singapore. In the event, only one day's flying was achieved between the UK and Cape Town. To keep the aircrew busy and amused, 801's senior pilot and closet-impresario, Lt Cdr Dickie Wren, devised a programme of after-dinner entertainment for the wardroom. The audience hailed the outstanding success of the evening, which confirmed 801 as a true outward-looking RN/RAF force to be reckoned with on board.

The day before the ship arrived in Cape Town I flew ashore in the COD Gannet with the mail to Ysterplaat South African Air Force Base, to be met by my wife and our three very young daughters. They had travelled out by sea to stay with her mother in Cape Town for the duration of 801's deployment. The ensuing port visit was memorable for many reasons; as far as is known, the squadron's activities were not recorded on any medium available at the time.

801 Squadron officers on HMS Victorious, *March 1969. CO,
Lt Cdr M Hornblower seated centre with Mike Bickley seated second from left.*

On Station

Eventually, almost a month after leaving UK waters, and after a further day's flying off Gan,
it was time to renew 801's acquaintance with Singapore from seriously long range. Two
aircraft launched at first light; Mike Hornblower and I led, with Lt Jonathan Tod and Flt
Lt Mick Whybro our number two.

Unfortunately, a hydraulic fault caused Jonathan and Mick to divert to the Royal
Australian Air Force (RAAF) Base at Butterworth. The CO and I landed at Changi after
three hours 20 minutes, dropped some practice bombs at China Rock in the afternoon
and cracked another two plus hours that night, finishing off with MADDLS to ensure that
everyone knew we had arrived. The following day we flew to Butterworth with bits for the
stricken aircraft, and then returned to Changi. We landed back on *Hermes* next day, having
achieved six sorties in three days in the same aircraft with minimal support.

During the next ten days, operating in the Penang area, a variety of weapon roles were
practised, culminating in the ship and squadrons successfully undergoing their operational
readiness inspection by the flag officer carriers and amphibious ships. The whole work-up
had taken almost three months from our first embarkation in May.

And so to Singapore and a fortnight disembarked at RAF Changi. The aircrew were
accommodated in hotels nearby, with self-drive naval Citroen 2CVs for commuting. Lt Fred
Secker demonstrated aquaplaning in one during an afternoon downpour and finished up

in a monsoon drain. A quiet squadron outing was made to savour the charms and ambience of Bugis Street, where Lt Lyn Faulkner rejoiced at experiencing smouldering firecracker paper in his hair.

Once re-embarked in mid-September, we concentrated on close air support at Asahan by day, and attacks under Glow Worm flares for the night-qualified team before setting off east to the Bismarck Archipelago and exercises with the Royal Australian Navy (RAN). Searching along island coasts for their fast patrol boats (FPBs) was fascinating: abandoned World War Two landing strips could be made out from the dense secondary growth in the midst of primary forest, but it was almost impossible to spot the boats. During exercise free play the CO and I carried out an opportunist medium-toss attack on the RAN frigate HMAS *Queenborough*. The practice bomb was spot-on for range, the aim off was happily in the right direction, and it splashed alongside the ship, to the relief and satisfaction of both parties.

As *Hermes* moved south into the Coral Sea in early October, Dickie Wren and I flew the ship's mail to Townsville in Queensland. No matter that we had been at sea for nearly three weeks, nor that we had flown at high level for an hour to get there, but the mayor of Townsville, the local beauty queen and the press were present on the airfield at 0645 to greet the first Buccaneer to land in Queensland, where the man with the insecticide flit gun was first up the ladder. What a welcome!

Exercise play with the RAN continued as we sailed further south, and an Australian journalist was embarked full of bright ideas. He suggested to the CO that, while searching along the coast for FPBs, we could perhaps take the opportunity to photograph someone, possibly female, on the beach. A suitable picture would be published in his newspaper and a prize offered for identifying the person. Nothing like a challenge of that nature to fire up the boss: the aircraft bomb-bay photographic pack was loaded and off he and I went, searching at very low level for targets on the glorious but deserted beaches on a clear, cloudless day. As we left the coast to return to the ship, we spotted a gaggle of light aircraft crossing well clear ahead of us heading inland.

Back on board, there was slight disappointment at the absence of a suitable beach photo, and a slightly one-sided discussion with commander (Air) about the light aircraft. A complaint had been received that we had intruded upon the Round Australia Air Race and upset some participants who were unaware of an aircraft carrier in the vicinity. It was, however, apparent that the ship had been unaware of the race, so a draw was eventually declared. We swiftly moved on to the next phase of the exercise, which gave us an unusual and welcome opportunity for close air support with live weapons on the Townshend Island bombing range off a remote part of Queensland.

The finale of the exercise was an early morning attack on Williamtown RAAF Base, north of Newcastle, New South Wales. Jonathan Tod took an Australian journalist with him, and 893 Squadron Sea Vixens escorted the Buccaneers. After a circuitous overland route at low level, we hit the target just as the opposition were scrambling their fighter defences. A reasonable outcome, but capped for ever by the journalist, euphoric at the debrief, publicly calling our steely AWI 'you beauty'.

After a busy month at sea we arrived in Sydney for two weeks. *Hermes* berthed at Garden Island, close to the many delights of King's Cross, the city, the beaches, spots around the magnificent harbour, and Harry's Café de Wheels for a restorative pie on the walk back to the ship. We were within striking distance of almost anywhere in south-east Australia. The ship's company scattered far and wide. During a long weekend trip well west of the Blue Mountains, I surmised to the owner in a remote roadside bar that they probably didn't see many sailors there. "Not since last night, when one of your chiefs fixed the lights for us," came the laconic reply.

It all had to come to an end and we refreshed for a few days flying off the RAN air base at Nowra before setting off northwards towards the Philippines with the intention of operating west of Manila, near the USN air base at Cubi Point. For some reason, however, this was not to be and the ship shaped course from east of the Philippines towards Okinawa where agreement to exercise had been obtained. Jonathan Tod and I flew to the USN air base at Naha to arrange the details, with Mike Hornblower and the ship's operations officer, Lt Cdr Ian Condie, as number two. The traditional Buccaneer low-level approach was made to the island, which caused a little concern in the air defence organisation. Once there, everything possible was provided, with great USN hospitality too. But this was a country at war. I watched the daily B-52 stream returning from operations over Vietnam to the nearby USAF base at Kadena; one every five miles for over 20 minutes. Our aircraft spotters were convinced that there were Lockheed SR-71 Blackbird aircraft on the island, in spite of all denials, and were rewarded when one flew low over the ship as we departed after ten days in the area. One reason for our presence there had been to carry out a programme of Bullpup air-to-ground missile firings, which were achieved successfully on the Tori-Shima Range to the AWI's delight, and maintaining night deck qualification. We also provided low-level targets for the USAF air defences, showing that our initial arrival profile had not been a one-off!

Hong Kong was our next port of call in late November for ten days, berthed alongside in the RN's shore base, HMS Tamar. As ever, Hong Kong offered something for everyone and the time flew by. Looking ahead, the CO suggested a maximum range sortie to Singapore once we sailed, but the route would take us over or near South Vietnam and intensive US operations wherever we launched, so the idea was shelved. We resumed flying for three days and nights when we reached Malaysian airspace, before disembarking to RAF Changi for four weeks over Christmas and New Year, while *Hermes* berthed in Singapore Naval Base.

We were now over halfway through the Far East leg of the commission and the opportunity was taken for family visits. A number of wives flew out to Singapore and all the aircrew were accommodated ashore. Most of the squadron ratings were also ashore, in accommodation at RAF Changi. Continuation flying from Changi carried on until 20 December. The squadron social secretary/entertainments officer arranged our Christmas dinner in the hotel. It was a great success until the after-dinner mints, which turned out to be the Fox's Glacier variety. He may eventually live that down.

During one of our disembarkations at Changi, the CO and I attended a late afternoon drinks party in the officers' mess in tropical white uniform, before going via the ship to change into plain clothes for an evening squadron run ashore in Johore Bahru. We left the party during a Singapore cloudburst with evening kit in our holdalls and set off in a naval Mini with the boss driving. In the downpour and darkness we passed someone by the roadside waving a red light but forced on. The next thing to appear through the murk was an army lorry broadside on across the road; we skidded and hit it, stopping with the smashed windscreen against the lorry's side. The CO emerged unscathed but I sustained a cut arm and was covered with glass. A passing taxi was flagged down, I was bundled in with my holdall and the driver told to go to the nearest hospital. A few minutes later I was delivered to RAF Changi hospital maternity entrance. My uniform was cut off, and I was given a shower to get rid of the glass: the end result was a naval officer in a maternity hospital clad solely in a towel. In remarkably short order I had my arm bandaged, retrieved my holdall, put on clean plain clothes, to general amazement, and was discharged. I did not get to Johore Bahru.

January brought an intensive period of day and night sorties with MADDLS in preparation for re-embarking in the middle of the month. After two DLP sessions with Lt Ted Hackett, I embarked with him as he made his first deck landing. The ship sailed to exercise areas off Penang and 801 Squadron got on with a heavy bombing programme, dropping or tossing more than 100 inert 1,000-lb bombs in two days, reportedly more than 809 Squadron's Buccaneers had dropped during the entire previous commission. Night work-up followed for a few crews, with rocketry and close air support on Penang Island by day for all. The CO and I carried out an attack on Butterworth, aiming to be on target at dawn. Letting down to low level over the jungle before first light was a real challenge, and it was still quite dark as we cleared the target. My logbook records the entire sortie as night flying with a night deck landing, so that experience was not to be repeated. The same day the first Malaysian to make rear admiral, and be appointed chief of staff of the Royal Malaysian Navy, visited the ship. He and I were the same age and had been in the same term at Britannia Royal Naval College Dartmouth just 11 years previously!

In early February we returned to Singapore for the last time. I knew that when I left 801 I would be going to either a frigate or mine-warfare vessel, so I got approval to spend a few days on board HMS *Ajax*, the frigate escorting *Hermes* to our next destination, Fremantle in Western Australia. After an informative and refreshing experience I returned to the carrier for the only two days flying possible on passage owing to the Indian Ocean swell before we entered harbour to an enthusiastic welcome from well-wishers. Some had apparently travelled from Sydney.

Fremantle and Perth lived up to all expectations, from the beaches and surroundings to the hospitality, entertainment and attractions in the city. There were narrow escapes too. Jonathan Tod and I spent a carefree afternoon haggling over didgeridoo prices but decided against purchase because the shop didn't have a current year model, and who wants last year's? After sailing from Fremantle on 27 February to head west, there was one day of flying and Fred Secker and I flew deep into the outback, seeing little sign of human habitation, and a stark contrast to the vibrant city on the coast. We landed on last and were told to shut down before clearing off the angle deck. Normally such an instruction indicated that the flight deck teams were about to exercise fire-fighting or rescue incapacitated aircrew from their aircraft. On this occasion, however, we were invited to vacate the aircraft.

*Celebration of Mike Bickley's 1,000 hours
on the Buccaneer. His pilot, Fred Secker,
is standing on a chair!*

The captain, Doug Parker, appeared on deck and, to my utter astonishment, presented me with a bottle of champagne to mark my achieving 1,000 hours in Buccaneers: a truly memorable final flight on station.

Homeward bound

Our passage across the southern Indian Ocean to South Africa was notable for long periods of poor weather. Flight deck sports and competitions were organised on the calmer days. A squadron mess dinner was arranged in the wardroom annex and someone remembered to tell the CO, who was relaxing on board an accompanying Royal Fleet Auxiliary ship. We managed one day's limited flying east of Durban before encountering big seas and high winds, with an unsettling ship's motion and some damage to boats and weather deck equipment, as we sailed along the South African coast. All that was forgotten as we arrived in Table Bay and entered Cape Town harbour on the calm, sunny morning of 12 March for a six-day visit that was as enjoyable as the one on our way out to the Far East. My family had already returned to Lossiemouth, leaving some things behind for me to stow on board for the final leg. The passage up the African coast and northwards was uneventful, suntans were topped up, some aircrew officers kept bridge watches, and we prepared to leave the ship. On Sunday 30 March 1969, all seven Buccaneers launched off Cape Finisterre in two waves and headed direct to Lossiemouth. We had been away from the UK for eight and a half months.

The remainder of my time in 801 Squadron was spent at Lossiemouth. The high point was our participation in a review of the Western Fleet and presentation of a new colour to the fleet by Her Majesty the Queen on 29 July 1969. The fleet would be anchored in Torbay. CO 801 Squadron was tasked with leading the jet aircraft flypast made up of 20 Buccaneers, 20 Sea Vixens and 9 Phantoms. The Sea Vixens and Phantoms would operate from RNAS Yeovilton, the Buccaneers from Lossiemouth. Mike Hornblower and I carried out three solo rehearsals, the latter two using Portland Bill Lighthouse as the rendezvous point and holding point for all aircraft. On the day, Buccaneers from 801, 809 and 800 Squadrons flew the length of the country in stream and rendezvoused as planned. The five Yeovilton squadrons joined us at Portland Bill and, after a five-minute timing delay, the formation crossed Lyme Bay into half a summer gale, rain and low cloud. We flew past the fleet in these miserable conditions then immediately dispersed in smaller formations to

801 Squadron line up at Lossiemouth in July 1969.

return to our bases. It had been a typical Fleet Air Arm flypast, with the only full rehearsal on the day itself, so it was with some relief that we recovered to Lossiemouth after almost three hours in the air. Two days later, Mike Hornblower and I left 801 Squadron after an eventful and exciting year.

Sequel

In 1988 I was serving in Gibraltar: the governor was ACM Sir Peter Terry. Lady Terry saw my observer's wings, we chatted about my times with the RAF, and she mentioned that they had been at El Adem. I was about to relate CO 801's encounter with the station commander there in 1968 when I realised that she and her husband must have been there at that time. A quick change of topic avoided re-igniting inter-service strife, but it had come close.

On an Indian Ocean cruise in 2002 I recounted this tale to a retired RAF officer. Another passenger overheard it and subsequently asked me to confirm that I had flown in Buccaneers. When I did so he asked me what the orange flag was for on the starboard side of the rear cockpit. I said it was on the tailplane trim fuse, which could be pulled out if there was a trim runaway. Credentials satisfied, it transpired that he had been a chief petty officer and we were both in 736 Squadron at Lossiemouth in 1967. Long live the Buccaneer fraternity!

CHAPTER NINETEEN

ENTER THE
LASER-GUIDED BOMB

NICK BERRYMAN

In the late 1960s, Texas Instruments in the USA began to develop a series of laser-guided 'add-ons' to enhance the accuracy of the 'dumb' iron bombs then in use. These Paveway kits, comprising a semi-active laser seeker, control canards at the front, and rear wings for stability, could be attached to a variety of existing warheads.

The introduction of an improved Paveway II to the United States Air Force (USAF) in the early 1970s, fortuitously coincided with an underspend in the RAF's annual budget, which paved the way (excuse the pun) for the UK to purchase a large number of Paveway I kits to fit to our existing stock of 1,000-lb medium capacity (MC) iron bombs, in order to develop a *relatively* cheap 'smart bomb' capability. Along with the Westinghouse Pave Spike laser-designator pod, these were destined for 208 and 216 Buccaneer Squadrons, then based at RAF Honington; the lead squadron for this being the recently formed 216, commanded by Wg Cdr Peter Sturt. Once operational, 216 was destined to join 12 Squadron to form a maritime strike/attack wing assigned to the Supreme Allied Commander Atlantic (SACLANT); the latter squadron being armed with Martel anti-shipping missiles, with 216 concentrating on LGBs.

In the autumn of 1979, the Central Trials and Tactics Organisation (CTTO) sponsored Trial Tropical to develop LGB tactics, using both 216 Squadron and Wg Cdr Graham Pitchfork's 208 Squadron (assigned to Allied Forces Northern Europe [AFNORTH] for operations over Norway and Denmark). For this trial, selected crews flew a series of sorties on the instrumented weapons range at the MOD West Freugh, and in co-operation with RAF Coltishall Jaguars. The trial culminated in October 1979 with a successful drop of live LGBs on the unsinkable Garvie Island off Cape Wrath in northern Scotland.

Unfortunately, in February 1980, the tragic loss of a XV Squadron crew on Exercise Red Flag in Nevada resulted in the temporary grounding of the entire Buccaneer fleet [see Chapter Eleven], and when the aircraft were once again cleared to fly in late July, the

AN/AVQ-23 Pave Spike laser-targeting pod and 1,000-lb Paveway bomb mounted on the port wing of a Buccaneer.

reduced number of serviceable Buccaneers inevitably resulted in 216 Squadron (by then relocated to RAF Lossiemouth) being disbanded, with its aircrew being transferred to 12 Squadron.

Meanwhile, back at RAF Honington, 208 Squadron recommenced Pave Spike training, but the Jaguar commitment had to be dropped. However, with the loss of 216 Squadron, the RAF now had a surplus of Paveway kits and Pave Spike designator pods, so it was decided that CTTO should investigate their use in overland operations in NATO's Central Region. The resurrected trial became Trial Tropical II.

And so it came to pass, in May 1981, that crews from both Buccaneer squadrons at RAF Laarbruch (XV and 16) were tasked to take part in Phase 1 of the trial, with an officer from CTTO evaluating the results. As weapons leader at the time, I was nominated as the 16 Squadron lead pilot, with Flt Lt Iain McNicoll for XV.

Phase 1

For most of the month of May, the RAF Germany (RAFG) Pave Spike crews from both squadrons (pilots Flt Lt Dan Findlay and myself, and navigators, Flt Lts Dick Aitken and Norman Browne on 16 Squadron) flew numerous sorties around the North German Plain, attempting to designate ('spike') various simulated targets, including hardened aircraft shelters and missile sites. This required a high level of skill from the navigators, as low-level overland Buccaneer navigation was done almost entirely with map, compass and stopwatch.

*Navigator's cockpit with the central screen for guidance
of TV Martel and Pave Spike laser target marker.*

As for the pilots, good eyesight was essential, as the summer visibility in northern Germany is often poor due to smoke and haze trapped below an inversion layer (fortunately, I had been issued with a pair of excellent flying glasses during my previous tour at the Tactical Weapons Unit in Wales).

With the Pave Spike laser and camera initially bore-sighted to the pilot's display unit (strike sight), the pilot had first to identify the target visually, and accurately aim the aircraft to enable the navigator to (hopefully) pick it out on a small monochrome video monitor in the rear cockpit. He then had to maintain designation (for safety reasons, the laser was not fired) while the pilot carried out a hard-level turn to avoid getting close to the target's defences. As the Buccaneer equipment was not capable of locking on to the target during the turn, the navigator had an extremely difficult job manually tracking and 'holding' it – even without objects like trees, houses and churches getting in the way.

Phase 2

The second part of the trial took place at RAF Lossiemouth from 22 June to 3 July 1981, with Wg Cdr Peter Sturt's 216 Squadron (in process of disbandment) kindly letting us share their hangar. The station commander also had us issued with the despised nuclear, biological and chemical (NBC) clothing, so that we wouldn't miss out if a station exercise was called. What a thoughtful chap.

While Phase 1 of the trial was a 'kill 'em with film' exercise, Phase 2 at the MOD West Freugh Weapons Test & Evaluation (T&E) Range in West Scotland entailed the delivery of inert Paveway bombs by 208 Squadron crews in a 'toss' manoeuvre from about 2.5 miles, while the 16 Squadron crews carried out the laser designation. This was a much easier proposition than Phase 1, as the raft, fitted with an acoustic laser-marking panel, was the only object in that part of Luce Bay, and entirely surrounded by water. Not only that, but the West Scottish visibility was miles (literally) better than that of the smoky and hazy North German Plain.

In order to practise co-ordination and timing with the bombers before going 'live', several attacks were planned to be carried out 'dry'; however, on one early attack, mistaking 'clear laser hot' for 'clear hot', the bombing crew tossed the first 1,000-lb bomb. Norman Browne, casually tracking the target and listening to the laser 'pings', got the shock of his life when the target suddenly disappeared in a huge splash. "Shit it's gone!" he said. "What has?" Dan Findlay asked. "The target!" Norman replied.

It had been discovered that the tossed bombs could pick up laser reflections from the target before reaching their apogee, and with the simple 'bang-bang' control system making large canard deflections for course correction, this resulted in a noticeable wobble, expending energy quickly, with the bomb(s) impacting short of the target. The bombs had to be delivered accurately, with the laser fired late in the weapon's flight to refine the impact point – precise timing and co-ordination with the bombing aircraft was crucial.

With two aircraft from each squadron, 208 and 16 carried out around 28 sorties during Phase 2, dropping a total of 26 inert Paveway bombs, and whilst we narrowly managed to avoid the station exercise at RAF Lossiemouth, we did make it back home just in time to take part in the Laarbruch exercise (MINIVAL) – and more NBC kit!

Phase 3

In 1981, the RAFG Buccaneer squadrons were to deploy to Nellis Air Force Base (AFB) in Nevada, USA, to take part in the annual USAF's premier air combat training exercise, Red Flag; 16 Squadron for the first two weeks, followed immediately by XV Squadron. As Phase 3 of Trial Tropical II coincided with the 16 Squadron deployment, immediately following the trial we were to travel from Canadian Forces Base (CFB) Cold Lake to Nellis AFB to be attached to XV for Red Flag (no way were we going to miss the best air exercise in the world). On 5 September, we returned to Lossiemouth for the 100 ft ultra-low flying training required by both the trial and the exercise. 1981 was turning into an ultra-low-level bonanza.

In early October, four Buccaneers deployed to Cold Lake; all being flown by 208 Squadron crews, as RAFG crews were either not qualified or not current in air-to-air refuelling (not very viable at 100 ft in the Central Region). The 16 Squadron aircrew, and all the detachment ground crew had to travel in significant discomfort in the back of a Hercules (Fat Albert) – a flight that could arguably be described as the definitive 'Flight from Hell'. Fat Albert was so full of ground equipment that we could not sit comfortably with our feet on the floor. Our main recreation during the long flight was playing bridge on top of the ground equipment, using sign language for bidding (the noise and vibration effectively preventing all speech). The air loadmaster had also thoughtfully left us a 'Lad's Mag' to read – the main article graphically illustrating the effects of syphilis in full colour – a useful deterrent to keep the lads on the straight and narrow for the duration of the detachment! When we finally arrived at Cold Lake, we understood just why we had been issued with

Armed with LGBs, two Buccaneers head for the weapons range.

mukluks and wolverine fur parkas, and why it was called Cold Lake – it was *very* cold.

A squadron leader from CTTO was the project officer in charge of the trial, aided by a sergeant and a very young LACW typist for admin duties. The 208 Squadron detachment was led by Sqn Ldr Geoff Frankcom and included all the required administration and engineering personnel. The 16 Squadron element comprised two crews – Dick Aitken and myself, with Norman Browne crewed with Dan Findlay.

The operations room was located in a freezing Portakabin situated pretty much in the middle of the also freezing airfield, and the targets at the freezing Cold Lake Air Weapons Range (CLAWR) were in the process of construction by a detachment of army engineers.

On 7 October, we carried out an initial range and target reconnaissance, but were unable to begin bombing sorties until the 13th, as the targets were not ready due to the very hard frozen ground making progress very slow for the engineers. The project officer insisted that the aircraft did no more flying until the targets were ready, in order to avoid any risk of aircraft going unserviceable. Unsurprisingly, this enforced inactivity soon began to affect the aircrews' morale, and severe friction began to build between one of the pilots and the man from CTTO. 'Words' were exchanged, and with the distinct possibility that physical blows might follow, the rest of us rapidly evacuated the freezing Portakabin to avoid being witnesses at any subsequent court martial. The middle of the airfield was even colder than the Portakabin, and we had to explain to our very young airwoman typist that it was quite normal behaviour for officers to let off steam in this manner.

Finally, Geoff Frankcom persuaded the project officer that a training sortie was abso-lutely necessary for us to maintain currency, so off we went for an hour's ultra-low flying – the formation being ably led by our most junior pilot, 'The Boy' Southwood. On return to the airfield, we had to climb from 100 ft to 500 ft, as this was the minimum run-in height stipulated for the main operating runway. However, as no minimum height was

Four 1,000-lb laser-guided bombs strike the bed-sheet target.

stipulated for the parallel 'outer runway', our intrepid formation leader brought us in for a very fast break from 50 ft. Whilst the other crews were most impressed by the dash and elan of this very young and relatively inexperienced pilot, the same could not be said for the CTTO project officer!

This episode prompted a renewed 'discussion' and handbag swinging soon broke out, with the project officer and our disgruntled pilot apparently disagreeing over the employment of air power. Once again, Geoff Frankcom found himself acting as mediator, my input of the RAF Germany perspective (as I saw it) merely helped to set off yet another explosion. This time, the admin sergeant (Swindles) was well prepared, with a trestle table outside the Portakabin covered in parkas for hire at CA$10 per half hour. With Sergeant Swindles (how very apt) making a fortune, and the LACW typist growing up fast, the situation was temporarily calmed by the arrival of the project officer's boss to referee the contest.

The trial finally got underway on 13 October, and we soon achieved great accuracy with the bombing – too accurate really, as the targets were completely destroyed whenever they were hit by the LGBs (which was just about every time), so we soon ran out of target materials. Fortunately, it was discovered that bed sheets from some empty rooms in the officers' mess served as pretty good substitute targets, and despite the army engineers' equipment tent reportedly being attacked by bears, we were able to continue as planned, although we were unable to return the bed sheets to the officers' mess at the end of the trial, as by then they had the appearance of a pile of tatty handkerchiefs.

On one sortie to the range, we noticed a single, large moose standing in a small lake within the training area; this made a nice alternative target for Pave Spike tracking practice (without bombing it, of course). After several runs, lower and lower each time, the moose never moved, and Dick began to think it might be a cardboard cut-out. After landing, having showed our videotapes to the Canadians, along with the moose's coordinates, we later discovered that the base commander had flown out in a helicopter to the range area and shot it!

On the 16th, after five 'spiking' sorties, Dick and I were given the opportunity of acting as bomber – dropping four LGBs. It had been worked out that we could drop eight bombs simultaneously from two aircraft flying in a fairly tight formation. The aircraft would then break outwards, away from each other; when almost inverted, it was then possible to see all eight bombs falling away and heading towards the target in close formation. Exhilarating stuff.

After an entertaining and sociable weekend playing 'crud' on the snooker table (a great Canadian tradition), with the assistance of Labatt's Blue and Molsen Canadian, we were able to carry out low-level sorties across the Great Plains of Alberta to the foothills of the Rocky Mountains (around 600 nautical miles round trip). A pleasant distraction from the daily trial sorties (although I'm not sure if we remembered to inform the CTTO project officer – why would we?).

On the 20th and 21st we carried out more 'spiking' sorties, and on the final day of the trial (23rd), Dick and I were able to finish off in style by tossing a further three LGBs to finally destroy the remaining bed sheet. At the end of the trial, OC 208 Squadron pitched up with his pilot Eddie Wyer to ferry back the fourth Buccaneer. He was completely unaware of the 'happenings' and walked straight into a tirade from the project officer's boss who had a bewildered OC 208 standing to attention, hat on, and on the end of an almighty rocket. One of the perks of being in command I suppose.

Fortunately, it was CTTO's job to write up the results of the trial, and 208's job to fly the Buccaneers back to Honington. Rumour has it that OC 208 was in such a hurry to escape the CTTO team he happily took off with a few aircraft snags, which were fixed once the four Buccaneers reached Goose Bay.

In order to fill in the time before reporting to XV Squadron at Nellis, Dan and I set off along the west coast of America via Vancouver, Seattle, San Francisco, Los Angeles, San Diego and Tijuana. Meanwhile, Dick and Norman attempted (but unfortunately failed) to route to Nellis via Hawaii.

However, that is a different story entirely …

Epilogue

When we eventually arrived back at Laarbruch, after an eventful Exercise Red Flag, I was instructed by a senior officer to write a report indicating that Pave Spike was not suitable for use in the overland role. Having spent the better part of six months proving the converse, I was not amenable to this 'suggestion', offering instead to write a report discussing its limitations. However, my offer was rebuffed. Bang went my career (if I ever had one), but much fun was still to be had, including tossing eight *live* Paveway bombs at Garvie Island (what a blast – literally) before being posted back to a mundane staff job in the UK.

CHAPTER TWENTY

MEDITERRANEAN TRAVELS ON 12 SQUADRON

BOB KEMP

During late 1983, the already dangerous situation in the Lebanon became critical and it was decided to provide air support for the small British land force contingent of the United Nations peacekeeping force. Known as 'BRITFORLEB' they were located in a block of flats near Beirut airport. To provide support and a visual deterrent, a detachment of six Buccaneers drawn from 12 and 208 Squadrons was deployed to RAF Akrotiri in Cyprus to be prepared to participate in Operation Pulsator. This peacekeeping role was perhaps a misnomer as we were heavily armed with Paveway laser-guided 1,000-lb bombs and the Pave Spike laser-designator pod. We also carried flare and chaff dispensers.

A warning order for Operation Pulsator to deploy to Akrotiri was received at Lossiemouth on 8 September 1983 and within 36 hours six Buccaneers had landed in Cyprus. The military position in the eastern Mediterranean was complex. The US Sixth Fleet was in the area, with around 100 strike aircraft embarked, as was the French aircraft carrier *Foch* with 40 aircraft and numerous escorts. There were hundreds of US Marines based in a military barracks in Beirut. We were, therefore, very much a token but potent force. The intelligence situation was vague with little or no detail of possible targets that included heavy artillery pieces operated by the Druze militia. Communications were also complex with a number of interested parties wanting ownership and control of our small force. We preferred to speak to no one once released.

We were a tiny UK contribution to what was a major US-led endeavour. Yet the Americans were always very supportive of our small force. One of the first actions was 'a show of force' aimed particularly at those in and around Beirut. Two Buccaneers were tasked to fly through the city and show the flag. This was a licence to thrill and the exercise was repeated a few times. Crews were cleared down to 100 feet and thereafter wore tee shirts with 'Real men fly through Beirut not over it'. But the real challenge was how to use the

Pave Spike over land rather than to attack ships. It was found that a steep diving attack from 11,000 feet would allow the pilot to point at a target and for the navigator to uncage the Spike and maintain the cross hairs on the target during the high G recovery and subsequent laser-guided bomb trajectory. Successful trials were carried out in 40-degree dive attacks on floating targets in Episkopi Range with direct hits being achieved. We kept our hands in by practising on telegraph poles simulating large artillery weapons positioned in the woods north of Akrotiri. Then we waited, holding two aircraft at a dawn-to-dusk readiness in anticipation of suitable tasking. We were poised to destroy artillery pieces used by the Druze militia or other factions in the hills around Beirut and in the Souq El Gharb region to the south of the city.

I took over command of the detachment in October just before a suicide bomber drove a truck into the US Marine compound in Beirut killing 241 US servicemen, 58 French military, six civilians and the two attackers. Tensions rose markedly and we sensed action. From time to time we would be tasked at no notice to bring two fully armed aircraft up to cockpit readiness and check in to Episkopi Control for take-off clearance. Another alert state, using a separate code word, brought two aircraft to cockpit readiness for release to fly into Lebanese airspace. Phantoms from 43 Squadron, also based at Akrotiri, would provide a fighter escort should we be bounced en route. This was getting exciting.

We flew at high speed to the Lebanese coast avoiding the Russian AGI (intelligence gathering ship) patrolling between Akrotiri and Beirut. Its task was to alert the Russians and the militia ashore of incoming aircraft. Our route invariably took us near the vast US fleet and to me that was the most dangerous part of any mission. Every fire control radar of the US fleet would lock onto us despite IFF procedures in place that should have identified us as a friendly force. We regularly expended our load of anti-missile flares and chaff in the face of an over-active and twitchy US fleet; and that was before we even got to the Beirut coast.

In order to try and clarify the UK/USA procedures in the hot spot of the eastern Med, I flew out by chopper to the USS *Independence* and met with the operational commander. Our meeting was held immediately underneath the launch deck of this amazing carrier and almost every two minutes we had to cease conversation as the roof above our head shook with the deafening noise of Tomcats, Prowlers and A-7s taking off. Walking across the deck of the carrier was another hazard as piles of live weapons, missiles and ammo trays were littered all over the place. I recall one of the straplines from the USN commander: "Success has a thousand fathers while failure dies an orphan." So true. What was impressive was watching the USS *New Jersey* firing her 16-inch guns into the heartland of Lebanon. At least they had found targets – or maybe not.

After the initial flights through Beirut we were wary of straying too close to Beirut itself as there were reports of many SAM 7 units there in addition to the deadly ZSU-23-4 anti-aircraft artillery (AAA). On one occasion just off the coast abeam Beirut airport we were locked up by an X-band transmission that I assessed to be a Gun Dish radar of a ZSU-23-4 gun unit. Units of the SBS were active in Beirut and in the surrounding area, but a suitable target for the might of the Buccaneer force was never identified.

We developed various tactics against the possible attack scenarios as vague intelligence

A Buccaneer flies 'through' Beirut and over the British Embassy.

situations were unfolding. One manoeuvre we practised involved three Buccaneers in close arrow formation. Flying a vari-toss manoeuvre, with nine seconds on the timer, we would release three 1,000 pounders simultaneously giving an impressive concentration of force. At bomb release the leader would continue with a roll off the top manoeuvre while both wingmen recovered left or right as per a steep long-toss recovery. I named it the 'Fleur de Lis' attack and it was rather nice to watch the formation attack from the ground.

One evening I was at a cocktail party in the Akrotiri sergeants' mess attended by the station commander, Gp Capt John Willis. A runner handed him a signal. Must be important I thought to gate crash a cocktail party with a signal. He read it and looked my way beckoning me across the room. "Bob," he said in a rather cold manner, "Take my car, go to the mess and round up all your boys. Be in the station HQ briefing room in 20 minutes." So off I charged in the station commander's car, complete with flag flying proudly on the bonnet. In the bar I found most of the team and the rest in their rooms. I filled the car with merry aviators and the rest hotfooted or cycled to the briefing room. At first the boys had second thoughts seeing me jump into the car with the flag and beckon them in. As we tore towards the briefing room every man and his dog saluted the car. A good start I thought.

In due course John Willis arrived in the briefing room still in mess kit and read the signal. Apparently the Soviet ambassador in London had complained to the Ministry of

Defence that the Buccaneers in Cyprus (us) had been dropping bombs on a Russian warship off the coast of Episkopi. John Willis had no alternative but to set up an immediate inquiry and tasked two members of 43 Squadron to carry out an investigation reporting back to him the next day. We had little sleep that night as we rushed around looking at all the authorisation sheets, what the boys had been up to, the number of practice bombs dropped and where. It transpired that a few days before, two Buccaneers had been bombing a splash target being towed behind a Royal Navy Leander frigate. There was a Soviet warship shadowing the Leander and clearly his report back to Moscow had been misconstrued somewhat. So we were squeaky clean after all and the Leander captain confirmed this. We heard no more about the 'incident'.

Morale on the detachment was high and we decided to take the mickey out of Akrotiri's squadron leader operations, a former Lightning pilot. He was always nagging us on procedures, low flying and anything else he could think of. Clearly he was a frustrated fast-jet jockey on a ground tour juggling with all the visiting crews who seemed to him to be on a bit of a holiday. So he wasn't totally daft. There had been a spate of complaints from the local army horse-riding club that jet noise was upsetting the horses, and some local farmer had threatened to fire his shotgun at low-flying aircraft if it continued. This was the setting for the wind-up. He had the habit of cruising up to our operations room with no notice – a bit like the deranged Sergeant Major Windsor Davies in 'It Ain't Half Hot Mum'. We made paper transfers of six bullet holes and stuck them across the tail of a Buccaneer that had just returned from a mission. Squadron leader ops was seen approaching the operations room and I grabbed a telephone with my back to his arrival.

Once he was in the room I started. "Listen to me brigadier, I don't care too much about your horses. I have an aircraft with bullet holes in the tail and clearly your guys are responsible for this. There is going to be trouble – it is lucky that the aircraft didn't crash." I turned round to see squadron leader ops flushing up at the neck. I put down the telephone and uttered a strained greeting. "Right," he said, "You guys have done it this time. Let me see this aircraft, call the station photographer." We walked out on to the pan to where the 'shot-up' Bucc was standing with a number of ground crew looking up at the tail. Sure enough the holes in the tail were very realistic – even matching the holes on the other side. The photographer arrived and snapped away. Luckily I had made sure there was no ladder available for the photographer to get any close-up views. Squadron leader ops marched off to the station commander's office promising me the end of the detachment for us all. It didn't take long before I received a call to report to the station commander who had the photographs in hand with squadron leader ops standing next to him – looking a little smug: "Tell me all about this Bob". I started, "Sir, squadron leader ops has been bugging us for a while and we decided to wind him up – a bit more than usual." I pulled out a paper transfer of bullet holes and handed them over to our frustrated Lightning pilot, and suggested he put them on his car. I think he saw the funny side but it did take him a while.

I returned from Pulsator in December 1983 and received the Campaign Service Medal with the Lebanon Clasp. This was quite a unique medal to the RAF and was awarded only to those aircrew who had made a minimum of three operational missions into Lebanon airspace within certain dates.

*A 208 Squadron Buccaneer, armed with Paveway bombs and
an AIM-9 air-to-air missile, on standby at RAF Akrotiri.*

This proved not to be the last of my visits to the island jewel of the Eastern Mediterranean. Towards the end of my tour on 12 Squadron, I started to fly with Willie Steele, a first tourist. On a sortie to Cyprus we stopped to refuel in Naples. We were flying in the tanker fit with a bomb-bay tank that gave us a total of 19,500 lbs of fuel. I checked the ODM to determine the take-off run at our all-up weight at a very high midday temperature and the length of useable runway. The ODM gave a 'go' condition for a blown take-off, but it was close. I must admit we did ponder delaying take-off a few hours to allow the temperature to drop a bit. However, we had not taken into account the rising ground after take-off.

At the end of the runway we checked the thrust of each engine at full power before take-off and all seemed okay. We started the take-off run at full power, but the aircraft seemed slow to accelerate at an indicated +40°C ramp temperature and, of course, we were bleeding air from the engines to augment the blown configuration. We rotated eventually and lifted off quite close to the end of the runway. We were airborne but our speed seemed to stagnate and we were not gaining height. The rising ground beyond was now very real and we were not reaching V2 – the speed at which the loss of one engine would not have resulted in the loss of the aircraft. This area over which we were uncomfortably near was covered in small shacks and temporary dwellings. As the ground rose in front of us, we were only just maintaining about 100 feet clearance from oblivion for them and for us. After a stressful few seconds, we gradually gained height but not speed. It had been a close one, and only Willie and I knew how close it had been. Lesson – trust the ODM, but if the margins are that tight think about other options. We didn't need to fill the bomb-bay tank, and that would have reduced our all-up weight by 3,500 lbs, and we could have waited until the temperature dropped.

Willie was developing well for a first tourist and we enjoyed many missions together. One day we were sitting on the end of the runway at Gibraltar awaiting take-off clearance. I was playing with the radar and was very surprised to find I could paint ships at a range of 220 miles. Normally the radar horizon at ground level was about 28 miles due to the curvature of the earth, and a range of over 200 miles should be impossible. After take-off, as we headed east down the Mediterranean, I noted that I had huge radar range when flying between 60 and 120 feet but this disappeared immediately above 120 feet or at 50 feet. With nothing much to do as we headed east at low level, except showing off to the odd cruise liner, I began experimenting with radar range against height. The range I was able to obtain on the wide band homer, a sensor that would pick up radar transmissions, also reinforced this data.

This phenomenon was due to thermal ducting when a layer of warmer air is sandwiched between two layers of colder air. It occurs in the Mediterranean more often than over the Atlantic, but it can give a military aircraft a huge advantage when in a duct searching for a target well outside the normal radar horizon or conversely hiding from an enemy by remaining outside a duct. And the passive wide-band homer was the sensor that could identify any duct very accurately without the need to use the radar at all. Over the next few weeks I developed a classified paper to highlight how to identify and exploit thermal ducting in the maritime theatre and submitted it to the Central Trials and Tactics Organisation (CTTO). Some discussion followed with CTTO but I was approaching my retirement and what happened to the paper I'll never know. But I do know that it was a tactical tool that offered a great advantage to any low-level attack aircraft.

Shortly afterwards I finished my last Buccaneer tour having clocked up just over 3,000 hours in that quite amazing aircraft.

CHAPTER TWENTY-ONE

MARITIME SQUADRON COMMANDER

MARTIN ENGWELL

From the time I joined the Air Training Corps, I knew I wanted to fly. After gaining my gliding certificate and completing a flying scholarship at Southend Airport on my 17th birthday, the die was cast. A visit to Hornchurch resulted in the offer of a direct commission and I arrived at South Cerney in May 1962 and graduated as an acting pilot officer when I was still 17 years old.

After flying training at Acklington and Valley, I found myself sent to the Vulcan OCU at Finningley before joining 50 Squadron at Waddington as a co-pilot; and I was still a teenager – just. I had had some great experiences on the Vulcan, including dropping a stick of 21 1,000-lb bombs on El Adem range and a 'bit' part as co-pilot of the Vulcan that appeared in the James Bond film 'Thunderball'.

After three years I volunteered for CFS and after completing the course at Little Rissington, I headed for Manby to instruct on the Jet Provost at the School of Refresher Flying. A couple of seasons flying No. 2 in the 'Macaws' formation aerobatic team was great fun, soon followed by more fun – I was given Gp Capt Peter Bairsto as one of my students. He was starting flying refresher training before heading for Honington as station commander. We would meet again.

At the end of my tour I too headed for Honington, via Chivenor, where I did the Hunter course. In May 1973, Buccaneer course completed, I joined XV Squadron at Laarbruch. A couple of years later, having been promoted to squadron leader, I left to join 12 Squadron as a flight commander. After a ground tour and a refresher course on 237

OCU I arrived at Lossiemouth in August 1983 to take command of 12 Squadron from the legendary Jerry Yates.

I was very quickly into the routine of becoming combat-ready flying maritime tactics, all types of overland and splash weaponry, night formation flying and air-to-air refuelling (AAR). The latter was a common feature of Buccaneer training and exercises and allowed a greatly increased range or radius of action. The type of refuelling aircraft varied and included Buccaneers, Victors, Vulcans and even Hercules. Whilst the fundamentals of AAR never changed, the experiences could often be very different – especially at night. This was demonstrated when Stu Smith, as No. 2 to Cas Capewell, was tasked for night AAR with a Vulcan tanker. He quotes:

"My first (and I believe the first-ever pairs) visit to a Vulcan tanker at night … when with only the upper grimes light as a visual reference due to the curved wingtip of the tanker, I found myself flying cross-controls, 1,000 feet above him, whilst Cas Capewell was plugged in, with 90 degrees of bank on! I completed a barrel roll over the top of them, losing several thousand feet in the recovery … the comments from Andy Hext in the back seat are not repeatable."

The aircraft had almost certainly got caught up in the wingtip vortex, which, because of the Vulcan's delta-wing shape, is particularly strong and wide.

My previous tour as flight commander on 12 Squadron in the 70s was very helpful in getting me up to speed as many of the tactics employed had changed little. In early November, this training quickly led into my first major maritime exercise; a Joint Maritime Course (JMC), operating from St Mawgan. During this period I was crewed with Dave Matthews, who had been Jerry Yates' navigator, and it quickly became clear that not only had I inherited an extremely competent navigator, but a very able and disciplined squadron together with a very lively social team.

Soon after my arrival, and during the early period of my combat-ready training, the maritime Buccaneer Wing had been tasked with supporting the British Forces in the Lebanon (BRITFORLEB) with a laser-guided bomb (LGB) capability. The Buccaneers deployed to Akrotiri for Operation Pulsator on 9 September and I took over as detachment commander on 20 December when I flew directly from Lossiemouth to Akrotiri, with in-flight refuelling from a Buccaneer, in five hours 20 minutes.

By now, a routine had been established, but I had to be given a rapid introduction to the overland LGB operations that had been developed for that particular role. I was crewed with Ron Wilder who introduced me to the tactics and I soon experienced a 'scramble' from standby to fly into Lebanese airspace – this was known as Exercise Tephrite. The multinational naval force stationed just east of Beirut was a truly impressive sight and I was pleased to know that all of the coordination procedures to avoid 'friendly fire' had already been 'ironed out' by my predecessors in theatre.

Simulated attack on USS Eisenhower.

At this stage, the overall situation was perhaps less tense, but flying into Lebanese air-space still gave pause for thought. This was demonstrated to me very clearly when I had to visit Beirut courtesy of a re-supply Chinook to discuss the latest situation with the ground liaison officer (GLO) responsible for providing targeting information to the Buccaneers if needed. I also had a chance to view the target area. The flight was uneventful but exciting. We coasted in at the mouth of the Beirut river, and dropped down to hug the river. The sight of the riverbank and accompanying trees above seemingly hanging over the Chinook was, even for a seasoned low-flying professional, somewhat awe inspiring. When we reached the relatively safe area adjacent to the Lebanese MOD we popped up to land on the car park.

I disembarked as the unloading process got underway and was welcomed by the GLO, who drove me to the south-eastern side of the city overlooking the Chouf mountains with the Beqaa valley beyond. This was where the Druze militias were situated and from which direction any attack might come. The army major was explaining this to me when a Jeep with two 'ragheads' and a huge machine gun on board drove up and stopped just a few hundred yards away from us. The machine gun was then directed across the valley and a loud salvo fired. At this point the major said, "I think that it is time we left". I didn't demur.

As the situation in Beirut had become less tense, the Buccaneer detachment was able to conduct more traditional maritime sorties in addition to maintaining a readiness to support the British Army.

One such maritime sortie happened in January 1984 when we were tasked to locate and observe the Soviet navy's new Kirov destroyer on its first major voyage outside Soviet waters.

Kirov had deployed from northern Russia and been tracked during its transit south past the UK and on into the Mediterranean. I led a pair of Buccaneers with Clive Lambourne as my navigator and Stu Morton with Harry Patrick as our No. 2. We flew to its predicted position in the southern Mediterranean; the intelligence community expected her to be en route to the Libyan coast, so we followed that general route looking, both visually and on radar, and listening to the radar warning receiver (RWR), for any sign of her. Finally, approaching Tripoli (but still over international waters), and without any contact, we climbed to improve the radar horizon as we probed the Tripoli coastline using the Blue Parrot radar when, suddenly, the RWR erupted with high-pitched notes, a sure sign that air defence radar systems were locking on to us. We had found Kirov on a port visit to Tripoli. This certainly got the adrenalin flowing and we immediately dropped back to low level, 'bustered out' (went to maximum speed), and headed directly away from the Libyan coast towards Akrotiri. Once at a safe distance we climbed out for our return. I left Akrotiri for Lossiemouth, via Decimomannu, on 31 January. Two months later the six Buccaneers and crews returned.

With Operation Pulsator behind us the squadron was able to get back into its 'normal' routine – but what a routine. Our flying consisted of major and minor NATO and national exercises, in addition to routine training for our maritime-attack role. Normal is, of course, a misnomer as these exercises were often very different and conducted over a wide area including the North Atlantic, North Cape, the Baltic, Atlantic and the Mediterranean, operating from a range of bases in the UK, in Germany and in Scandinavia. Additionally, although predominantly a maritime-attack squadron, we also had to remain proficient in our 'strike' role as part of the national nuclear-deterrent force. This involved long-range 'high-low-high' overland navigation and bombing exercises which often involved landings at an overseas base.

In May 1984, the squadron deployed to Eggebek, Germany for Exercise Bright Horizon. We were hosted, most appropriately, by MFG2 (Marinefliegergeschwader 2) of the German navy. On landing, we were welcomed with schnapps and raw herring. Bright Horizon was a coastal maritime exercise involving anti-FPB (fast patrol boats) operations as well as more familiar open-sea anti-shipping attacks. Anti-FPB operations were very demanding as not only were the FPBs able to navigate the coastal waters and inlets, but also were highly manoeuvrable making achieving weapons release parameters very tricky. Unfortunately, the Buccaneer force no longer had rockets in its inventory so, for our simulated attacks against FPBs, we used a shallow dive-bombing technique; the weapon for these attacks would have been 1,000-lb retard bombs. Not only was it difficult to maintain the aiming sight on the target, but also the time of flight of the bombs allowed an FPB to take evasive action.

The JMOTS (Joint Maritime Operational Training School) organised JMCs, which were regular events in our exercise calendar. JMOTS was a joint Royal Navy and Royal Air Force organisation that planned and conducted these major exercises every year. JMCs provided joint collective training in a multi-threat environment for UK maritime units, and those from invited NATO and other allied countries. JMCs were held three times a year and were controlled by the JMOTS staff at Rosyth, Edinburgh. The primary purpose

Flt Lt Willie Steele (left) and his navigator Flt Lt Dave Skinner with the Wickenby Sword.

of these exercises was for the training of RN ships' crews, but they also provided an important training opportunity for all maritime forces including the Buccaneers. They gave us an opportunity to practise our maritime attacks and regularly included 'splash' bombing against a towed target, in-flight refuelling and, if the RN contingent included a carrier, fighter affiliation training. In one memorable JMC, in June 1984, the RN provided a small trawler-type target for the Buccaneers to drop live 1,000-lb bombs. I led a six-ship with Red Thompson on that 'Sinkex' mission, and each aircraft had four 1,000-lb bombs, which were delivered by a 'toss' manoeuvre from an Alfa 3 co-ordinated attack. This was a unique opportunity for all of us.

In early 1983 the Wickenby Register, an association commemorating those who died during World War Two flying with 12 and 626 Squadrons from RAF Wickenby near Lincoln, renewed their links with the squadron. They presented us with a ceremonial sword and dagger for annual presentation to, respectively, the most deserving aircrew and ground crew members for that year. The first aircrew recipients of the Wickenby Sword were a young pilot, Willie Steele and his navigator Dave Skinner with the Wickenby Dagger presented to Junior Technician Tony Leek.

Willie went on to complete the qualified weapons instructor (QWI) course, became a six-ship formation leader, and had completed over 1,000 hours on the Buccaneer. Tragically, on 14 June 1985, he perished in a crash on final approach into Lossiemouth. The week after Willie's loss, the station and the squadron were subjected to a Tactical Evaluation (TACEVAL). It was a great tribute to the training, professionalism and dedication of the entire squadron that they were able to put in an outstanding performance under these very difficult circumstances.

On 12 October 1984, we deployed to Gibraltar for the major maritime exercise Autumn Train. The RN contingent included the aircraft carrier *Illustrious* along with its supporting warships and this gave us the very best opportunity to test our tactics and procedures. The highlight for us was to be a 'free play' event in which the *Illustrious* Group would be given an opportunity to 'hide' in the western approaches to the Gibraltar Straits, and use all its assets to protect against attack. The attack package included a Buccaneer armed with AR (anti-radar) Martel, and in long-range fit, to operate in the 'probe' role, a six-ship combined TV and AR Martel formation of Buccaneers, two Nimrod MPA, and a Fleet Requirements and Air Direction Unit (FRADU) Canberra fitted with Blue Parrot radar to act as a decoy.

The Nimrod was airborne well before the attack force and, operating covertly, managed to provide a good SURPIC (surface picture) and confirm the carrier's position. The AR Martel Buccaneer 'probe' was the first attack aircraft airborne, and with its increased range was able to fly around the Task Group to attack from the north-west. After take-off, the

Approaching Gibraltar.

six-ship operated completely radio and radar silent (except for some mandatory air traffic calls), departed at low level and, when away from prying RN eyes, climbed rapidly to just beneath the civil airway off the west coast of Morocco, simulating civil air traffic, before making a rapid descent to low level. Using the Nimrod surface picture, the main attack formation positioned to attack from the south-west. Meanwhile, the AR Martel 'probe' aircraft, somewhat ahead of the main formation, attacked from the north-west as the decoy formation approached on a direct route from Gibraltar using its Blue Parrot radar to simulate a Buccaneer searching for its target.

The main attack formation, using the latest information from the Nimrod, timed its pop-up and radar sweeps to locate *Illustrious* and initiate its coordinated AR and TV missile attack. The combined probe and main attack Buccaneers would have delivered six AR missiles, which would have significantly degraded the target's ability to respond, having launched its Sea Harriers against the decoy group. With no Sea Harriers to worry them, the six Buccaneers, simulating TV Martel missiles, flew past the carrier with the Vangelis tune 'To the Unknown Man'[1] playing at full volume on the safety frequency.

It wasn't all work and no play, of course, and 12 Squadron personnel took part in the annual 'Inter-Services Olympiad' with at least one representative in every sport. We only came first in one event but amassed so many points for our second places (although we were not used to coming second) and for getting points in every one of the sports, we

[1] Theme tune for 12 Squadron used in a training film made in 1978 whilst operating from Gibraltar.

Armilla Patrol work-up at Gibraltar with Martin Engwell in centre.

retained the 'Mini-ships Trophy' for the fourth successive year. The organising Royal Navy PTI commented: "If all teams entered the Olympiad with the same enthusiasm and spirit as did 12 Squadron then one year, perhaps, there may be a different winner."

Whilst in Gibraltar for Exercise Autumn Train 84 I heard the shocking news that Jerry Yates had been killed in an accident whilst flying in a Hunter in the Oman. His wife Linda was keen that Jerry's ashes be scattered into the Moray Firth, an area that they both loved. I discussed this with Bob Kemp, our navigator flight commander who had served with Jerry before I had taken over, and we agreed a plan. Jerry's ashes were carefully packed into a large manila envelope with 'On Her Majesty's Service' stamped on both sides – he would have liked that. The envelope was placed between the airbrake petals at the rear of Buccaneer XX864 for this special sortie and, armed with the committal reading prepared for us by the Lossiemouth padre, Niall Griffin, we were ready. To mark Jerry's time on 12 Squadron we decided to commit his ashes at 12 seconds past 12 minutes past 12 o'clock on 9 November; it was a beautiful day. At 100 feet and 550 knots, and at the precise time, Bob read the committal and I opened the airbrake to commit Jerry's ashes into the Moray Firth. Jerry was home.

Later in November 1984, we were tasked to commence training for low flying down to 50 feet above sea level at 540 knots. The RN had recognised that ships and crews about to deploy to operational areas, such as the Falklands and the Gulf/Middle East, needed more

Squadron exchange to RDAF Aalborg, April 1985.

realistic anti-cruise-missile-training opportunities. We incorporated this training into our regular maritime-training missions and crews had to have completed this training before exercising with RN ships. This was known as Exercise Armilla and regularly took place out of Gibraltar with RN ships about to commence deployments to these operational areas.

Squadron exchanges were another regular event and in April 1985 I led a team to Aalborg for an exchange with 723 Squadron RDAF recently equipped with the F-16. No. 723 Squadron was a multi-role (air defence/attack/training) squadron and much of the flying was with the F-16s providing fighter affiliation and evasion training. Our detachment included a Hunter, as well as Buccaneers, providing the opportunity to offer our Danish hosts flights in a Hunter in exchange for flights for our aircrew in an F-16. I was privileged to fly in a two-seat F-16 tasked to oppose a Buccaneer formation and was truly impressed by its performance and amazing cockpit visibility. In return, I was pleased to be able to offer two sorties in our Hunter for two of their pilots. (Perhaps not a fair exchange, but they were delighted). Socially, 723 Squadron were fantastic hosts and, as with squadron exchanges generally, there was much eating and drinking and, on this occasion, a friendly football match.

After almost three years at the helm my time as OC 12 Squadron came to an end in June 1986. Keith Moore arrived to replace me, and I flew my last sortie on 19 June with Chas Wrighton in the back. It finished with me leading a 12-ship combined Buccaneer and Hunter formation in a flypast over Lossiemouth, a fitting end to a memorable last flying tour, and with 1,748 hours on the mighty Buccaneer in my logbook.

CHAPTER TWENTY-TWO

TWO TOURS ON MARITIME BUCCANEERS

GORDON NIVEN

After flirting half-heartedly with civil aviation, I applied to the RAF to become a pilot. To my disappointment, they offered me navigator as their need for pilots was lower than usual that year. I could, however, reapply in two years' time. Well, guess what I did? In hindsight, I could have saved everyone a lot of time and trouble if I had accepted their first offer. The last words having been spoken to me in pilot training being "the best you'd have made is a Herc co-pilot". Enough said.

On arriving at nav school, a very grumpy re-tread from basic flying training, I noted a model of a Buccaneer on the desk in one of the classrooms. I felt a surge of well-being and a sense that the mighty jet may get to play a part in my story. To this day I have no idea whose desk it was or even if they made it to the Bucc themselves. But it was the boost I needed just at the right time. On graduation, we were given a pint mug with our posting stuck to the bottom. So, down in one, turn it over, BINGO, BUCCANEERS!

So, there I was in September 1981 on 237 OCU at RAF Honington. Even typing these few words has brought a smile to my face, nah, let's be honest, a broad grin. However, there were a few disquieting signs. As you entered the building there was a board containing all the course photographs going way back. Not so strange you might think. Except that for the graduated courses, there was an axe drawn embedded in each of the poor individuals who had failed and for the current course, an axe poised over the heads of a few. Designed to inspire or intimidate? Given that the Bucc's genesis was navy carrier operations, where bad weather and night ops would only favour the committed, it's not surprising that the standards were set very high.

Trip one was a local area famil just to get used to the beast. I take my hat off to the 'better than Herc co-pilots'. Being a navy design, there was no dual-control Bucc. So, the first time the pilots got airborne, they were completely in charge, albeit with a no doubt

The 237 OCU detachment to Akrotiri in November 1981.
Gordon Niven standing at the front in the cockpit.

tense pilot instructor in the rear seat. Immense respect for both. Trip two was where we were shown the finer points of the aircraft's performance. Sinking lower and lower over the sea, the surface becoming a blur, we were at max chat, 580 knots or so, about 30 feet above the sea. Once stable, the instructor took his hands off the controls and held them above his head, gobsmacking or what? The aircraft was sitting on a cushion of air, quite incapable of hitting the sea. Presumably on the understanding that the 'man-in-front' has the jet trimmed out first. Being the first on my course to fly, the other navs were curious to hear how it had gone. I enthused at length about the wave-top dash in particular only to be invited into a quiet corner of the hangar by my instructor where he commended me on my performance but then reminded me of flying regulations, flight authorisation and the importance of keeping schtoom.

We were approaching winter where the weather could have a severe impact on our course progression. So, we decamped to RAF Akrotiri in Cyprus for three weeks. We did get quite a bit of flying done, but I'm not convinced that the main driver was for the instructors to have a whale of a time in the sun whilst downing kokanelli (a real rust eater) and hoovering up kebabs. As students, it also gave us an insight into what squadron life might be like. Our return was cast in doubt as the UK was being bashed by one of the worst winter storms in years. On landing at Honington, the snow was piled three feet high on either side of the runway.

The Soviet navy Udaloy-*class destroyer at speed.*

One day I was crossing the hangar and noticed a bunch of crusty old blokes being shown over a jet. I assumed it was the local Rotary Club or the like, but was informed it was a group of Mustang pilots who had been stationed at Honington during the war. What a pity we didn't have a chance to speak to them. It would have been great to hear their war stories. Years later at a Bucc Association dinner at Lossie, the barman said how amazed he was at how much booze we old guys could pack away. Old guys I thought, staggered at his impudence. I thought back to those 'old guys' in the hangar in Honington, we would be the same age now as they were then. And indeed, we old guys were stacking it away.

There were three possible postings for us, stay at Honington and join 208 Squadron, go to RAF Laarbruch in Germany and join XV or 16 Squadron, each of them in the overland interdictor/strike role declared to SACEUR, or 12 Squadron at RAF Lossiemouth providing maritime strike/attack declared to SACLANT. I had no idea what any of the postings would entail and was just genuinely happy to be heading for my first squadron.

So, for me the north of Scotland beckoned. Arriving on 12 was a bit of a shock. There were quite a few of the squadron who had served on secondment with the navy Bucc fleet, so the carrier ethos of work hard play hard was very strong. My acceptance ride with the boss was to find a Soviet destroyer, the *Udaloy* off the Norwegian coast. No pressure there then. I embarked on the combat ready syllabus, a series of maybe 30 sorties/disciplines one had to master to be declared combat ready to SACLANT. You received all the necessary briefings, but by Jove you had better have absorbed it first time round, as there was no second briefing. Exercises were very common, both station-generated and from higher commands.

As a recently married young flying officer with no kids, I wasn't eligible for a married quarter provided by the RAF. The only option open to us was to get our first mortgage and we bought an idyllic cottage a mile or so from base. Best move we ever made. We had many family members visit. On one occasion as we relaxed after dinner the telephone rang. It was about ten o'clock in the evening; it was a station call-out practising our reaction to an unprovoked attack by the massed forces of the Warsaw Pact (WP). Our house guest thought it was a joke until I donned my flying suit, got my bike out and cycled, a little unsteadily, off to work.

Our standard formation was a six-ship with four aircraft armed with TV-guided Martel missiles, which were fired, between 10–7 nautical miles and two aircraft with the radar homing version, the AR Martel. The TV missiles were data-linked to the aircraft and the missile guided by the navigator onto the target. All aircraft had four 1,000-lb bombs in the bomb bay.

Day-to-day, training would entail practising our tactics against some unsuspecting vessel plying its merry way around the shores of northern Scotland. However, there was also a series of more formal exercises. These ranged from squadron-to-ship arrangements through to full blown NATO-wide maritime exercises.

The bigger exercises were indeed enormous. They would often start with a USMC carrier battle group forming off the US eastern seaboard and then 'fighting' its way across the Atlantic to a simulated landing somewhere in Norway or Denmark. Hundreds of ships, submarines, and aircraft from all NATO nations took part. These provided us with training in an environment that was as close to the real thing as possible. This included flying in quite atrocious weather, certainly in my early days well outside of our normal peace-time limits – conflict with the WP would not have waited for the weather to improve. As junior crews, we would be No.3 in each element. We would stay with the formation gaining experience in flying in adverse weather, then be ordered to RTB before the formation attack. The remaining four aircraft would then execute a specific pre-planned attack, splitting to permit safe separation, with each aircraft executing a 4G pull up into the low cloud base, simulating the release of their bomb load before pulling half inverted by 2,000 feet to recover back to low level; nerve-tingling stuff and not for the faint-hearted. Had anyone ejected at any point in those conditions, it is almost certain they would not have survived. An hour later, we would be back in the crew room enjoying coffee, but the ships would still be out there being tossed around like corks. Tragically, about 18 months into my tour, we lost the lead crew of a formation executing this very manoeuvre during a station exercise. No trace of the crew or aircraft was found. A very sobering experience.

All the while, numerous Soviet units gathering intelligence of NATO operations were observing our activities. On occasions we were tasked against the US carrier group, which was invariably a complete waste of time. We would flog out into the Iceland-Faroes gap, only to be completely ignored by the carrier air safety cell. On one occasion we had an aviation photographer with us. Inbound to our elusive target we spotted a splodge on the horizon. Now if you see a fighter, it is a dot, if you see a Nimrod, it is a slightly bigger dot. This was a splodge, so something quite a bit bigger than anything we had ever seen before and well worth investigating. We detailed our subordinate element to continue towards our elusive target, whilst we set off to investigate the splodge. As we closed, it became clear it was a Russian Bear, a four-engine, eight-propeller behemoth capable of quite astonishing speeds. Being face-to-face with Ivan for the first time was quite something. Our other element never saw the carrier.

The aircraft's bombing system was exercised daily, so rarely gave any problems when delivering 1,000-lb'ers. Not so the Martel. In my seven years at Lossiemouth, we only had two occasions in which to fire these 13-foot monsters. The first was a one-month

Martel against the de-commissioned frigate HMS Galatea.

deployment to the US Navy base in Roosevelt Rhodes, Puerto Rico. The second was off the west coast of Scotland.

The Caribbean deployment operationally was a complete disaster as the target we were firing against was not sufficiently radar significant, which made manoeuvring to our missile firing point virtually impossible. We never found out if the target would have shown up on the TV screen. We did manage some weapons training, using 1,000-lb inert and practice bombs and fighter affiliation against the resident USN A-4 Skyhawk squadron. Socially, though it was quite a trip. One of the guys met the crew from the RN frigate deployed to the area. He got the contact details for some Brits 'house-sitting' for the extremely rich in the British Virgin Islands. Getting there was easy. The USN base flying club had a wide range of aircraft available to it; the result of confiscations during drug busts in the area. So, an eight-seater was hired at very reasonable rates for the short hop. The house our hosts lived in was spectacular – imagine a Caribbean lair for a James Bond movie set and you'll get the idea. We were invited back to go scuba diving the following weekend. But such was the embarrassment at the complete failure of the primary reason for the deployment, the boss decided it would be bad form to enjoy ourselves too much!

And so, to the firings off the west coast of Scotland. This was as big a deal for the engineers as it was for us. As missile firings were so rare, there was little current experience. At least the engineers practised loading and testing the real missiles each time we had a station exercise. The navs also had a ground trainer to practise mid-term and terminal phase guidance. We also had a TV airborne trainer wing pod, so whilst the pilot flew the missile flight profile, the navs called out flight path corrections including the terminal phase guidance of the missile, though not quite up to the moment of impact.

A decommissioned Leander Class frigate HMS *Galatea* was moored out to sea to be used by a variety of platforms for live firings. We were allocated a slot to fire four TV Martel. We flew a six-ship formation with my man-in-front and I leading the second element. The weather was ideal, slight sea state, high cloud base. The lead designated the target at 30 miles, but as we approached the firing point at ten miles, we were converging with the lead element. I decided to hold our firing to seven miles to permit the lead element to enter their terminal manoeuvre to the right. I don't recall noticing or hearing our 13-foot 1,500-lb beast leave the aircraft, but I soon picked up the frigate bang on the nose, perfect line-up. No requirement for any mid-course corrections. The fewer inputs made to the missile, the less likely there were to be any malfunctions. The flight profile took about

70 seconds. As I selected terminal guidance, I noticed there was a large plume of water just beyond the ship. I placed the cross hairs on the superstructure one-third way up from the waterline while experiencing the sensation that the vessel was racing towards me – then the screen went blank.

On return to base I had quite a range of emotions, primarily euphoria at having had a successful firing. But then I began to think about how it would have been for real. The kinetic energy of the missile doing 500 knots would drive it into the heart of the ship, the effect of the relatively small warhead exploding though the Misnay-Schardin plate causing catastrophic devastation. The effect on the crew, Jesus, the effect on the crew! We would be at war; we would have just attacked one of their combatants who themselves would be out to sink our ships. It was the first time I had ever really contemplated the effects of our weapons. But at least, on this occasion, the ship was undoubtedly empty. Interestingly, years later, I would go through the same emotions, but this time for real, having just delivered two Paveway II weapons through the roof of a building in Kosovo.

On the transit back Rob and I discussed what had transpired. It was odd that we converged with the lead pair at firing. However, pressing in to seven miles hadn't been an issue and the target had appeared on my TV screen pretty much on the nose. Of concern was the lack of missile hits from the lead pair. We could be pretty sure we had hit the target. However, in the last few seconds of missile flight the TV image blurred, so we couldn't be certain. The videotape would reveal all, and No. 2's video should show our impact. As we walked back to the crew room there was an excited group waiting for us. Our No. 2 was already in and had viewed his tape. It clearly shows our missile impact squarely in the centre of the frigate. The resulting explosion and blooming of his TV screen caused him to twitch inadvertently, the movement of his joystick causing his missile to rise slightly, cresting the superstructure of the ship and impacting harmlessly on the sea beyond. For a very experienced nav, this was a most unexpected outcome. A sure sign that we needed to have more regular firings. Had his missile followed mine, it is quite possible the ship would have been sent to the bottom of the ocean there and then.

Lead and his No. 2 hadn't faired any better. Lead's missile never established data link and was therefore never guided. It presumably flew on until it ran out of fuel then crashed into the sea a short distance beyond the target. His No. 2, a junior nav who later became a well-respected QWI, explained he believed he had been briefed to aim high on the superstructure. It was the plume from his missile impact I had seen on my screen. So, we had one hit out of four and all this in a benign environment. Not the fog of war, no enemy air defences targeting us or intercepting our missiles flying a relatively easy profile; 1,000 ft at a little over 500 kts in a dead straight line. Thank goodness Sea Eagle was on its way, where we would be firing 24 sea-skimming missiles from over the horizon. The Nimrod MPA supporting the firings sent a series of photographs of the frigate showing a plume of black smoke pouring out of a large section of the ship's hull, which had peeled back like a tin can. From my perspective job done.

Having failed to sink the ship, our sister squadron was tasked to drop Paveway laser-guided bombs. This they did with devastating effect stripping the superstructure off the ship. They delivered their bombs from a toss manoeuvre from three miles. It is anybody's guess whether the defenders or attackers would come out on top in that one. But still the frigate refused to sink. The remnant of the hull was tracked for another 24 hours before the sea swell finally swamped it and it sank beneath the waves.

Seven years and 1,500 hours flying later, it was time for a move, off to the mighty swing-wing Jaguar; sorry, Tornado. But my connection with the Bucc wasn't quite over. I had been deployed to Bahrain as part of the UK attack force in support of Operation Desert Storm. Standing in the bar of the Diplomat Hotel (big advantage over the other two bases) I had just suggested the Buccs deploy to provide much-needed precision bombing. Not a popular comment given the company I was in. Undeterred, the next day I sent my old muckers on 12 Squadron a postcard suggesting if they were going to go to war, this was the place to be. Quite prophetic as it turned out.

CHAPTER TWENTY-THREE

AAR – THE PRE-WAR SHORT COURSE

JOHN 'FRAS' FRASER

When Iraq invaded Kuwait in August 1990, I was a pilot instructor on the Buccaneer Operational Conversion Unit, No. 237, based at RAF Lossiemouth. The OCU's secondary war role was laser designating at low level in the European theatre of operations for Dutch F-16 and RAF Tornado aircraft delivering Paveway II smart bombs. The two other Buccaneer squadrons at RAF Lossiemouth were also trained in the laser designation role, albeit for the maritime theatre of operations. We were all therefore expecting to be used in the Gulf from an early stage in the conflict, but were still at Lossiemouth when the war started in January 1991. On the Tuesday of the second week of hostilities, AOC 18 Group flew up to Lossiemouth to 'clarify matters and remove any doubt', and to personally reassure us that: "Your presence would not be required in the war, and you should make plans for being at home." It was therefore a bit of a surprise to arrive at work on the Wednesday morning to be told that a signal had arrived, and we were to get out to the Gulf as quick as we could – the plan had changed.

The engineers immediately started working flat-out to modify the aircraft for the required desert fit. New secure radios, new IFF and a variety of other essential equipment was fitted whilst the aircraft were repainted during a frantic three-day period during which the first 12 crews to deploy were selected, myself included. The first thing we all had to do was to report to the station medical officer who admitted he didn't have a clue what inoculations we should have, so he decided to give us eight of the ones he thought would be most useful. Goodness knows what they were, but we received two injections in each arm and two injections in each buttock, which resulted in everybody returning to the briefing facility walking around like John Wayne, having just got off his horse carrying a sheep under

Stabilising behind a Buccaneer tanker.

each arm. It was in this surreal atmosphere that we started discussing the tanker trail to deploy to the Middle East.

My previous operational experience on the Buccaneer had been in RAF Germany where there was no requirement for air-to-air refuelling due to the nature of the role, so the refuelling probes were not fitted to the aircraft. I pointed this out to the assembled team, and apologised for throwing a bit of a spanner in the works. After a quick think, it was decided that I would do a very short AAR conversion course in-house, starting first thing the next day. We retired to the bar that evening for a light refreshment where I was 'comprehensively' briefed by a squadron mate on the technique and the essential need-to-knows. As a reference for me, he also very kindly drew the stabilised position behind the tanker on a bar chit. I was now all set for the next day's task.

We launched first thing the next morning as a pair, a Buccaneer in AAR configuration with me flying on its wing. The aim of the exercise was to do some general manoeuvring to acquaint myself with the formation position for tanking, and then to have a few dry plugs to practise the art itself. My back-seater, Redvers Thompson, although an experienced Buccaneer navigator, had recently returned from a US exchange tour on the F-111 at Mountain Home AFB in Idaho so, although he wasn't particularly current himself, he had seen enough AAR in his time to know when we were in the right position and when we were not.

Now, a few words of explanation for the uninitiated. Having spent most of one's flying career desperately trying to avoid making contact with another aircraft, AAR reverses that concept, which initially feels quite unnatural. Many colourful terms have been used over the years to describe the black art such as, 'trying to shove spaghetti up a wild cat's arse' or 'taking a running f**k at a rolling doughnut'; however, most of the time, like a lot of other things, it is fairly straightforward as long as you follow some basic disciplines.

On a Buccaneer configured as an AAR tanker, the refuelling pod is carried on the inner station of the starboard wing, and it trails a conical 'basket' comprising, in simple terms, a receiving valve with attached metal spokes all held together by a canvas ring about two feet in diameter at the end of a three-inch-thick hose about 30 feet long, down which the fuel flows. The canvas ring is studded with beta lights, which are essentially glow-in-the-dark marbles for reference during night AAR. The basic concept is to establish a stabilised position behind the tanker with the AAR probe about two feet behind the basket. It is important not to focus on the basket but rather formate on the tanker. Having achieved the stabilised position, two or three per cent of engine power is added and the probe will engage with the basket with just enough forward momentum for it to lock into position in the valve. Once locked into the valve, it is necessary to continue to move forward, pushing the hose about five feet back into the pod, and this allows the fuel to flow. Sounds straightforward enough.

So there we were, on a delightfully clear, crisp, January morning flying at about 8,000 feet over the Moray Firth and "cleared to join on the right, heading 040 degrees, 280 knots". I quickly achieved a loose echelon starboard position and then moved into what my back-seater adviser confirmed was a pretty good stabilised position. We sat there for a few minutes to take stock, wiggle toes and fingers (you don't want to be too tense) and let everything settle down. Once we were both happy, I added a few per cent on both engines and, as described in the mess bar theory lesson, the aircraft moved gently forward, and we made a perfect contact. I then continued to advance a few feet further and we were there – success first time! Rather pleased with myself, we held the position as per the brief for some gentle manoeuvring before disengaging to have a short break before having another plug.

Now flushed with confidence, the next attempt wasn't nearly as pretty as the first. From the loose echelon position, we quickly moved into the stabilised position once again. However, on this occasion I didn't stay there for quite as long as I had done before, so it would probably be better described as a 'transitory stabilised' position. I then added the required few per cent to engage, but at light weight the Buccaneer had an abundance of power so, in my enthusiasm to re-engage, I perhaps applied just a bit more than the ideal. Red was already on top of the rapidly developing situation and, as his sphincter snapped instantaneously from f2.8 to f16, he apparently uttered a spontaneous, but fairly non-standard alert of something like "WHOAH NEDDY!" quite loudly over the intercom – but it fell on deaf ears. As we surged forwards, the basket rose up in the aerodynamic bow wave of the aircraft nose and, quickly realising that my closing rate was too high, I closed both throttles and pushed the control column forward in an attempt to duck underneath. Alas, all was in vain.

The aircraft probe caught the rim of the basket at around the six o'clock position and, as momentum continued to push the aircraft forward, it penetrated the spokes. The aircraft was also still pitching down so, as I skewered the spokes, the basket doubled back on itself and, with a quick snap, the whole assembly broke free from the hose and slid to the bottom of the probe at the base of the windscreen. Rather frustratingly, the comprehensive brief in the bar the previous evening had failed to cover this eventuality, and also the correct terminology for informing the tanker pilot that the basket was now on the receiver aircraft so I chose to transmit "spokes", which was the best I could think of at the time, to which the tanker pilot replied, "clear to withdraw slowly". To fully clarify the matter I then decided to break with R/T discipline and transmitted, "You don't understand mate, I've got the basket!" to which he replied "Er … Roger".

Having our own basket was also a new experience for my back-seater, although the novelty was wearing off very quickly for us both as it thrashed around wildly in the slipstream, and the refuelling valve smashed repeatedly into the armoured glass of the front windscreen. Thankfully, it shook itself free of the basket after several very loud attempts to penetrate the cockpit, and we were also relieved that it didn't sound as if it had impacted on any other part of the aircraft as it flew away into the Moray Firth below – one good reason why AAR is conducted over the sea whenever possible. We were then just left with the metal spokes, but not for too long because they also detached themselves fairly quickly afterwards, and disappeared down the starboard engine, together with all the beta lights, leaving just the canvas material wrapped in knots around the base of the probe.

The Rolls-Royce Spey engines fitted to the Buccaneer were remarkably reliable, and also very resilient to the frequent bird strikes that were one of the many hazards of operating at low level. This resilience was undoubtedly due to the combination of there being a fixed stator stage at the front of the intake just prior to the moving parts, and also to it being a bypass design, so most foreign object debris tended to be routed into and then through the bypass by centrifugal force, thus avoiding damaging the central core. In fact, very often the first indication of a bird strike was a thump followed by the smell of roast seagull in the cockpit.

Undoubtedly, the starboard engine hadn't anticipated an early-morning breakfast of basket al fresco, but it initially seemed to cope well, munching through a selection of metal spokes and beta lights with enthusiastic aplomb. However, as we turned to route back towards Lossiemouth, with our tanker aircraft now visually inspecting us for damage and shadowing in support, it started to show signs of mild indigestion so I throttled it back to idle initially, where it seemed a lot happier. Shortly afterwards though, it did start to grumble and complain a bit more so I shut it down completely, and we declared an emergency as we recovered to base in single-engine configuration, where we landed uneventfully.

Naturally, the banter level of the crew-room choir was very high when we arrived back on the squadron for a post-sortie coffee, and it was standing room and tickets only in the

*The hard-working ground crew prepare
a Buccaneer for another mission.*

coffee bar as every available comic genius was in attendance, waiting eagerly to deliver their one-liner. Those of us in 'The Club' know exactly where sympathy lies in the English dictionary, and there's certainly none of it on offer within the Royal Air Force in these types of circumstances! My crew-room roasting was brought to an abrupt end however, when the word came through from squadron operations that the engineers had managed quickly to re-configure another aircraft into tanker mode, and we were scheduled to get airborne again as soon as possible for the re-match. Thankfully, the next sortie went to plan, I had learned all too graphically from the folly of my previous 'bull in a china shop' approach, and that stood me in good stead for all my future AAR events.

The next day we were airborne with a Buccaneer tanker for another consolidation sortie, and the day after that was my first experience jousting with a Victor K2. The evening of the same day saw us airborne once again, this time for my first experience of night AAR from a Buccaneer tanker; darkness adding a whole new dimension to the already steep learning curve. It's an experience that really does concentrate the mind and, for obvious reasons, it was always deemed by most sane and sensible souls to best be avoided whenever possible. On this occasion, the whole squadron was flying for routine currency, and so the team cunningly elected to send me off first in the hope that I would clobber the basket once again, and they could all then cancel and retreat to the safety of the mess bar.

Alas, all was not to be and the disappointment of the squadron junta was palpable when I returned to land immediately after take-off since the undercarriage had failed to retract; the subsequent change over to the spare aircraft then meant that I was now at the end of the queue for the tanker's services. However, when we did get up there, the bright moonlit night enabled me to tank without incident, much to Red's relief – he was putting a professionally brave face on it but I'm pretty sure he really wasn't looking forward to the experience very much. After landing, my short AAR course was deemed to be complete; I was declared AAR competent and Redvers and I positioned out to the Gulf in a Hercules C-130 only 30 hours later to join the war where we flew 13 missions together, with AAR on each mission.

The Buccaneer detachment was based at Muharraq Airport, Bahrain, during the first Gulf War and AAR was an integral part of each sortie, which was normally in excess of four hours

'Fras' Fraser (right) with his navigator 'Red' Thompson in Gulf War fighting dress.

long. Typically, two Buccaneers would fly in a formation with four Tornados supported by either Victor or VC10 tankers, and it was normal to tank outside Iraqi airspace on the ingress to the target and, if required, on the egress as well. Depending on how close the target was to Bahrain, Tornados often tanked both ways, but the Buccaneer's famously long legs meant that we never needed a top-up on the return.

On our first mission, the formation launched pre-dawn and, as the sun rose, we rendezvoused with the tanker as it tracked north-west on the Saudi side of the Iraqi border. After filling up, we continued on track and monitored secure radios as our F-15 fighter escort and SEAD (Suppression of Enemy Air Defence) F-4G Wild Weasel and EF-111A Raven formations checked in with the coordinating AWACS aircraft. Once the team was assembled, the package turned on to a north-easterly track to ingress towards the target, flanked by Wild Weasels with the fighter escort clearing the airspace ahead. Approaching the target the Tornados and Buccaneers moved into their attack formation; two Tornados flying in close echelon, with the laser-designating Buccaneer following one to two miles behind. A similar group were about two miles in trail. Having identified the target, and whilst illuminating the DPI (designated point of impact) with laser energy, the designating Buccaneer transmitted a code word to clear the Tornados to release their weapons once they were within the parameters. Thereafter, the Tornados turned to egress whilst the Buccaneer manoeuvred, illuminated the DPI until bomb impact before following the Tornados outbound on their egress track.

The attack was a complete success and the bridge was destroyed. We turned for home and re-joined the other Buccaneer, taking great pleasure in overtaking the Tornados as they prepared to meet the tanker once again. We were already changed and waiting in operations as our swing-winged colleagues landed; and after debriefing we were soon on our way back to our hotel, ready to enjoy a light refreshment and a cool swim – a satisfying way to wrap up a very busy first day at the office.

After the war ended on 28 February, Red and I were spared the nine-hour Buccaneer transit home and headed back to Lossiemouth in the relative comfort of a VC10, bringing our first Gulf War experience to a conclusion in mid-March 1991. It was certainly a baptism of fire, but applying the invaluable

Laser marker on the Ar Ramadi bridge seconds before it was destroyed.

lessons learned during my short pre-war AAR course at Lossiemouth made things a whole lot less stressful for all concerned during the conflict. However, without doubt, my introduction to AAR as a precursor to war is certainly an experience that I, for one, haven't forgotten.

As a postscript, I include the timeline of our 1991 AAR conversion, which highlights the urgency/rapidity of the process from AAR conversion to first operations:

Tuesday 22 January – Stand-down, you're not going

Wednesday 23 January – Depord (Deployment Order) received

Saturday 26 January – Monday 28 January – Six AAR day and night conversion sorties in three days

Wednesday 30 January – Position to theatre of war

Friday 1 February – First Op Granby flight – area familiarisation and Pave Spike training (i.e. inside a week of starting AAR conversion)

Monday 4 February – Only role-training mission (Pave Spike and Tornado GR1s)

Tuesday 5 February – First operational mission with VC10 AAR – As Samawah Road/River Bridge: DCO!

This graphically illustrates what can be achieved when operational necessity dictates.

CHAPTER TWENTY-FOUR

END OF AN ERA

NIGEL HUCKINS

I never expected to fly the Buccaneer. I had done two tours on the Jaguar, one operational at Brüggen and the other on the OCU at Lossiemouth. I then converted to Tornado and, after a tour on the Tornado Weapons Conversion Unit, I returned to Brüggen as squadron QWI on 17 Squadron. The fun time was then terminated by Staff College and a tour in the Ministry of Defence Directorate of Training. After months slogging on a paper for future fast-jet training, I escaped to Riyadh in late 1990 as wing commander operations for Op Granby, which is where I had my first real operational dealings with the Buccaneer force. Prior to that, I had been aware of them as fierce competitors in the RAF Germany's annual Salmond Trophy competition in the late 1970s.

The arrival of the Buccaneer at Bahrain was prompted by a lack of RAF laser-designation capability in a war that was rapidly being waged with precision-guided munitions. The Tornado force had just received the only two experimental trial TIALD pods, which were insufficient to provide for all aircraft in theatre. Then some bright staff officers had suggested that the Buccaneer with Pave Spike might fill the gap. After arrival, the Buccaneer detachment rapidly developed operational procedures for buddy-buddy designation for Tornados. The small, but very professional, Buccaneer detachment made a great contribution to the success of the RAF's operations against Iraqi forces.

In the late 1990s the chance of commanding any of the reducing number of Tornado squadrons was very slim. The appointments' staff had dangled some OC Ops posts but they all fell through, so a flying tour seemed unlikely. I was therefore very surprised to receive a call asking if I would be prepared to take over 208 Squadron and see the Buccaneer out of service in 1994. I did not hesitate in replying in the affirmative.

Wg Cdr Nigel Huckins and his 208 Squadron personnel at Lossiemouth.

*

I arrived at RAF Lossiemouth in October 1991. Although I had been off flying for over three years, I was not offered a Hawk refresher course as Hunters were used as part of Buccaneer conversion, and I could refresh on that aircraft. The refresher course consisted of 12 sorties of general handling, instrument flying and low-level navigation, all flown with Sqn Ldr John 'Fras' Fraser who was a long-time QFI and ex-Buccaneer OCU instructor. After a total of nine hours on the Hunter, I started on the Buccaneer conversion in January 1992. The Hunter T8B was equipped with the same airstream direction detector (ADD) as the Buccaneer. Fras and I flew a few sorties practising the Buccaneer approach, and other techniques, using the ADD before he accompanied me in the rear seat for my first Buccaneer flight. With no flying controls of his own, this required a very special type of instructor, and he managed the trip without his voice ever taking on any urgent or high-pitched patter. We practised approach techniques at medium level before Fras was happy that I wouldn't blow it, so he allowed me to do it for real.

There followed a couple of familiarisation sorties with Flt Lt John Tait, another very experienced Buccaneer pilot, in the back seat. I was passed fit to be let loose with a real navigator and Flt Lt Carl Wilson was given the honour. The rest of the conversion course proceeded in good order with some excellent Scottish weather. The Hunter was used for instrument flying, formation and night flying before these events were flown in the Buccaneer. Next came the weapons events including 'bunt' dive-bombing, laydown and toss followed by the full range of maritime tactics by both day and night. The final part of conversion, and the purveyor of the highest adrenalin, buttock-clenching experience to date, was night maritime tactics, which involved close formation at medium and low level with simulated multi-aircraft coordinated Sea Eagle missile attacks. For those brought up in the era of night-vision goggles with compatible cockpit and navigation lights, the Buccaneer had none of that.

Night formation was done using the leading-edge navigation lights as well as the single white formation light on the trailing edge of the wing. This got quite tense when you were in cloud, and is still one of the most difficult and draining flying experiences I have ever had. Nevertheless, I appeared to have convinced the doubters, who were still muttering in the dark corners of the crew room, that someone without a Buccaneer background should not take the squadron. With a final handover check in the Hunter with the departing squadron commander, Wg Cdr Bill Cope, and an arrival check on the Buccaneer with Sqn Ldr Mike Scarfe, I passed the conversion and took command of 208 Squadron on 31 March 1992.

One of the most impressive things about the Buccaneer was how steady it was at very low level. The Jaguar was quite twitchy and needed watching all the time; the Tornado was reasonable even if the radar altimeter sometimes stuck, but with the Buccaneer it was like riding on rails.

I was soon into the real thing. The Royal Navy required its ships heading to the Persian Gulf to join the Armilla patrol to carry out counter-air training. Buccaneers operating from Gibraltar provided this, and I was part of a small detachment tasked to work with HMS *Liverpool*, which was heading for the Gulf. I led a two-ship on the first day when *Liverpool* was practising live firing and anti-air operations. We simulated a Sea Eagle launch at about 20 miles then took on the role of the sea-skimming missile by flying as low as allowed. The next day I was invited to spend the day on *Liverpool* to look at things from the other side. We were given an excellent tour of the ship and, while clambering round the mast to look at some electronic equipment, I saw that the top of the bridge was decorated with a very large union jack. While passing close to the ship as a simulated missile the previous day, I had never seen this large flag. On enquiring how high the top of the bridge was, I was told 35 feet. Either they were being economical with the truth or maybe my radar altimeter was suffering from Tornado sticking!

Another memorable feature of life on a Buccaneer squadron was the strength of the navigators' union. Although I enjoyed my single-seat days on the Jaguar, the Tornado had convinced me that two seats were definitely the way to go. I had met a number of Buccaneer navigators who had transferred to the Tornado and was impressed by their professionalism and their obvious enthusiasm for their previous aircraft. In the Buccaneer, there was no computer-aided system, and back-seaters had to use pure navigating skills to complete

'Skids' Harrison's arrival at Leeming.

a mission successfully. There was an inertial platform provided, but purely for Sea Eagle missile targeting and its latitude and longitude readout was not a great aid to navigation.

Shortly after I arrived on the squadron, the Ministry of Defence released some funds to buy a few satellite navigation systems. These disappeared into the rear cockpit, as navigation in the Buccaneer was absolutely a back-seat issue. We had been invited to the RAF Gatow closing weekend and spent a very enjoyable few days with other NATO and Russian air force guys. Having done a bit of navigating in single-seat fast jets, I decided that I would like the satnav box in the front in order to practise my airways flying on the way back from Berlin. This seriously upset my back-seater who saw it as an intrusion into his sphere, and he refused to say a word to me all the way back apart from informing me that he would not sing out if I got off track. A wise pilot never should upset his man in the back.

As time went on, the aircraft began to show its age and it started to suffer from problems. Fatigue was always an issue and we found that the more experienced pilots could fly evasion sorties with much lower fatigue counts. When evading, newcomers tended to hunt around 2½ G, which clocked up a month's worth of counts, while the more experienced guys pulled through and held steady G with minimal counts on the G meter.

We did have a few other issues. On one occasion I returned with the airbrake hanging off the back of the aircraft rather like a bee that had lost its stinger. The hinges had sheered leaving the brakes hanging by their actuator rod. On another occasion, I was the last one

'Skids' Harrison was awarded a Green Endorsement for his actions in saving his aircraft.

to land after a night sortie. After touchdown, I tested the starboard brake, but it remained on. Despite using the nosewheel steering, the aircraft trundled off the runway onto the grass.

A more serious mishap occurred to Flt Lt 'Skids' Harrison. We were a four-ship tasked to carry out simulated attacks on an American task group led by a Ticonderoga Class cruiser off the west coast of Ireland. We had just let down from a high-level transit and I was looking at the radar altimeter, which was oscillating by about 50 feet due to the height of the waves, when we picked up a warning on the radar receiver. As we turned starboard, I looked over at Skids and noticed a plume of vapour from his aircraft. He then announced that his undercarriage had suddenly lowered for no reason and he thought he had lost some fuel. In fact, the undercarriage doors had ripped off, destroyed one under-wing tank, holed the other and punctured the bomb-door fuel tank.

Within seconds he was reduced to internal fuel only, and we were a long way from home. After pulling up and turning east as we made a Mayday call, we started to consider where to divert. The weather in Ulster, and most of Scotland, was appalling so we settled on RAF Leeming in North Yorkshire as the best bet. On arrival, the cloud base was fine but there was a crosswind. From the outset of the incident, Skids had had greens for nose and one main undercarriage leg but not for the second main leg, although the leg appeared to be in the down position. Despite all his attempts, he could not get a green to confirm the leg was locked down. He made an excellent approach and touchdown, but the recalcitrant main leg collapsed on the roll out. It is a testimony to the rugged build of the Buccaneer that the nose and other main landing gear leg had lowered at 500 knots and were still working when he arrived at Leeming.

Finally, on the negative side, and more tragically, we lost an aircraft and crew, which crashed into the Firth of Forth. The previous squadron commander, Bill Cope, was appointed the president of the Board of Inquiry and insisted on salvaging as much of the aircraft as possible. As a result, it was determined that a rudder position feedback rod had failed, which caused the rudder to go hard over. This, at high speed and low level, induced a rapid roll leaving the crew no chance of ejecting.

On a happier note, we did have some new and unique experiences. HQ 1 Group phoned to say that a slot had come up for a detachment to Decimomannu in Sardinia. I think the UK paid a contribution and they wanted to get their money's worth. Deci had been frequented by RAF Germany squadrons, and I had been there with both Jaguar and Tornado. While Germany-based Buccaneer squadrons had used the Capo Frasca bombing range and NATO facility at Deci, it was completely new to UK-based maritime squadrons, and there were many mutterings of 'we don't do that here'. Nevertheless, I convinced my execs that all would have a good time and we duly departed. The boys had a lot of fun with short four-ship sorties to the range for a wide variety of bombing events. After we had been there a couple of days, we had a visit from the resident Italian air force F-104 squadron asking if we would be interested in sharing some air combat manoeuvring instrumentation (ACMI) range time for some dissimilar two v two air combat. After some perusal of the relevant orders, we duly agreed and, while it was like two old girls going to a disco, all had a great time. The 104s had to be sharp as they ran out of fuel very quickly – we of course could have stayed all day.

Another highlight was the 1993 Queen's Birthday flypast. In June, after a tremendous effort by the engineers, 20 Buccaneers and two Hunters arrived at RAF Manston to position for the flypast. Sqn Ldr Rick Philips and Wg Cdr Nigel Maddox led an immaculate diamond 16 up the Mall and over Buckingham Palace. We also just managed to get the formation over HQ Strike Command at High Wycombe before low cloud forced us to break up and head back to Lossiemouth.

I had always admired the photographs of various 208 Squadron aircraft flying past the pyramids at Giza in honour of the unit's long association with Egypt and the Sphinx on the squadron crest. So, I thought it would be good to get a final version before the squadron disbanded. Lossiemouth was a great place to be based with excellent weather and low flying; however, it did suffer from having no night during the summer, which made night flying currency an issue. To get round this, for many years the squadron deployed to Cyprus for two weeks each in the summer. This seemed the ideal place to launch our last photo operation with the pyramids. After much correspondence through our embassy in Cairo, we achieved approval. On 19 July 1993 we set off as a five-ship with a cameraman, Sgt Rick Brewell, aboard.

Notwithstanding all the advanced work, and monumental pleading by Neil Devine in the back seat, Cairo ATC had never heard of us and sent us off on a desert voyage to the south of Cairo. We wandered round our planned route at low level through some fairly murky weather when, to my surprise, we flew over a SAM site, which many years of recce training told me was a Russian-built SAM 2 Guideline set out exactly as in all the intelligence diagrams I had studied. Not a peep on the RWR luckily. Eventually we returned to Cairo when they let us do an ILS into Cairo International, which routed us by the pyramids so we got the photo, but not as close as we would have liked. Doing a five-ship ILS to a major international airport was another first.

As I had done my operational conversion to the Buccaneer on the squadron, I thought we could use the same system and take on more first tourists before the aircraft was retired in 1994. Conducting operational conversion on a squadron saved considerable flying hours as we did not need staff continuation training to keep up with all the skills required. In addition, a bounced four-ship could be considered part of normal squadron training. This idea was approved and, as result, we trained two *ab-initio* pilots, Ned Cullen and Steve Reeves. I have met both in later life and they very much appreciated the opportunity to fly the Buccaneer and become one of the 'Buccaneer mafia'.

There was one more time before the squadron disbanded when the Buccaneer reminded me that it could bite. Returning from a night three-ship maritime-attack sortie we rendezvoused with a Buccaneer tanker off the east coast. I was the number three and had just plugged in when the tanker pilot called that he needed to turn left to head towards Lossiemouth. Night tanking from a Buccaneer was a challenge as it had minimal lighting with just navigation, formation and the basket 'beta' lights to keep you orientated. As we came round in a gentle turn to point up the Moray Firth, the lights from the ground and the stars all merged and I was suddenly completely disorientated.

I immediately closed the throttles to disengage from the basket. As we slid back, I rolled right to clear the tanker but as I did so, we hit the tanker's jet wash when my aircraft stopped flying normally. It seemed to rotate 270 degrees left before repeating this to the right as well as descending. Any rearward movement on the stick produced severe juddering. Altitude was decreasing, but not too rapidly. Remembering spin recovery from my early days on the Chipmunk, I called my back-seater to eject if we did not recover by 8,000 ft. I applied corrective controls and we emerged with the aircraft still feeling sensitive at about 11,000 ft. As I looked out, I could see Lossiemouth's runway approach lights on the nose so we completed a straight-in approach. It was not long before we repaired to the 'Bothie Bar' for a restorative drink. Next day I admitted our experiences to the station commander and, after some muttering about allowing non-Buccaneer experienced pilots to command Buccaneer squadrons, he suggested that I should re-qualify at night tanking, and I duly complied.

As April 1994 approached, we needed to plan for the disbandment of the squadron and retirement of the Buccaneer from RAF service. The undying enthusiasm of the large number of navy and RAF crews who had flown the aircraft was well demonstrated by the large numbers turning up at the annual 'Buccaneer Blitz'. A final event would obviously have to be a substantial affair. I decided that Fras was the best man to put in charge of planning a weekend of events, while I hatched my own plan for the end of the Buccaneer era. I had decided that I wanted to re-badge our aircraft with the squadron markings of every RAF squadron that had operated the Buccaneer. I had to obtain permission from the active squadrons to use their insignia as well as from 18 Group. Although the hard-working engineers were initially sceptical of the idea, this was replaced by enthusiasm. The *pièce de résistance* was to repaint one aircraft in the full livery of the last Royal Navy Buccaneer squadron, No. 809. The painting

Wg Cdr Nigel Huckins leads the walk out for the squadron's farewell flypast 26 March 1994.

The final fly-by.

task was completed, and we got a fine airborne shot of seven aircraft in echelon.

I was lucky to lead this unique formation, and the final nine-ship during the Buccaneer reunion weekend. Fras did an amazing job with over 900 people turning up at Lossiemouth for the aircraft's swansong, a magnificent tribute that emphasised the huge affection for the 'Last All-British Bomber'. The effort in the repainting scheme was fully justified by the profound and emotional reaction of the navy personnel on seeing a Buccaneer in navy livery leading the final flypast. I feel very privileged to have commanded a great squadron, and to have joined the exalted ranks of 'Buccaneer Boys'.

CHAPTER TWENTY-FIVE

BUCCANEER
TO CAPE TOWN

KEITH HARTLEY

First some background: Buccaneer XW988 had been bought from MoD Disposals by Mike Beachy Head, a serious South African enthusiast who had already bought and was operating a Canberra T.17 and two Hunters (a T.8 and an F.6A) from his base in Cape Town. He was keen to add a Buccaneer to his collection with its obvious South African connection. I got involved when he asked us – the 'us' being the Classic Jet Aircraft Company (CJAC), who had already prepared and delivered his other ex-RAF aircraft – to do the same for the Buccaneer. Not being a true Buccaneer expert (my time comes from Boscombe Down and BAe), I asked Warton colleague Peter Huett (2,500 hours Bucc on 12 and 16 Squadrons and a couple of RN exchanges, etc.) if he'd care to join me – being a mature, responsible and cautious individual, he played hard to get for at least three seconds before consenting.

XW988 was one of the three 'specials' built for MoD(PE) use. Essentially an S.2B, it had been extensively kitted out with instrumentation and special trials fits but was otherwise pretty standard. Externally, the most obvious difference was the special outboard pylon fit, small pylons specifically for carriage of cameras for recording weapons release from the normal wing pylons. On purchase, the aircraft was clean apart from these pylons, although standard wing overload tanks were fitted for subsequent flying. There were no bomb-door or bomb-bay fuel tanks – the bomb bay was well cluttered with flight trials instrumentation (FTI) wiring and brackets, but plenty of space remained for equipment stowage.

Similarly, the nose was devoid of radar, the space being occupied by racking and a few leftover bits of FTI, but still provided a great space for easily accessible en route stowage. The cockpits were only slightly modified, with additional FTI dials; there were no radar or

Buccaneer S.2 XW988 during its days with the RAE before leaving for South Africa.

RWR displays in the rear cockpit, so Pete had to keep himself occupied with the standard fuel switchery and an ADF. With the indicator in the rear cockpit we anticipated an intriguing bit of crew co-operation if we ever needed to do an NDB approach during the delivery. There was a VOR with displays in both cockpits, an ILS onto the OR946, and TACAN, as usual also on the OR946. The other outstanding feature of the aircraft was its age – even after delivery to Cape Town, it had less than 1,400 hours total time – used, not remaining!

The initial game was to prepare the aircraft for flight (it had not flown for about nine months) and deliver it to the CJAC hangar at Exeter. Technically, this was simple – a primary-star, full-seat servicing, and the already excellent condition of the aircraft made it all very straightforward.

Administratively, it was potentially much more difficult. We had prepared and delivered the earlier Canberra and Hunters on the UK civil register, and had had to obtain UK certification for the aircraft. The UK CAA had considerably more heartache over the prospect of a civil-registered Buccaneer – they regarded the aircraft in the same class as the Lightning and several other heavy metal ex-military aircraft that they refused to countenance. We therefore discussed the aircraft directly with the South African CAA who agreed that the aircraft would be certified if operated and maintained in the manner proposed. A South African CAA engineer visited Boscombe during the primary-star servicing, expressed himself satisfied and issued the C of A.

However, we still needed to fly the aircraft in UK airspace, for delivery to Exeter, air tests and any necessary ferry shakedown flying. The legal position was unclear – we may have been entitled to just wave our fingers at the CAA – but we chose for obvious reasons to seek the UK CAA's approval for such flying. As you might guess, they were far from happy, being well aware that giving approval would seriously damage their arguments against a UK-registered aircraft flying, but eventually the combination of irrefutable technical argument and political pressure from the South African CAA persuaded them in favour.

Accordingly, the aircraft, still in MoD(PE) green and yellow paint plus RAF roundels, plus the South African registration ZU-AVI, was moved from Boscombe Down to Exeter on 19 April. The trip was just a ferry plus a brief check of services and handling. The following day we completed the air-test schedule without problem and left it to the engineers to prepare the aircraft with the overload fuel tanks and preparations for the ferry. The shakedown went well with the fuel flows and transfers all working as advertised, and apart from an intermittent IFF reported by ATC, the aircraft was ready to go.

The route, planned by Peter, took advantage of BAe Warton's general experience in deliveries through the Middle East and Africa. In Africa, the legs were largely determined by the available airfields, rather than utilising the maximum range of the aircraft, hence we were never short of fuel.

The route was:

Day One: Brindisi; Luxor night stop.

Day Two: Djibouti; Nairobi night stop.

Day Three: Harare; Jo'burg; Cape Town.

The other two main drivers for landing and diversion fields were the availability of air starters and – if possible – LOX. All the airfields planned had air starters for some civil jets but the only uncertainty was the compatibility of their connectors with the Buccaneer.

After some research, we thought that most would be OK, and made up an adapter to cater for the one case we were worried about. The adapter was stowed in the bomb bay, and was needed only once, at Djibouti. LOX was a problem, since we couldn't get the mod kit to carry a spare LOX container in the bomb bay. We set off full, Djibouti (French navy) said they'd have some, but in the event their connectors were incompatible, and we finally ran out halfway through Tanzania – but flying the rest of the way below 12,000 ft cabin altitude made little difference to the range requirements.

Diary of Events

Day One

1 May 1996. Wet dank and early start, off on time from Exeter. ATC report IFF garbled, so 'Trusty Man in Back' begins long litany of surprised innocence, promised recycles, etc. to persuade ATC to let us through the airways. DME from TACAN dead, VOR and ADF OK. Thank God for triplex handheld GPS, two for him, one for me. Lots of haggling with French ATC over route and lack of IFF, get re-routed around Switzerland. Winds less painful from Genoa onwards.

Land Brindisi after two hours 40 minutes. I do the turn round and Peter does ATC. He returns and announces that even though Greece originally said no diplomatic clearance required (civil aircraft) they've changed their mind. Lose two hours in sorting, including discovery that our man in embassy who said he'd fix it for us has gone home. In the end, just re-file the plan without clearance, get accepted, and go.

Hit Luxor at sundown, following run down abeam the Nile in unusual weather. Peter and I have been through Luxor many times, and it's always CAVOK or, at worst, 5 km visibility in blowing sand with no significant cloud. This time, however, there's almost an overcast at 20,000 ft, with scattered around 11,000 ft, visibility not special but OK.

Land, wind light and variable, sky yellow, temperature over 40°C and quite humid for Luxor. Flight time to Luxor 2.30. We have the usual argument with ATC over parking next to fuel point (ground refuelling at Luxor, and they just love to make you re-start and taxi somewhere else) – we lose. Re-fuel, and wait for air starter to move aircraft to next parking spot on an empty pan. I disappear into radio bay to disconnect LOX pack while Peter takes bags out of nose.

While tucked inside the radio bay, something smacks me on the back of the legs, and at the same time lots of whistling noises: back outside to find a good 40-knot wind and the visibility less than 50 metres in thick dust. All the locals have legged it for the safety of the bus. I spot the canopy is still open and rush to the nearest overload tank where a ladder was parked for access onto the top. Note use of past tense, ladder is now heading for the Red Sea.

Peter, meanwhile, noticed the locals scarpering and wondered why, then noticed huge wall of sand converging fast; initially he tried to close nose but soon decided he'd probably die in the attempt, so put it back on the parking latch and hung on. The storm lasts for five to ten minutes and then returns to light and variable, but still a heavy, sticky, static-filled air; it then rained. I'd got the canopy closed by then, so the net result was to provide the jet with a very pretty dimpled-effect finish of raincratered dust. Unlucky says local agent – this stuff only happens once a year, for about three to five days.

We eventually start one engine, move, and stack to the hotel. There are still no faxes awaiting us on Ethiopia, Eritrea and Kenya diplomatic clearances, which we hadn't received before departure. Peter tries the phone and fax to Warton, but without success, have to try again in the morning.

Day Two

In the morning, still no diplomatic clearances. We go to the airport to use agent's phone, and find it is in fact the phone box in airport concourse. After phoning Warton, again without success, Peter goes back to hotel to make a significant contribution to Egypt Telecom's, and the Sheraton's profits by contacting embassies direct, while I go out to the aircraft to try and protect it from heat.

I decline use of the proper ladder – $96 per hour – and use the fuel truck steps instead in exchange for a $10 note. Cover the canopy as best I can but can do nothing for the rest – aircraft looks lonely and apprehensive on glaringly white, exposed pan and the temperature is climbing through 40°C. Fortunately, the high overcast keeps the worst of sun at bay.

Get back to hotel to find Peter has sorted diplomatic clearances to get us to Nairobi, but it's now too late to go and get there in daylight. Also, leaving now would mean transiting Djibouti in the hottest part of the day, so we stack for the day, looking for lunch and cooling session by pool. This is interrupted by a call from Mike Beachy Head, urging us to press on now because we need to get to Cape Town by Saturday for monster celebratory thrash. We thank him for suggestion but decline the offer of night in Djibouti (no visas) followed by a four-leg day to Cape Town. Further interruption to serious relaxation when BAe Warton team delivering PC9s to Riyadh arrive for night stop.

Day Three

Early start out of hotel, and quick clearance through the airport, including paying a serious bill for agent's and ATC charges. In spite of early start, it is already very hot.

Start and taxi, get held at the end of the runway and argue with ATC who insist we return to dispersal, no diplomatic clearances, same old thing, not military etc. etc. Gave them all the same answers as yesterday and eventually brazen them out.

Uneventful journey to Djibouti over ferocious scenery; a lot of northern Eritrea is just serious mountains slashed with ravines, everything fractured, tortured rock – we won't walk out of there if we need to use Martin-Baker. Eritrean ATC confused by aircraft type, they finally acknowledged Peter's polite "Buccaneer/Bucc/NA.39" and replied, "Aah, OK, Tupolev, yes?" We agreed, it was less hassle. Flight time to Djibouti 2.10 with a no-pain arrival, everyone very helpful, although the handling agent didn't pitch up until we had already done most things. Very hot – mighty bomber sits on the pan and bakes quietly. French air force very helpful and take away LOX tank, otherwise a quick refuelling, painless ATC and lots of spectators. French could not fill LOX – pity since we had lost about a quarter during the enforced stop at Luxor, so we were down to less than half.

As anticipated, the air starter in Djibouti has a short nozzle that cannot connect to the Bucc's recessed nozzle, so we need to use our cunning adapter. Since we'd never trust the local ground staff to connect and disconnect the starter, and close the door properly, start requires Peter to be outside to do it. Getting the engines started and the doors closed is easy: the first fun comes with stowing the adapter back in the bomb bay, because it is now very hot: RAF flying gloves offer only limited insulation. The second fun for Peter is clambering up the vehicle parked near the wingtip, up the wing and then sliding, legs astride, over the canopy elegantly into his seat. I love working with professionals!

Local military man asks for flyby on departure but I tell him only if he clears it with ATC and the military. To my surprise he does, so it's the dumbbell turn after take-off and whizz past the tower and depart on track, no diplomatic incidents.

Another quiet leg – what a contrast to Europe – mostly spent looking at big cumulo-nimbi looming over the horizon, roughly where we'd expect to find Nairobi. On arrival we find two huge storms, one atop Mount Kilimanjaro and one over Mount Kenya with Nairobi wide open and visible from 100 miles. So fat for fuel we had to dump some – I'm glad Mr Shell was giving it to us for free. Flight time was 1.50 and a pleasant late afternoon in Nairobi's lovely climate.

Ground support quite good, with a quick refuel and lot of interest from the locals.

Have a minor worry about a bit of hydraulic fluid coming from the aircraft in various places, but a close look doesn't show anything untoward – it is a Buccaneer after all.

Stack to the excellent Norfolk Hotel where we take afternoon tea on the terrace while studying the ODM for tomorrow's take-off. The aircraft is quite light but Nairobi is high and hot, so Peter persuades me that a blown take-off is a better option than speeding up close to the tyre-limiting speeds.

Day Four

Another early start in anticipation of three legs' worth of potential bureaucratic hassle. The blown take-off proves uneventful. Sadly, Kilimanjaro is hidden in cloud, and cloud cover persisted for the first half hour over Tanzania. Thereafter, the scenery changes to green, rolling savannah and quite well populated. The oxygen runs out as we approach the Tanzanian border, so we let down to cruise the rest of the way at FL 120; we are fat for fuel. Easy arrival into Harare with excellent weather and the runway visible at 50 miles. Locals very friendly and helpful and aircraft draws, as usual, a good crowd.

Another blown take-off, followed by a pretty direct route to Jo'burg. However, on arrival in South African airspace an intimidating lady tells us that we wouldn't be allowed to take off again unless the IFF was fixed. We consider diverting but it all gets too difficult – let's land at Jo'burg and let Mike Beachy Head sort it out, coming to escort us out in the Hunter if necessary.

Thanks to some admin hiccup, the handling agents are not expecting us, so we taxi round the airfield for a bit while we find somewhere to park. The airfield's huge, a couple of 12,000 ft runways and enough taxiways to keep Tarmac in business for years.

Eventually get to the agents and contact Beachy Head, who calls the airport manager and briefs him on his acquaintance with the head of the South African CAA. This results in a rapid agreement to a special VFR departure, everyone's happy (well, almost). Meanwhile we have to start up and taxi elsewhere for refuelling. Further delays paying extra parking and ground-handling fees, plus a long wait for fuel. Eventually, we get airborne on a confusing VFR departure procedure that basically involves overflying the centre of Jo'burg at 1,500 ft fighting for airspace with a million little bug smashers.

Once clear of the Jo'burg CTZ, the airspace is wonderful – take a straight line to Cape Town (700 nm) and follow it. You can chat to odd radar units along the way, but it's not necessary: when you do, they're interested, helpful, and efficient. Approaching Cape Town, we're joined by Beachy Head's two Hunters, who close up for some photos, and then formate on us for the recovery. And that's another thing – it may be an international airfield of some size and traffic, but they readily cope with a military three-ship run and break: I can't quite remember when I last did that at Heathrow or Manchester.

Finish with a couple of circuits and landings and bring aircraft to rest on its dispersal surrounded by a crowd suitably awed by the huge, rumbling, vibrating, shrieking monster that does funny things with its wings when it taxies. Peter and I climb out feeling tired but satisfied, and greatly impressed with the aircraft, which has behaved flawlessly throughout – we had no more snags than when we left (IFF) in spite of the harsh climate and distances travelled. By the time we descend the steps, the table is in place by the nose

XW988 transformed into ZU-AVI flies over Cape Town.

of the aircraft, white cloth, crystal glasses, plenty of ice, Chivas Regal, right let's get started.

For the stats gatherers, we did 14 hours 25 minutes, in seven legs. Generally, we cruised at FL330, although on occasion we got up to 370, cruising at Mach 0.88 or even 0.91.

Day Five

The following day I take Mike Beachy Head for an area recce (or, for him, a chance to experience and show off his new aircraft). It proves to be a stunning trip – I'm not sure who enjoyed it most, he or I. Peter gives him a heavyweight back-seat brief, while the engineers fix the IFF. The weather, as seems completely usual, is outstanding, with infinite visibility and a brilliant blue sky. Departure is simple enough, even for me – straight ahead to 1,500 ft, and at three miles we're clear of the zone and purely VFR. Down to 200 ft over the sea, 500 kts and surfing. Round Cape Aghulas (the southern tip of Africa and the first time for me) and then east to the Overburg test range and airfield. Fast low flyby, slow flyby and orbit, followed by fast low departure back out to sea. Smoke back around Cape Point; see Table Mountain from the seaward side for the first time (that's the view you get on all the postcards), and up the coast to the air force training base at Langebaan. Another fast flyby, slow flyby over the line of PC7s and back for the fast-rolling departure. Back to Cape Town after short hold, a single circuit with low overshoot for photos, and final landing. Just enough time to change and for Peter and me to get to the terminal and depart for London.

When we deliver the next one (yes, he bought XW987 as well), we must try and spend a bit more time there.

CHAPTER TWENTY-SIX

THE SPIRIT LIVES ON

GRAHAM PITCHFORK

The final days of the RAF Buccaneer force at the end of March 1994 marked the end of an era. The farewell to the aircraft at Lossiemouth, organised by the last Buccaneer squadron commander, Wg Cdr Nigel Huckins, and attended by some 500 air and ground crews and their families, was spectacular, emotional and brilliantly organised and executed. It marked the end of 32 years of operational service in the British military, but the Buccaneer brethren were not going to allow this sad occasion from keeping alive the spirit created by our involvement with this great aircraft.

As recounted in the previous edition of *Buccaneer Boys*, an Aircrew Association was created and, within months, over 500 former aircrews from the Royal Navy, the Royal Air Force and the South African Air Force had signed up. Company test pilots soon joined us, together with others who had flown the aircraft at Boscombe Down.

Since the formation of the association our affection for the aircraft has strengthened, brought about by our memories, our twice-yearly newsletter and the numerous gatherings, which take place all over the country. The legendary Buccaneer Blitz, established in the 1980s, attracts members from far and wide at our annual gatherings in London. The biennial Ladies Night brings together 200 people when we re-visit our old watering holes at Yeovilton, Lossiemouth and Honington. In recent years we have added Gosport to our venues. A number of our ground crew began meeting annually in Norwich, and this event has expanded and now includes those who flew the aircraft.

Amongst the many memorable reunions, no-one will forget the amazing visit in 2008 hosted by our South African members. With 70 UK members and their partners travelling to Pretoria, no event could better epitomise the spirit of the Buccaneer Boys.

The Gilroy Trophy on display in the Honington officers' mess.

We have been immensely fortunate to have incredible 'top cover'. ACM Sir Michael Knight was our first president and served for 20 years with Vice Admiral Sir Ted Anson giving great support for much of that time until he passed away. ACM Sir David Cousins held the reins for a number of years before handing over to our current president, AM Sir Peter Norriss. Capt

Ted Hackett, a founder member, has served as our active vice president for many years. Few associations can have been so fortunate to have such 'hands-on' support from the top.

As the years pass, and we have more time on our hands, so the golfing fraternity expands with numerous events each year. Under the expert stewardship of Dave Wilby, we meet every year in Rutland to remember our great friend Mike Bush when we play to support the charity set up by his widow Sarah. In recent years, Peter Norriss and Dave Wilby have established the Buccaneer Ryder Cup when two teams of 12, drawn from the east and west of the UK, meet at a central location to play 36 holes and enjoy a dinner and an evening of banter. A prestigious event held at Bath competes for the 'Mrs Warren's Teapot', a household relic given a stay of execution by Pete Warren.

A centrepiece of our association remains our Gulf War veteran Buccaneer, XX901, housed at the Yorkshire Air Museum together with an array of weapons 'acquired' over the years. It has received a new coat of paint and Graham Henderson, nephew of a founder member of 12 Squadron, and later its CO, Ian Henderson, faithfully re-painted the aircraft's nose art, which looks immaculate.

Finally, I want to mention the Gilroy Trophy instituted in 1972 in memory of my great friend Sqn Ldr 'Jock' Gilroy, the wing weapons officer at RAF Honington. An outstanding ground-attack pilot, he was killed on a night-bombing exercise on Jurby Range in January 1972. He was held in such high regard that his colleagues wished to remember him in an appropriate manner, and so his memory lives on with the Gilroy Trophy. A weapons competition amongst the Buccaneer squadrons and the OCU based at RAF Honington, and then at RAF Lossiemouth, was held annually with the winning unit retaining the sword. Today, it resides in its display cabinet in the front entrance to the officers' mess at RAF Honington, now the depot of the RAF Regiment.

Together, all these activities and events continue to cement the unique nature of the 'Buccaneer brotherhood'. It is 60 years since the aircraft entered service with the Fleet Air Arm, and 27 years since it was retired from service. Sadly, our ranks are starting to thin and we remember those we lost. Yet, the aircraft continues to bind us together, our friendships strengthen and we all remain immensely proud to have flown and serviced:

The Buccaneer – the Last All-British Bomber.

THE BUCCANEER BOYS

Sir Peter Norriss

Sir Peter Norriss joined the RAF in 1966 whilst studying Modern Languages at Magdalene College, Cambridge. After his first tour as a QFI at the RAF College Cranwell he embarked on the first of three tours on the Buccaneer. First he served on XV Squadron at Laarbruch in Germany before becoming the chief flying instructor on 237 OCU when he was awarded the AFC. After Staff College and an MoD tour, he commanded 16 Squadron back at Laarbruch where inter alia he formed the only ever RAF Buccaneer display team, the five-ship Black Saints. He was station commander at RAF Marham with Victor tanker and Tornado GR 1 squadrons. In 1988 he began his long association with the world of procurement, first on the operational requirement's staff and then with the Procurement Executive. He was Controller Aircraft on the Air Force Board from 1996–2000. He is president of the Buccaneer Aircrew Association.

Graham Pitchfork

Graham Pitchfork trained as a navigator at the RAF College Cranwell before serving on a Canberra photographic reconnaissance squadron in Germany. In April 1965 he started a three-year exchange tour with the Fleet Air Arm and spent a year with 800 NAS embarked in *Eagle* before becoming an instructor on 736 NAS. On his return to the RAF, he served two tours on Buccaneers at Honington before being appointed as OC 208 Squadron in July 1979. After tours at MoD, and as director of the Department of Air Warfare at RAF Cranwell, he was the station commander at RAF Finningley. His final appointment was as director of Intelligence (Commitments) in the MoD. He retired in 1994. He was chairman of the Buccaneer Aircrew Association for 25 years.

Michael Clapp

Michael Clapp joined the Royal Navy as an executive officer cadet in 1950. He saw service off Korea in the cruiser HMS *Ceylon*. After more sea time he joined No. 1 Long Observer Course before being appointed to a Skyraider AEW squadron. After completing the RAF Staff Navigator course he was seconded to Ferranti, where his career on the Buccaneer began. He served on 700Z Flight, the Buccaneer Initial Flying Trials Unit before joining the first Buccaneer squadron, 801 NAS in *Victorious*. After command of a minesweeper in the Far East he assumed command of 801 Squadron operating the Mark 2. The squadron won the Boyd Trophy for its contribution to naval aviation. He commanded two frigates, and his last job as a commodore was in command of the Falkland's Amphibious Task Group, his services recognised when he was appointed CB.

John Harvey

John Harvey joined the RAF as a technical cadet at RAF Henlow. His first appointment was as the junior engineering officer on 74 Squadron operating Lightnings from Coltishall and then Leuchars. A similar tour with 19 Squadron in Germany followed before he was selected for pilot training under a scheme to train a few engineers as pilots. As he finished his advanced training at Valley, he was sent to Lossiemouth to form and command the RAF Buccaneer Element on the Fleet Air Arm's 736 Squadron. In 1972 he returned to RAF engineering duties at Swanton Morley. In 1975 he joined the Jaguar project office and two years later he was part of the Nimrod AEW project office. He left the RAF in 1979 to pursue a career in computing, finally working for General Dynamics.

Peter Gooding

Peter Gooding's first front-line tour in 1970 was on 12 Squadron Buccaneers. He had two further tours on Buccaneers: first as an instructor on 237 OCU, and then in 1974 as a flight commander on 16 Squadron at Laarbruch, Germany. After Staff College and two years in Hong Kong, in 1982 he commanded IX Squadron, the world's first Tornado squadron. He was awarded the AFC. Later, in 1990 he was station commander of RAF Linton-on-Ouse, Yorkshire. After leaving the RAF in 1990, he instructed for ten years as a civilian on the Slingsby Firefly 260 at RAF Barkston Heath.

Peter Sturt

After three years as a flight cadet at the RAF College Cranwell, Peter Sturt converted to the Hunter and flew with 8 Squadron from Khormaksar in Aden. He was an instructor at 229 OCU at Chivenor before beginning his three years on exchange with the Fleet Air Arm. He later converted to the Harrier and was a flight commander on 20 Squadron based at Wildenrath in Germany. He served as OC 216 Squadron at Honington before converting to the Tornado and serving at Marham as OC Operations Wing. After operation's staff tours at HQ 1 Group and the MoD, he was the commander British Forces for Operation Warden based in Incirlik Air Base, Turkey, retiring from the RAF in 1996.

David Ray

After graduating from the RAF College Cranwell, Dave Ray began his long career on the Buccaneer in 1971 when he joined XV Squadron at Laarbruch. He qualified as a QWI and started another tour on XV in 1976 as weapons leader. He served as the Buccaneer member of the Central Trials and Tactics Organisation. He later served in MoD in the operational requirements branch when he staffed the Buccaneer avionics update programme.

His final association with the Buccaneer was as the commanding officer of the OCU at Lossiemouth in 1987. He was the station commander at RAF Valley, served on the Joint Maritime Operational Training Staff and retired in 2002. He is the vice chairman of the Buccaneer Aircrew Association.

Tom Eeles

After training as a pilot at the RAF College, Cranwell, Tom Eeles served on a Canberra bomber squadron in Germany. He was one of the first RAF pilots to serve on exchange with the Fleet Air Arm converting to the Buccaneer in 1966. He joined 801 NAS and was embarked in *Victorious* and *Hermes* before becoming an instructor on 736 NAS. He attended CFS and trained as a QFI before returning to the Buccaneer world to complete a tour on 12 Squadron and three on 237 OCU, culminating in 1984 when he was appointed as the chief instructor. He later served at the Central Flying School and was the station commander at RAF Linton-on-Ouse. He retired in 1997 and then served as a reservist on Cambridge University Air Squadron for ten years. He is chairman of the Buccaneer Aircrew Association.

David Herriot

After completing his training as a navigator, David Herriot started his 'Buccaneer Life' in 1971 as the first RAF-trained first-tour navigator to join the force. He completed four tours, all on different RAF squadrons (XV, 12, 237 OCU and 16) and flew almost 2,500 hours on the aircraft. He completed the QWI course and subsequently became the weapons leader on 16 Squadron. He later flew with 17 Squadron on Tornados and, later, was the weapons standards and evaluation officer at RAF Brüggen. Apart from a tour as wing commander cadets at the RAF College, all his ground appointments were associated with air warfare training and operational requirements. He served as a RAF detachment commander in Italy during the Kosovo War. Before retiring in 2007 he commanded the training wing of the RAF's Air Warfare Centre at Cranwell. He was the founding member and honorary secretary of the Buccaneer Aircrew Association for 26 years.

Mal Grosse

Mal Grosse was educated at Lancaster Royal Grammar School and joined the Royal Air Force in 1962. During the next 27 years, as a pilot he flew eight types of aircraft, mainly Hunters and Buccaneers, including four years' service in the Middle East. He attended the Royal Australian Air Force Staff College. He was awarded the Queen's Commendation for Valuable Service in the Air and the AFC, retiring in 1988. He then joined British Aerospace with responsibility for Eurofighter Typhoon marketing, spending his last four years in Canberra as director of the Eurofighter sales campaign. Giving up full-time work in 2000, he has maintained his aviation interest through oil painting, with the occasional commission funding his continued bad habits.

Dave Ainge

After joining the RAF at the RAF College in 1982 as a pilot, Dave Ainge trained on the Gnat at Valley before converting to the Hunter at Chivenor. After a first tour on 1 Squadron at West Raynham, he joined 234 Squadron at Chivenor, initially as a tactics instructor before qualifying as a PAI (weapons instructor later known as QWI). A third Hunter tour as squadron PAI and flight commander on 8 Squadron at Bahrain was followed by a ground tour at Honington as the wing PAI. He then returned to the Hunter as flight commander of the Weapons Instructional Flight on 79 Squadron, firstly at Chivenor, then Brawdy. His final flying tour was on Buccaneers with 208 Squadron at Honington, first as squadron weapons leader then as a flight commander. Finally after a short ground tour as wing weapons officer at Honington, in which he still flew the Hunter, he retired to commercial aviation in 1981.

Ken Mackenzie

Ken Mackenzie joined BRNC Dartmouth in 1964 as a seaman officer and relished two training appointments in minesweepers in the Far East. After observer training he served on an assault helicopter squadron, and then an ASW squadron before qualifying as an RAF navigator and serving on 12 Squadron. He then joined 809 NAS for the final commission of *Ark Royal* and was in the last-ever naval Buccaneer launch in November 1978. Subsequent aviation appointments included operations officer at RNAS Portland and operations officer of the carrier *Hermes* with Sea Harriers embarked. He commanded HMS Gannet with two helicopter squadrons at Prestwick and finally as the RN liaison officer at CTTO Boscombe Down. He retired from the RN one month before his 65th birthday.

Paul Smart

Paul Smart joined the RAF in June 1975 as a LMech(air communications). After basic training at RAF Swinderby and trade training at RAF Cosford, his first posting was first line with 39 Squadron on Canberra PR.9s. After three years at RAF Wyton, his first overseas posting was to RAF Laarbruch and 16 Squadron. Since leaving the RAF in 1982 he has kept in contact with many of his former colleagues, re-visited RAF Laarbruch twice for reunions and maintains a healthy interest and affection for both marques of aircraft worked on. He is an active member of the RAF Association.

Peter Browning

Peter Browning began his RAF career as an aircraft apprentice at Halton in October 1966, graduating three years later as an aircraft technician. His long career on the Buccaneer started at Honington until 1981 when he moved between Germany and Honington every three years, serving on 237 OCU, 12, XV and 16 Squadrons. In 1983, as a chief technician, he joined the Tornado force at Marham serving on 27 Squadron before two tours at Brüggen, first on 31 and then IX Squadron. From 1987 until his retirement in 2003 as a flight sergeant, he served at Wyton and at Halton.

Frank Cox

Frank Cox joined the Fleet Air Arm in 1962 and, on completion of his flying training, served in 800 NAS embarked in *Eagle*. In 1967 he joined 738 NAS flying Hunters and served as a tactical instructor and air warfare instructor (AWI). In 1967 he returned to the Buccaneer world flying in 809 NAS from Lossiemouth and *Ark Royal*. He joined the staff of 764 NAS (AWI School) in 1971 and a year later joined 237 OCU at RAF Honington as a weapons instructor. After an exchange tour with the US Navy flying the A-6 Intruder, he returned to 809 NAS in 1976, becoming senior pilot in 1977 until the squadron was decommissioned in December 1978. He later served at Brawdy and at Yeovilton, where he also flew the Firefly and the Sea Fury for the Naval Historic Flight displays. After leaving the navy in 1983, he continued to fly Hunters until 1985 for Airwork Ltd and subsequently Flight Refuelling Ltd. Since then he has been flying corporate jets worldwide.

Dries Marais

Dries Marais began his pilot training in 1964 and after graduating from the South African Military Academy at Saldanha, he joined 8 Squadron to fly the Harvard. After a year, and attendance at the Central Flying School, he became an instructor at AFB Langebaanweg on the Aermacchi Impala in 1970. Three years later he became the PAI on the base. In 1976 he converted to the Mirage III and a year later joined 24 Squadron at AFB Waterkloof to fly the Buccaneer S.50 as the squadron training officer. In 1980 he became the PAI at 85 Advanced Flying School at AFB Pietersburg. From 1987 to 1990 he was the staff officer electronic warfare at SAAF Headquarters in Pretoria. He resigned after the Angolan War ended. He spent 37 years as an aircraft accident investigator and specialist witness.

Malcolm Ward

Malcolm Ward was commissioned in 1979 and joined the Buccaneer force in 1981 as the junior engineer officer on 208 Squadron. Subsequent tours included the Phantom, Harrier, Nimrod, Sentinel, VC10 (twice) and Eurofighter Typhoon (three tours), all of which benefitted from the lessons he learned from the mighty Buccaneer. After attending the German armed forces staff college as an exchange student, he undertook staff appointments in the MoD, HQ Air Command, Abbey Wood, Munich and Kandahar. His final tour was as an exchange officer in the German MoD in Berlin, where he represented Germany on arms control issues. He never returned to the Buccaneer force, but he did revisit 208 Squadron, by then operating the Hawk T.1 from RAF Valley, where he finally got to fly with 208, three decades after leaving the squadron. He retired in 2014.

Michael Bickley

Michael Bickley joined the Royal Navy as an executive branch cadet at Dartmouth in 1954. After training as an observer, he flew in the AEW role, initially on Skyraiders and then the Gannet. In 1962 he joined 831 NAS, the RN's electronic warfare squadron at RAF Watton. He later became the naval advisor to the RAF Central Signals Establishment. He trained on the Buccaneer in 1965 before joining 800 NAS as the electronic warfare officer and executive officer. After a year at sea in *Eagle*, and a brief period as an instructor on 736 NAS, he joined 801 NAS in 1967 as the senior observer embarked in *Hermes*. Two non-flying jobs followed before he assumed command of 809 NAS embarked in *Ark Royal*. He later served in MoD, was the naval attaché in Bonn, served in Gibraltar and his final appointment was as the air attaché in The Hague. He retired in 1993.

Nick Berryman

Son of a wartime Spitfire pilot, Nick Berryman graduated from the RAF College Cranwell in 1964, and after a tour flying reconnaissance Canberra PR.7s on 58 Squadron, he completed two operational tours in RAF Germany on XV and 16 Squadrons, and one as a qualified weapons instructor (QWI) on 237 Buccaneer OCU. Between Buccaneer postings, he served on No. 2 Tactical Weapons Unit at RAF Brawdy as a QWI on Hunter and Hawk aircraft. Finally, after three staff tours, Staff College, and 27 years in the RAF, the flying bug returned, and he joined Monarch Airlines flying the Airbus A300-600ER for another 16 years. At the age of 74, he is still in the aviation business as a synthetic flight instructor at CAE (UK) Ltd, training civilian pilots on the Bombardier Global Express, and RAF pilots on the Raytheon Sentinel R Mark 1.

Bob Kemp

Bob Kemp joined the RAF on a direct entry commission. Following flying training he trained with 736 Squadron at Lossiemouth on the Mark 1 Buccaneer. He qualified as a weapons instructor on the first Buccaneer Attack Instructors' Course and amassed over 3,000 hours in both the maritime and overland roles on 12, XV and 208 Squadrons. On retirement from the RAF, he took up a commission as a reservist in the Royal Auxiliary Air

Force. He commanded the City of Edinburgh Squadron for eight years before becoming inspector of the force, a position he held for seven years. Later he was appointed Director Scotland of the RAF Benevolent Fund and currently he is a trustee of a number of military charities. He was appointed CBE in 2007.

Martin Engwell

After completing a flying scholarship, Martin Engwell joined the RAF in May 1962 and trained as a pilot. After a tour on Vulcans, he became a flying instructor and was a member of the Macaw aerobatics team. He joined the Buccaneer force in 1972 and served on XV Squadron at Laarbruch. In 1975 he became a flight commander on 12 Squadron at Honington. After a series of ground appointments, in August 1983 he assumed command of 12 Squadron, which had moved to Lossiemouth. He continued to be involved in the Buccaneer force serving at HQ 18 Group and in the MoD followed by a tour at HQ SACLANT, Norfolk, Virginia. His final tour was with CINCEASTLANT at Northwood. He retired in September 2001 having been appointed OBE.

Gordon Niven

Gordon Niven joined the RAF as a direct entrant in 1978. After completing navigator training at RAF Finningley, he was posted to Buccaneers and in 1982 joined 12 Squadron at RAF Lossiemouth. On completion of two tours on the maritime wing, he converted to Tornado joining 31 Squadron at RAF Brüggen in Germany. In 1993, he was posted to Denmark as an attack planning officer in a NATO headquarters. He returned to 31 Squadron in 1997 as a flight commander and flew six combat missions over Kosovo in 1999. During a staff tour at Strike Command, he oversaw the closure of RAF Brüggen and the return of the RAF's last flying units back to the UK from Germany. For six months he was the deputy force air component commander for Operation Northern Watch at Incirlik Air Base in Turkey before taking up his last tour as a staff officer at JFC HQ, Naples, Italy, which included oversight of air operations in the Balkans. He retired from the RAF in 2006.

John Fraser

John Fraser joined the RAF from Glasgow University where he was a member of the UAS. After completing his flying training, he converted to the Buccaneer and served in Germany on XV and 16 Squadrons. After a tour as a QFI at Linton-on-Ouse, he returned to the Buccaneer world at Lossiemouth, served on 237 OCU, commanded the Buccaneer Training Flight and was a flight commander on 208 Squadron. He flew on operations in the First Gulf War. He was the project officer for the spectacular 'Farewell to the Buccaneer' party held at Lossiemouth in March 1994. He commanded Bristol University Air Squadron and served in MoD before retiring in 2000 to continue a flying career in commercial aviation.

Nigel Huckins

After completing fast-jet training in 1975, Nigel Huckins went to the Jaguar force first-ly on 14 Squadron in RAF Germany and then to 226 OCU at RAF Lossiemouth. This was followed by a posting to the Tornado force, firstly as a QWI on the TWCU at RAF Honington and then as squadron QWI of 17 Squadron back in RAF Germany. Then he completed RAF Staff College and a staff tour in MOD, which included detachment to Riyadh as wing commander operations on Operation Granby. He finally converted to the Buccaneer in 1992, taking over as the last Buccaneer squadron commander on 208 Squadron. Subsequently, he served tours with the Air Warfare Centre, as liaison officer to US European Command in Stuttgart before his final tour as an instructor on the USAF Air War College in the United States.

Keith Hartley

Keith Hartley entered RAF College Cranwell in 1967, and after completing his training as a pilot, he converted to the Lightning. He served on squadrons in Cyprus and in the UK before attending the one-year course at the Empire Test Pilots' School in 1976. He joined A Squadron at A&AEE at Boscombe Down testing fast jets and advanced jet trainers. In 1979 he joined British Aerospace at Warton as an experimental test pilot on the Tornado, Jaguar, Buccaneer and Hawk. In 1988 he was a test pilot tutor at the International Test Pilots' School at Cranfield. He returned to Warton in 1992 and was the experimental test pilot on the Typhoon. After six years in Australia, he became the chief test pilot and chief operations officer at the Test Flying Academy of South Africa.

Abbreviations

A&AEE	Aeroplane and Armament Experimental Establishment	CTTO	Central Trials and Tactics Organisation
AAR	Air-to-Air Refuelling	DFGA	Day Fighter Ground Attack
ACMI	Air Combat Manoeuvring Instrumentation	DH	Direct Hit
ADD	Airflow Direction Detector	DL	Deck Landing
ADF	Airborne Direction Finding	DLP	Deck Landing Practice
		ECM	Electronic Countermeasures
AEO	Air Engineer Officer	FAA	Fleet Air Arm
AEW	Airborne Early Warning	FDO	Flight Deck Officer
AF	After Flight	FL	Flight Level
AFB	Air Force Base (South Africa/USA)	FOB	Forward Operating Base
		FPB	Fast Patrol Boat
AFB	Air Force Board	FRA	First Run Attack
AFNORTH	Allied Forces Northern Europe	FRADU	Fleet Requirement and Air Direction Unit
AMCO	Air Maintenance Control Office	GAT	General Air Traffic
		GLO	Ground Liaison Officer
AOB	Air Order of Battle	GPU	Ground Power Unit
AOC	Air Officer Commanding	HAS	Hardened Aircraft Shelter
APC	Armament Practice Camp	HE	High Explosive
APU	Auxiliary Power Unit	HF	High Frequency
AR	Anti-Radar	HUD	Head-Up Display
ATC	Air Traffic Control	IFF	Identification Friend or Foe
AWI	Air Warfare Instructor		
BAI	Buccaneer Attack Instructor	IFTU	Intensive Flying Trials Unit
BF	Before Flight	ILS	Instrument Landing System
CA	Controller Aircraft		
CAA	Civil Aviation Authority	IP	Initial Point
CBLS	Carrier-Bomb Light Store	IRT	Instrument Rating Test
CFS	Central Flying School	JMC	Joint Maritime Course
CHAG	Chain Arrestor Gear	LACW	Leading Aircraftwomen
CLAWR	Cold Lake Air Weapons Range	LCR	Limited Combat Ready
		LGB	Laser-Guided Bomb
COD	Courier on Deck	LOX	Liquid Oxygen

LPAST	Low Pressure Air Start	RSO	Range Safety Officer
MADDLS	Mirror-Assisted Dummy Deck Landing	RWR	Radar Warning Receiver
		SAAF	South African Air Force
Martel	Missile Anti-Radiation Television	SACEUR	Supreme Allied Commander Europe
MC	Medium Capacity	SACLANT	Supreme Allied Commander Atlantic
MDSL	Manual Depressed Sight Line	SAM	Surface-to-Air Missile
MRG	Master Reference Gyro	SAR	Search and Rescue
NAS	Naval Air Squadron	SBAC	Society of British Aircraft Constructors
NASU	Naval Air Support Unit		
NBC	Nuclear, Biological, Chemical	SEAD	Suppresion of Enemy Air Defence
OCU	Operational Conversion Unit	SEATO	South-East Asia Treaty Organisation
ODM	Operation Data Manual	SFD	Strike Force Dispersal
ORP	Operational Readiness Platform	SNCO	Senior Non-Commissioned Officer
PAI	Pilot Attack Instructor	SOBs	Senior Observer
PE	Procurement Executive	SSB	Single Sideband
PEC	Personal Equipment Connector	SURPIC	Surface Picture
		SWAPO	South West Africa People's Organization
PNR	Point of No Return		
PSP	Pierced Steel Planking	TAC	Tactical Air Command
QFI	Qualified Flying Instructor	TAS	True Airspeed
		TCA	Terminal Control Area
QRA	Quick Reaction Alert	TIALD	Thermal Imaging Laser Designator
QWI	Qualified Weapons Instructor		
		UHF	Ultra High Frequency
RAAF	Royal Australian Air Force	USMC	United States Marine Corps
RAFG	Royal Air Force Germany		
RAN	Royal Australian Navy	USN	United States Navy
RDAF	Royal Danish Air Force	USS	United States Ship
RHAG	Rotary Hydraulic Arrestor Gear	UWT	Under-Wing Tank
		VOR	VHF Omnidirectional Range
RNAS	Royal Naval Air Service		
RP	Rocket Projectile		

Index